# Cases in Canad

Second Edition

# Cases in Canadian Business Law

## Second Edition

David C. McPhillips

*Faculty of Commerce and Business Administration*
*University of British Columbia*

Irwin Davis

*Faculty of Commerce and Business Administration*
*University of British Columbia*

Gerald G. Smeltzer

*Faculty of Commerce and Business Administration*
*University of British Columbia*

Prentice-Hall Canada Inc. Scarborough, Ontario

Canadian Cataloguing in Publication Data

McPhillips, David C., 1946-
    Cases in Canadian business law

ISBN 0-13-115254-8

1. Commercial law — Canada — Cases. 2. Business
law — Canada — Cases. I. Davis, Irwin, 1917-
II. Smeltzer, Gerald G., 1946- III. Title.

KE918.5.M32 1984    346′.71′07    C84-098862-1

ISBN 0-13-115254-8

Prentice-Hall, Inc., Englewood Cliffs, New Jersey
Prentice-Hall International, Inc., London
Prentice-Hall of Australia, Pty., Ltd., Sydney
Prentice-Hall of India Pvt., Ltd., New Delhi
Prentice-Hall of Japan, Inc., Tokyo
Prentice-Hall of Southeast Asia (Pte.) Ltd., Singapore
Editora Prentice-Hall do Brasil Ltda., Rio de Janeiro

Production Assistant: Alan Terakawa
Cover Design: Jo-Ann Jordan
Typographical Design: Julian Cleva, Jo-Ann Jordan
Production Editors: Scott Olson, Charles Macli

Typesetter: ART-U Graphics

Printed and bound in Canada by Webcom Ltd.

1 2 3 4 5 WC 89 88 87 86 85

# Table of Contents

# Table of Cases

# Preface to the First Edition

This casebook contains forty-six cases which have been chosen, for the most part, from various Canadian jurisdictions. The purpose of the book is twofold: to give students of Business Law an opportunity to read actual decisions which will offer an insight into the methods the courts use in applying legal theory to actual cases; and to serve as a vehicle for classroom discussion.

The cases are self-explanatory and deal with various areas of Business Law. In a book of this size, it would be impossible to cover all the critical issues, but we have chosen cases that cover many of the more important ones.

The book has been designed to complement the major Canadian texts in the field. Some of the cases have been edited to exclude discussions of points of law that are not relevant for students of Business Law. We have attached notes at the conclusion of many cases explaining particular legal terms contained therein with which the students may not be familiar.

We have also included an introductory section entitled General Explanatory Notes. This section should be read before beginning the discussion of the cases, as it contains explanations of issues and terms that arise very frequently, if not in every decision.

The cases have been selected, where possible, on a representative geographical basis from across Canada; but as these cases deal mainly with fundamental principles, it is important to stress that they are equally applicable in each of the common-law provinces. Where statutes are referred to, the provisions are, again, generally similar in those nine provinces.

We hope that the users of the book will find it helpful, and we welcome any comments from them.

We are indebted to our colleagues here at the University of British Columbia, to our own teachers, and particularly to our students, who made this effort most worthwhile.

*David C. McPhillips*
*Frank R. Taylor*
*Irwin Davis*

# Preface to the Second Edition

The five years since the publication of the first edition has been an active period in Canadian business law. Certain areas of the law have changed through a process of evolution, while other changes have occurred to keep pace with the demands of a modern business community. Many of the cases in the second edition have been selected to illustrate these developments.

Specifically, over the last five years the appeal courts in Canada have increasingly applied the doctrine of unconscionable transactions to commercial cases. At the same time, we have included cases to demonstrate, among other things, the strength of the doctrine of privity of contract as between parties who are dealing on relatively equal terms in business transactions, the relevance of the area of *non est factum*, and the widening scope of tortious liability for professional or occupational groups. Lastly, we have added three cases to illustrate the general principles of the law of bankruptcy and have expanded the section on business organizations.

We would like to thank the following reviewers for their constructive comments on the first draft of this edition:

Professor E.A. Braid, of the University of Manitoba; Professor S. Gunz, of the University of Waterloo; and Mr. Bill Hooker of the British Columbia Institute of Technology.

Once again we are indebted to our students, who continue to make this effort worthwhile.

*David C. McPhillips*
*Irwin Davis*
*Gerald G. Smeltzer*

# General Explanatory Notes

Many of the cases in this book contain a number of similarities, which include references to case citations, courts, statutes, certain legal terms, costs, and third party proceedings. In order to facilitate reading and understanding the materials, each of these terms is explained here.

## 1. Case Citations

Selected decisions of the judges are collected and published in book form by various reporting agencies. The importance of a case will be determined not by the amount of money involved but by the legal principles considered and the effect of the decision upon our law. These series of reports are identified either by the year in which the book was published or in a numerical order. In the first instance the year is shown in square brackets [1984], in the second where the year is used merely for added information it will be in round brackets (1984) e.g., [1984] 3 W.W.R. as contrasted with (1984) 150 D.L.R. In the latter the series number is 150 while in the former the 3 indicates that the book is the third issued in 1984. Frequently, of course, the same case will be reported in more than one series. For speedy reference the page number is always indicated as the last part of the citation. For convenience, the titles of the series are always abbreviated. Following is a list of the services from which the cases in this book have been obtained.

| | |
|---|---|
| All E.R. | : All English Reports (English) |
| Ch. D. | : Chancery Division (English) |
| C.P.R. | : Canadian Patent Reporter (Canadian) |
| D.L.R. | : Dominion Law Reports (Canadian) |
| M.P.R. | : Maritime Practice Reports (Canadian) |
| Nfld. & P.E.I.R. | : Newfoundland and Prince Edward Island Reports (Canadian) |
| O.R. | : Ontario Reports (Canadian) |

S.C.R.                : Supreme Court Reports (Canadian)
W.W.R.            : Western Weekly Reports (Canadian)

# 2. Courts

The various provinces all have the same basic courts for hearing civil actions although they do not have exactly similar names. The courts of first instance, or courts where actions are started, are basically the Supreme Court, Superior Court or Court of Queen's Bench; these have unlimited jurisdiction within the province. There are also county or district courts whose jurisdiction is limited by the geographical area over which they have authority and by the amount of the claim which they can hear. From these courts an appeal lies to the provincial Court of Appeal or the Appeal Division of the high court. Finally the court of last resort is the Supreme Court of Canada in Ottawa to which appeals from any of the provinces may be directed. It is now necessary to obtain the consent of that court before an appeal may be launched; this consent can only be obtained where a point of law of special interest or importance is involved.

# 3. Statutes

In several of the cases specific statutes are quoted. Where this occurs they are either federal Acts, such as the *Lord's Day Act,* or provincial Acts which are common to all or many of the provinces. This is especially true in those situations dealing with the sale of goods. It should be realized that the section numbers of similar statutes may vary from province to province because the subject matter is in different order, but often the wording is identical or, if it is not, the effect is the same. The corresponding sections may be easily identified by reference to the appropriate provincial statute.

# 4. Legal Terms

a) *Estoppel* arises as a rule whereby a party is not allowed to give evidence to deny something he has previously maintained by word or deed.
b) *Prima facie* simply means "on the face of it" or "apparently". Generally it refers to something which can be accepted as correct until the contrary is proved.
c) *Specific performance* is an equitable remedy sometimes granted by the courts wherein a defendant is ordered to carry out the terms of a contract. It is frequently used in cases involving the sale of real property wherein the vendor is directed to convey the land to the purchaser. The courts are reluctant to give such orders, for a breach of them amounts to contempt of court, which may lead to possible criminal prosecution.

# 5. Costs

Every legal action involves various legal expenses for all parties to the litigation. There are fees paid to lawyers and expert witnesses, charges for filing documents, travel expenses of witnesses and so forth. Most of the expenses are recoverable in whole or in part when they are included as part of a court award of costs. However, lawyer's fees are a matter of separate contract between a lawyer and his client and usually the fees charged will exceed any costs which are awarded. A client must pay these fees regardless of any court award.

Normally, the court orders the losing party to pay the costs incurred by the winning party, which is often referred to as "costs following the event". The court has a discretion here though, and may award costs to any party or to none at all. Any other valid reason may also influence the judge in his disposition of the question of costs; for example, fairness or equity.

In order to calculate these costs, some courts have a table, called a tariff, which has various provisions or columns in it for each item that is recoverable. For instance, a successful plaintiff might be allowed a certain amount for issuing the writ of summons, a different amount for a statement of claim or as an allowance for each day spent in trial. Again, these costs are frequently less than the actual charges and the difference will be borne by each individual party. Should any party not agree on the proper items or amounts to which the successful party is entitled, they may be submitted to an officer of the court for taxation or review. Disagreement with the latter's decision may then be resolved by an appeal to the courts.

The different provisions or columns represent varying amounts which may be charged in respect of each item. Usually, the applicable column is decided by the amoun awarded; that is, the higher the aard, the higher the recoverable costs. But even this is subject to the discretion of the court.

Where a court decision is appealed, the ultimately unsuccessful party usually has to pay the costs of the other in all courts (but again, at the discretion of the court). Thus if a decision is rendered by the Supreme Court of Canada, the unsuccessful party would likely be responsible for the costs in that court, the provincial Court of Appeal, and the court of first instance. Sometimes where there is a cross-appeal (that is, where both parties are objecting to some aspect of the judgment), the courts will not award any costs for the cross-appeal on the grounds that they are already provided for in the result of the main appeal.

Since a counter-claim is in effect a separate action, the court may award costs to both parties, should each be successful. At other times the judge may feel that one of the claims did not materially increase the expenses and only award one set of costs.

In some situations, as where two cars collide and one of them is knocked onto a sidewalk injuring a pedestrian, the plaintiff may not be sure which of the other two parties is responsible and so will claim from both. Should the judge decide that one of them was in no way to blame, that party is normally entitled to have the action against him dismissed with costs. Where the plaintiff has been reasonable in suing both, the court may allow the plaintiff to also charge the unsuccessful defendant for those costs which he has to pay to the successful defendant.

Where an action was reasonably brought against an estate, the court may decide, whatever the result, that the costs of all parties should be paid by the estate.

Generally speaking, the judges frown on a person bringing an action in a higher court than necessary, especially if the object is to obtain larger costs. Where this happens the costs are usually awarded on the scale of the court in which the action should have been brought. Since this is a matter of discretion, exceptions may be made.

# 6. Third Party Proceedings

Should a defendant feel that another person, not a party to the action, is responsible for the claim, he may take third party proceedings, claiming that if he is found liable, the third party should be required to reimburse him for what he has had to pay the plaintiff. Such an award will usually include the amount of costs required to be paid to the plaintiff. In addition since the defendant was successful in the claim against the third party, the defendant's costs may be levied against the third party.

# PART ONE

# Torts

# A. Intentional Torts

## Bahner v. Marwest Hotel Co. Ltd. et al.

*(1969) 69 W.W.R. 462*
*B.C. Supreme Court*
*June 13, 1969*
*Upheld on appeal (1970) 75 W.W.R. 729*

WILSON C.J.S.C.: The plaintiff sues all defendants for damages for false imprisonment.

I said at the end of the trial that in so far as there were conflicts of evidence, and the conflicts were not, except in the case of the witness Muir, great, I accepted the plaintiff's evidence throughout in preference to that of witnesses called for the defendants and that I found the defendant Marwest Hotel Company Ltd. liable. Counsel for the defendant, Cst. Muir, had already admitted liability. The plaintiff has said he is not pressing his claim against the city of Vancouver and it is clear on authority that the city cannot be held vicariously liable for the acts of the defendant, Cst. Muir.[1]

While the questions of liability were decided by me at the trial I said that I would at a later date give reasons for judgment and assess damages.[2]

The plaintiff is a young, lively, educated and intelligent German immigrant to Canada. On August 13, 1967 he took two friends, Mr. and Mrs. Duggan to dinner at a restaurant operated by the defendant Marwest at the Bayshore Inn in the city of Vancouver and called Trader Vic's. The evidence shows that this has generally been regarded as a superior sort of eating place. The three of them commenced their dinner at the continental hour of 10:30 p.m. to 10:45 p.m. The plaintiff, as host, ordered a bottle of wine to accompany the dinner, a respectable French wine for which the restaurant charged about $8. No other drinks were served to this party until 11:30 at night and there is the clearest evidence (apart from the evidence of Cst. Muir which, for reasons given later, I reject) that this was an entirely sober and decorous party and that the plaintiff, particularly, drank only three to four wineglasses of wine with his meal and was not in any way or at any time even slightly intoxicated.

At 11:30 p.m. the party had consumed the main part of their dinner and about half their wine. Their waiter, James Gee, than asked the plaintiff if he would like another bottle of wine. The plaintiff said that he would and at 11:35 p.m. a bottle was brought, opened and left in a receptacle on or by the table. The plaintiff and guests continued their dinner and by 11:50 p.m. had consumed the wine left in their first bottle but had not touched the second bottle. At this time, the waiter Gee, came to their table and told the plaintiff that he must, as provided by provincial law, consume the entire contents of the second bottle of wine before 12 midnight as after that hour it was illegal to drink wine in the restaurant. The plaintiff said "We can't drink a bottle of wine within ten minutes without getting drunk." The waiter said. "You will have to pay for the wine anyway." The plaintiff refused to do so.

The waiter then called the manager, Harvey Chinn, who came to the plaintiff's table at 11:45 p.m. The following dialogue ensued:

"Chinn: You ordered the wine and must pay for it.

"Plaintiff: There is not enough time. I was not told I must finish it. I refuse to pay for it. If I have to pay for it, then since there is no time to drink it here, I will take it and drink it elsewhere.

"Chinn: You can't take it away from here. That also is against Provincial law."

I state here that I have little doubt that the waiter and the manager were correct in their statements as to the effect of the liquor laws and regulations of this province and that to those of us brought up under and enured to those aboriginal edicts there might be nothing astonishing about the unreasonable demands made upon the plaintiff. But one can easily imagine the effect on a person accustomed to more tolerant customs of a demand to pay for a bottle of wine he could neither drink nor take with him.

It may be that the plaintiff was wrong and that he was under a civil liability to pay the hotel for wine he could neither consume on the premises nor take away with him. But, even if this is conceded, it can be no stretch of the imagination be conceived that he was guilty of any criminal act. He had made no false pretence, he had used no force, he had simply, as all of us are entitled to do, refused to pay a sum he did not think he owed. The fact that he may have been wrong was irrelevant where the refusal to pay was made as here in honesty and in good faith.

There followed more talk between the plaintiff and the manager. It culminated in this exchange:

"Manager: If you don't pay for the bottle of wine I am going to call the police.

"Plaintiff: I am not going to pay for the bottle of wine."

The plaintiff then offered to give the manager his name and address.

At this point there appeared on the scene another actor, a security officer, so called, who must have been summoned by the manager. This gentleman was employed by Pinkerton's Detective Agency, which agency was in turn engaged by the hotel company to provide security services for the hotel. He has since left Canada and cannot be found; nothing is known of him save that he bore the formidable nickname "Rocky."

This person told the plaintiff he was a security officer. There was some talk in which Rocky explained the position taken by the hotel management to the plaintiff and the plaintiff reiterated his refusal to pay for the wine. Rocky then said "You must pay for the wine or I will call the police." The plaintiff paid his dinner bill of $50 to $60, and even tipped the waiter, an extraordinarily magnanimous gesture in the circumstances, but he did not pay for the second bottle of wine.

Next the plaintiff and his guests got up from their table and commenced to leave the hotel. When the plaintiff reached the exit for which he was headed he found it blocked by the security officer who said "You cannot leave." There was more talk, the plaintiff still refused to pay. The security officer said "I am going to call the police." Since he was not permitted to leave, the plaintiff sat down at another table nearer the door and his guests joined him.

I cannot take very seriously the argument of counsel for the hotel company that there were other exits from the cafe unbarred and that the plaintiff might have escaped through one of them. The plantiff, commanded by a security officer to stay, and prevented by that officer from leaving by the ordinary exit, behaved with admirable restraint in making no forcible attempt to pass the security officer. After what the officer had said and done he could reasonably expect to be restrained by force if he tried to leave by any exit and he was not required to make an attempt to run away.

Two uniformed policemen arrived. One of them was Cst. Muir, a defendant in this action, and it was he who took charge of the matter and conducted all subsequent dealings between the police and the accused.

Muir spoke first to the manager and was presumably told of the circumstances. Then he came to the plaintiff and asked, "Did you have this dinner and wine, what is this all about?" The plaintiff told Muir that he had ordered the wine at 11:30 p.m. and had been told near midnight that he must drink it before midnight and that he had, in those circumstances, refused to pay for the wine. Muir said, "If you don't pay I will take you along." The accused then asked if he might go to his car and get a toothbrush before he was taken away. This request was refused. Muir said, "You are under arrest." He did not say what the charge was but the preceding discussions show clearly that the plaintiff was being arrested for refusing to pay for the wine. Muir's assertion at the trial that he arrested the accused to prevent a breach of the peace and because he was intoxicated in a public place is a mendacious afterthought devised at a later time to try to defend an indefensible position, totally unsupported by and indeed contradicted by the other evidence.

The patrol wagon was called and the accused was placed in its barred interior and taken to the police station where he was relieved of the contents of his pockets and of his necktie and placed in a dirty, smelly cell with two unpleasantly drunken persons.

Muir went off and talked to a justice of the peace who, on hearing the facts, told Muir that the accused could not on those facts be charged with the offence of obtaining goods by false pretences.[3] Muir then went to the plaintiff in his cell and told him that he would not be charged with the offence of obtaining the wine by false pretences but would be charged with being intoxicated in a public place. This was, I am convinced, the first intimation that the plaintiff had received that he was thought to be drunk and, as I am further convinced, the first time that there had occurred to Muir the idea of so charging him. Muir had found from the justice of the peace that he had made a grave error and, instead of admitting it and releasing the accused with appropriate apologies as he ought to have done, he sought to protect himself by laying a baseless charge not previously mentioned or thought of, a sorry course of conduct and one which it saddens me to discover in a member of our usually fair-minded and well-conducted police force.

The plaintiff was removed to another cell and kept there until the next morning when he was released on bail. He was subsequently tried in Vancouver city police court on Muir's charge of intoxication in a public place. Muir was the only person who gave evidence. Although a dozen restaurant guests, as well as the restaurant staff, were present at the restaurant on the night of August 13, and must have seen what was going on and had full opportunity to observe the conduct of the accused, not one of the them was called by the crown as a witness and the magistrate, having heard Muir's evidence, and doubtless formed much the same opinion of it that I have, dismissed the charge without calling for a defence.[4]

It seems to me that there were here two false imprisonments. When Rocky, the Pinkerton man, barred the exit from the cafe and told the plaintiff he could not leave, there was false imprisonment by the defendant Marwest Hotel Company Ltd. When Muir, without a warrant, took into custody and gaoled the plaintiff, who was not committing an offence, and whom the constable had no reasonable cause to believe to be guilty of an offence, there was a second false imprisonment. There was no reasonable and probably cause for imprisonment in either case. As I have said, it must be assumed that the reason in Muir's mind justifying the arrest was the plaintiff's refusal to pay for the second bottle of wine, and the plaintiff also knew that his refusal to pay was almost certainly the reason for his arrest. But I find as a fact that Muir did not, at the moment of arrest, disclose to the plaintiff the reason for his arrest. I think that Muir had in his mind some confused notion that a failure to pay for a thing ordered was a crime, but did not know what crime it was. The attitude of the manager and house detective of this grand caravanserai, both of whom seemed to have thought that failure to pay was a crime, may have influenced Muir's thinking.

I have considered whether or not the hotel company is responsible not just for the false imprisonment of the plaintiff by its own agent. Rocky, but also for the further or continued false imprisonment of the plaintiff by Muir. Certainly the company's employees summoned the police, and certainly if they had not done so the plaintiff would not have been arrested by the police. But I have no evidence that the hotel authorities actually handed over the plaintiff to the police or that they did anything more than tell Muir what had happened, leaving it to him to make the decision as to arrest. Muir himself says he acted on his own judgment in making the arrest. Having these facts in mind I apply this statement of Collins, M.R. in *Sewell v. Nat. Telephone Co.* [1907] 1 KB 557, at 559, 76 L.J.K.B. 196: "If a person desires to obtain a judicial decision from a proper tribunal, and for that purpose states the facts to a police officer, and the latter, acting on his own initiative arrests the person implicated, no trespass is committed by the person who gives the information to the police officer." I think the hotel company is only liable for the false imprisonment by its security officer but, in assessing damages, I do not propose to forget that the hotel authorities were responsible for the totally unnecessary presence of the police on their premises and for the completely unjustified public interrogation of this German Hampden by uniformed policemen, and this during the period of his restraint by the security officer and before his arrest by Muir. The arrogance and stupidity of the conduct of the hotel authorities cannot be overstated.

The plaintiff is, as I have said, young, personable, lively and intelligent. His father is leader in Germany of the Bavarian liberal party and Mr. Bahner has assisted his father in elections and other political activities. He qualified in Germany as a commercial pilot, has a Canadian licence to operate single-engined commercial aircraft, and owns, in Canada, an aircraft of that type. He has, since 1963, spent most of his time in Canada, but has visited Germany each year. He intends to visit Germany again at the end of this year to assist his father in a political campaign. In 1967 and 1968 he has unsuccessfully sought employment as a pilot in British Columbia, the Yukon and the Northwest Territories. His attempts in 1968 were all, of course, made after the Bayshore incident. Any suggestion that he was intemperate in the use of alcohol or had been arrested for intoxication would, he says (and I believe him), if made known to a prospective employer, be fatal to his chances of employment as a pilot. I am asked to infer from the fact that at least a dozen guests as well as the hotel employees saw his arrest at the Bayshore, that the news of this happening must have reached the persons whom he had asked for work and have defeated his applications. This is certainly a possibility, but it is not a probability and I cannot make the inference. Therefore no part of the damages to be assessed is allowed on the basis of loss of employment.

But the fact that he was publicly humiliated by detention by the security officer in the hotel in the presence of the staff and a dozen guests, and by subsequent interrogation and arrest by a uniformed policeman was known to a considerable number of people, who have in all probability and very naturally told other persons about it. It is hard to calculate how far news of this kind may spread and what harm it may have done. Few persons who witnessed his arrest are likely to be aware of his subsequent acquittal. The ripples from the boulder thrown into the water by the defendants may spread far. The degradation consequent upon the experience suffered by the plaintiff is sore and not easily forgotten.

I have been asked to award punitive, exemplary or vindictive damages. Defense counsel refer me to *Rookes v. Barnard* [1964] A.C. 1129, [1964] 2 W.L.R. 269, [1964] 1 All E.R. 367, a decision of the House of Lords in which it was held (Lord Devlin, at p. 410) that exemplary damages should only be awarded in three classes of cases. It is clear that this case would not fall into either of the first two categories defined by Lord Devlin at p. 410, but it may well fall into the class of cases he refers to in these words at p. 412:

> ...When this has been said, there remains one class of case for which the authority is much more precise. It is the class of case in which the injury to the plaintiff has been aggravated by malice or by the manner of doing the injury, that is, the insolence or arrogance by which it is accompanied. There is clear authority that this can justify exemplary damages, though (except in *Louden v. Ryder* [1953] 2 Q.B. 202, [1953] 2 W.L.R. 537, 97 Sol.J. 170) it is not clear whether they are to be regarded as in addition to, or in substitution for the aggravated damages that could certainly be awarded.

But in *McElroy v. Cowper-Smith and Woodman* (1967) 60 W.W.R. 85, [1967] S.C.R. 425, Spence J. has said, at p. 93: "I am of the opinion that in Canada the jurisdiction to award punitive damages in tort actions is not so limited as Lord Devlin outline in *Rookes v. Barnard*." Hall J., in the majority judgment in the same case, said at p. 86: "Defamation of a professional man is a very serious matter and ordinarily would be visited with an award of substantial damages, including punitive or exemplary damages if the circumstances so warrant." The effect of these two opinions given in a case which did not fit into any of the classes defined by Lord Devlin in *Rookes v. Barnard* must be that *Rookes v. Barnard,* in so far as it deals with the law as to punitive damages, is not applicable in Canada.

In awarding damages here I am influenced by the nature of the conduct of the hotel authorities which I consider to paraphrase Lord Devlin's words, to have been arrogant. I prefer to call the damages I assess in this case aggravated damages, damages which I think are due to the plaintiff in recompense for the humiliation and degradation to which he was exposed. But, lest they be thought excessive in that light, I am content that the damages should be considered, to the extent of $1000 in each case, punitive. As Lord Devlin has suggested, the line is not easy to draw.

In the case of Cst. Muir, I think the damages which would in any event be payable by him for the false initial imprisonment of the plaintiff, beginning at the hotel and continuing to the city gaol, must be enhanced and aggravated by Muir's subsequent conduct. At a later time, when he must have known full well that he had no grounds for detaining the plaintiff, he did not release him but chose to detain him on another charge known to him to be false and baseless, in effect yet another false imprisonment.

I think the defendant Marwest Hotel Company Ltd., the instigator of the proceedings, and the defendant responsible for the greater part of the public humiliation of the plaintiff, should pay him $3500 in damages and I think that Muir should pay him $2500 in damages.

The plaintiff claims $75 special damages, as counsel fee to the lawyer who defended him in police court. Footnote (k) at p. 770 of *38 Halsbury, 3rd ed.,* says:

> The fact that the plaintiff…was put to expense in defending himself is not a matter to be considered in assessing the damages in an action of false imprisonment; but such matters form the subject of damages in an action for malicious prosecution.

The authorities cited are of some antiquity: *Chivers v. Savage* (1855) 5 E.&B. 697, 25 L.J.Q.B. 85, 119 E.R. 641, and *Guest v. Warren* (1854) 9 Exch. 379, 23 L.J. Ex. 121, 156 E.R. 161.

The plaintiff here was imprisoned and released on bail. In order to protect himself against the possibility of further imprisonment he retained a lawyer to whom he paid a fee of $75 for defending him in police court. With the greatest respect to contrary opinion I think that he is entitled to recover from defendant Muir the sum so paid, as damages following from his false imprisonment and necessary in order to prevent its continuance.

Both judgments will carry costs.


NOTES

1. *The City of Vancouver was not liable for the acts of the constable, where he was enforcing the general laws of the community and not acting specifically for the benefit of the city. This rule is an exception to the principle of vicarious liability introduced so that our laws can be properly enforced.*

2. *At the conclusion of a trial the judge may deliver his judgment or decision immediately together with his reasons, or he may reserve his decision and hand it down in writing after he has considered the evidence and the law. Here he found the hotel company and the police officer liable, but handed down his reasons and determined the amount of the damages later.*

3. *The fact that Mr. Bahner may have been liable to pay for the wine he had ordered and opened did not mean that he had committed a crime for which he should be arrested. He had not ordered the wine with no intention of paying—which would have been obtaining goods by false pretences—but rather a civil dispute had arisen as to whether he should pay for wine he could not consume.*

4. *When the magistrate heard the evidence on the charge of being drunk in a*

*public place, he found that the crown had not proved that Mr. Bahner was drunk and so dismissed the charge without calling for him to make any defence.*

## Booth et al v. British Columbia Television Broadcasting System et al.

*(1982) 139 D.L.R. (3d) 88*
*B.C. Court of Appeal*
*May 7, 1982*

LAMBERT J.A.: This is a defamation[1] case. The words were spoken in 1972. They were recorded on tape and broadcast on television and published all in 1972. The trial took place in 1975 and this appeal is from the trial judgment at that time [summarized [1976] W.W.D. 78].

In 1972, there was a change in the law affecting prostitution and the defendant television system or one of its employees conceived the idea of interviewing a prostitute. The defendant, Margo Wong, was interviewed by the defendant, David Rinn, on television in a programme produced by the defendant, Clapp, and broadcast by the defendant British Columbia Television Broadcasting System Limited.

The words that are in issue in the case are set out in the reasons of Mr. Justice Hinkson, the trial judge, and they are these:

Q. What are policeman like in Vancouver?
A. Some of them are O.K. and some of them are not. There's good ones and crooked ones.
Q. Are they any payoffs in Vancouver?
A. Yeah there's about—in one night maybe twelve cops get paid off from different squads.
Q. You've paid them off?
A. I've paid them off quite a few times.
Q. How much?
A. Ummm—if it goes Vag "C" charge usually you have to pay them maybe half a bill—fifty dollars. If it's for narcotics you usually up a hundred—two-hundred dollars.
Q. Could you name individuals involved?
A. Oh I could—yeah—but I'm not gonna name them—cause that would just get me up a creek without a paddle—but there is, I'd say three on the Morality Squad that are quite high for payoffs and I know two on the Narc Squad that are high up—right up on top that take payoffs, and there's a

few other ones on—like Traffic—you know they're special squads that take some.

The interview was broadcast by the defendant, British Columbia Television Broadcasting System Limited, at least twice, I understand on the same day, and then had a wider dissemination after that, but the scope of any wider dissemination was not in issue at the trial or before us.

The plaintiffs are 11 members of the Vancouver City Police Force, or they were in 1972. They are all members of the narcotics squad. There was in 1972 a vice department in the Vancouver City Police Force, and within that department four separate squads: the narcotics squad, the liquor squad, the morality and gambling squad.

• • •

Counsel on the appeal referred very largely to the same leading authorities in relation to defamation that consists of statements referring to more than one person without naming particular persons, and those leading cases are *Knupffer v. London Express Newspaper, Ltd.*, [1944] 1 All E.R. 495; *Morgan v. Odhams Press Ltd., et al.*, [1971] 2 All E.R. 1156. Counsel referred to other cases but those are the principal cases relied on and those were the principal cases relied on by the trial judge. There is no significant dispute between counsel as to the broad legal concepts that are applicable and, as I understand their arguments, neither counsel takes objection to the statements of law by the trial judge but rather takes objection both on the appeal and the cross-appeal to the application of that law to the particular words in this case and the circumstances in this case.

The overriding issue in cases of this kind where the words are clearly defamatory in themselves is whether the words were published of and concerning the particular plaintiff who is claiming, and in addressing that question Viscount Simon says in the *Knupffer* case at p. 497:

> There are two questions involved in the attempt to identify the appellant as the person defamed. The first question is a question of law—can the article, having regard to its language, be regarded as capable of referring to the appellant? The second question is a question of fact, namely, does the article in fact lead reasonable people, who know the appellant, to the conclusion that it does refer to him? Unless the first question can be answered in favour of the appellant, the second question does not arise, and where the trial judge went wrong was in treating evidence to support the identification in fact as governing the matter, when the first question is necessarily, as a matter of law, to be answered in the negative.

In the *Morgan* case we were particularly referred to the judgment of Lord Morris of Borth-y-Gest which indicates that the dual nature of the test grows out of the practice in charging juries in cases of defamation.

The trial judge deals more extensively than I have with the law, but I do not think that it is necessary to go further than I have done. He adopts the test set out by Viscount Simon and he applies it to eliminate all of the 11 plaintiffs except two, Booth and Donald. As I understand his reasons, he is saying that the words referring to "two on the Narc Squad that are high up—right up on top", are capable when considered in relation to the facts of this case of being considered as being published of and concerning only Booth and Donald.

The trial judge also considers that the remainder of the words are, as a matter of law, not capable of being considered as published of and concerning any of the other plaintiffs other than Booth and Donald.

The trial judge then goes on and considers the evidence of 12 or 14 witnesses who gave the view that they took when they heard the defamatory statements or heard about the defamatory statements, and he concludes that a reasonable person on hearing these statements would think that they were said of and concerning Booth and Donald, and on that basis the trial judge finds liability of the defendants to Booth and Donald.

In his assessment of damages he awarded $7500 to each of those plaintiffs as compensation and $5000 to each of those plaintiffs by way of exemplary damages. The exemplary damages, therefore, totalled $10 000 and were awarded after careful consideration and a listing of those factors that justified such an award, particularly the prospect of profits being made by the broadcasting defendant from the excitement generated by a story of this nature, and the assistance of all the defendants in publishing the defamatory statement after being requested not to do so until an opportunity had been given to the police departments to investigate the truth of what was alleged.

An appeal[2] has been brought by the defendants British Columbia Television Broadcasting and Clapp, the only two defendants who were represented at the trial. Their appeal is as to liability.

A cross-appeal has been brought by the plaintiff, Donald, and by the nine other plaintiffs, other than Booth, who did not recover on their claim.

In relation to the appellant Donald, the cross-appeal asks for a higher award of exemplary damages. In relation to the other cross-appellants the cross-appeal asks for a finding that the defendants are liable to them and then asks for damages, both compensatory damages and exemplary damages.

I turn first to the appeal. Three points were argued.

The first was whether the words were capable of being considered as being published of and concerning the plaintiffs Booth and Donald.

The submission of counsel for the appellant was that they are only capable of referring to the staff sergeant who was in charge of the narcotics squad and the sergeant who was his second in command.

As I have said, the actual phrase was: "two on the Narc Squad that are high up—right up on top". In my opinion, we are not concerned with what the speaker subjectively meant to say; we are concerned with the meaning that reasonable men would take from what was said. But words, of course, are merely a mode of communication and all the circumstances of the communication must be considered as well as the mode that was used. The kind of person that the speaker was, and the kind of knowledge that people would anticipate that the speaker would have are relevant factors in determining the content of the communication. The circumstances in which the words are used are also relevant. So is the general audience to which the statements might be considered to be directed, and the special audience with special knowledge of the organization of the Vancouver Police Department. These too are relevant factors in deciding whether reasonable people generally, or whether reasonable people with special and particular knowledge, would find that the defamatory statement was published of and concerning the particular plaintiff.

The speaker was Margaret Wong, a prostitute with some knowledge but clearly not any detailed knowledge of the organization of the drug squad. There is no reason to believe that she would know of a transfer or personality of the second in command a week before she spoke. There is no reason to believe that when she says that she is referring to someone right on the top that she was referring to an inside administrator of the department who has overall supervision.

The trial judge found that those words were capable of referring to Booth and Donald. He found that those words were not capable of referring to the junior members in seniority and in work of the squad and, indeed, he found that the words were only capable of referring to Booth and Donald. He reached that conclusion on the basis of the words themselves, but also on the evidence that had been led and, of course, where the trier of fact and decider of law are the same there is no reason for any precise separation of the functions or decision of the two questions that have been raised by Viscount Simon. The ultimate question remains whether the words were published of and concerning the plaintiff. After considering all the evidence the trial judge decided that they were capable of being considered as published of and concerning Booth and Donald and that they were no capable of being considered as published of and concerning anyone other than Booth and Donald. I agree.

The second point in the appeal raised by counsel for the appellant relates then to Booth and Donald and is that even if the words were capable of being considered as published of and concerning them that reasonable men would not have concluded that they were published of Booth and Donald and that even on the basis of the evidence that particular people did consider them published of Booth and Donald that, on the whole of the evidence, it should not have been concluded that a reasonable man would consider them as published of Booth and David.

Counsel for the appellant took us through the relevant parts of the evidence of 12 or even 14 witnesses on this point, and indeed there were considerable variations in their reactions to the story. However, counsel for the appellant concedes that he is not asking us to reassess on the balance of probabilities the conclusion reached by the trial judge on the question of fact, whether a reasonable person would be led to the conclusion that reference was to Booth and David. He said on the basis of the evidence the trial judge was clearly wrong in his conclusion.

In my opinion, on the basis of the evidence that was read to us, the trial judge was not clearly wrong. He reached a conclusion on a question of fact and, in my opinion, there was ample evidence to support that conclusion, that a reasonable person who knew Booth and Donald might well conclude that the defamatory words were uttered of and concerning them.

The third point related to the pleadings. In my opinion, para. 19 of the statement of claim was an ample pleading to support the conclusion of the trial judge, notwithstanding that the judgment of the trial judge did not come within the more particular pleading in para. 18 that I have recited and, indeed, as I understood his argument, counsel for the appellant did not press this third point.

For those reasons I would dismiss the appeal.

I turn now to the cross-appeal. It comes essentially to two points.

The first is that the defamatory words were uttered of and concerning all 11 of the plaintiffs and not just Booth and Donald. The major ground on which this is put is that all were members of the narcotics squad, that the words should not be construed as if they were a statute, but should be considered as a communication made orally and that in considering that communication the true question is what would reasonable people take from the words as an impression, as well as or coupled with the more precise content of the words, but not limited to the precise grammatical content of the words.

I do not disagree with counsel for the plaintiffs on the cross-appeal with his view as to the proper way of considering the words spoken. It is the impression that they convey that is crucial. But, in my opinion, the words "two on the Narc Squad that are high up—right on top" and the other words that surround them do not, in law, have a link with the other nine plaintiffs. It is true that the evidence indicates that there was immediate suspicion of all of the members of the narcotics squad and indeed there may well have been suspicion beyond that into the morality squad, into the vice squad as a whole, but that suspicion is more a matter of the mind of the person who heard the statement and his or her association with particular members of the police force. A neighbour who knows only one police officer, for example, and hears something about the police force would think immediately of that police officer, whether the words that are used have any real link to that police officer or not. So, an immediate suspicion is not necessarily an indication that the words are capable of being considered as published of and concerning the particular plaintiff. I think a good deal of the evidence was in that category.

After considering the evidence to which we were referred and considering both the precise words that I have quoted and the surrounding words, I agree with the trial judge that the other nine plaintiffs were not included and not capable of being included as being referred to in the words that were uttered.

A second point was made in relation to the members of the trafficking subgroup of the narcotics squad.

The trial judge dealt carefully with the evidence of how traffic and trafficking were used by the police witnesses and by other witnesses and he reached the conclusion that, again, the words were not capable of being considered as referring to the two plaintiffs, Simmons and Larke, who worked in the trafficking subgroup. On the basis of the evidence I agree with the trial judge.

The second point on the cross-appeal related to damages. Very fairly, counsel for the plaintiffs on the cross-appeal said that he was not asking us to reassess in 1982 and by 1982 standards the award that had been made by the trial judge in 1975 with respect to defamatory words uttered in 1972. His submission was that by 1975 standards the award of a total of $10 000 as exemplary damages was inordinately low. He did not refer us specifically to any cases decided in this jurisdiction and, indeed, my recollection of those cases indicates that they would not support a submission that 10 000 was inordinately low for a case such as this. The case was clearly an appropriate one, in my view, for an award of exemplary damages[3] but, in my opinion, an award of $10 000 in total was a fit award and it was appropriate to divide it as to $5000 to each of the two plaintiffs in whose favour judgment on liability had been made.

For those reasons I would dismiss the cross-appeal.

*ANDERSON J.A.: I agree.*

*MACFARLANE J.A.: I agree.*

*LAMBERT J.A.: The appeal and the cross-appeal are dismissed.*

NOTES

1. *There are two types of defamation—libel which is in written form and slander which is spoken.*

2. *Appeals can be made on questions of law only and not on questions of fact. A cross-appeal means that the other parties or at least some of them are also appealing portions of the lower court award.*

3. *Exemplary or punitive damages are awarded only in cases where the defendant has acted in a particularly irresponsible manner and serve as a type of punishment beyond the real damages which were incurred. They are awarded only in very limited circumstances in Canada in tort or contract cases where damages are basically compensatory. The criminal law system is considered the proper forum of levying punishment.*

# B. Negligence

## Schanuel v. Hoglund

*[1980] 3 W.W.R. 544*
*Alberta Court of Appeal*
*February 15, 1980*

LIEBERMAN J.A.: On 27th June 1974 the respondent (plaintiff) was injured while riding "as a guest without payment for the transportation" in a motor vehicle owned and operated by the appellant. At trial the learned trial judge found that the appellant was grossly negligent, that the respondent was not *volens*, that the respondent was not contributorily negligent and, finally, that the injuries complained of by the respondent were the result of the gross negligence of the appellant and of the accident that occurred as a consequence thereof. Special and general damages in the total sum of $123 240.29 were awarded to the respondent. This is an appeal from that judgment.

In his judgment the learned trial judge made findings of fact with respect to the circumstances surrounding the accident, which in the main are not in dispute. I repeat them herewith.

On 27th June 1974 the plaintiff, Irene Schanuel, her husband, Ed Schanuel and the defendant, Doug Hoglund went fishing at a spot near the junction of the Red Willow and Wapiti Rivers near Beaverlodge, Alberta. They went to the fishing spot in the defendant's 1965 Jeep four-wheel drive stationwagon vehicle which he had recently purchased and which he alone drove at all times during the fishing trip. The road to the fishing spot leads down a steep winding hill on a dirt road to a flat area at the bottom of a valley.

Shortly after arriving at the fishing spot, it started to rain and they took shelter in an abandoned fishing shack while waiting for the rain shower to clear up. The plaintiff suggested that perhaps they should abandon the fishing trip and leave for home because the road would be slippery and it would be difficult to drive up the hill. The defendant assured them that the four-wheel drive Jeep that he had recently acquired could go anywhere.

The plaintiff raised no further objections at this time, the rain subsided and they started fishing. They fished for two to three hours, during which time there was a series of intermittent showers, and then they decided to leave for home. The defendant, driving his vehicle, made four unsuccessful attempts to go up the hill and in each attempt the wheels spun without the vehicle moving forward. After each attempt the defendant backed some distance downhill in order to prepare for the next attempt. The plaintiff became more frightened at each attempt. She suggested that they abandon the vehicle and walk home and pointed out that farther up the hill the road slopes off to the right into a steep gully. She was seated in the middle of the front seat between the driver and her husband. She did not insist on leaving the vehicle nor was she prevented from doing so.

On the fifth attempt, the defendant progressed further up the hill and arrived at the place where the road slopes off to the right. At this point the vehicle commenced to slide sideways, the defendant then turned the front wheels in an effort to prevent the slide and, in a further attempt to control the vehicle, shifted it into reverse gear.

The vehicle backed down over the embankment, travelled backwards down a steep slope for some 25 to 30 feet and came in collision with a clump of trees...

Shortly after the rainfall started, the plaintiff suggested they leave because the hill would be slippery; she was assured by the defendant that his four-wheel drive Jeep would go anywhere. Later on, after the first attempt to climb the hill, she pointed out the fact that farther up, the road sloped off to the right into a steep gully and suggested that they abandon the vehicle and walk home. Her advice was ignored by the defendant.

To these facts I would add that the road in question was only nine feet wide and that just downhill from the point where the Jeep went off the road there is a curve in the road that obscures the area in which the accident took place. This is the area about which the respondent said she warned the appellant. I quote from the examination in chief of the respondent:

Q. Now before making the fifth attempt, did you have any thoughts about where on the road you were going to be going with that vehicle? A. Yes, we did.
Q. What were your own thoughts about that? A. Well, I knew that we would get to the portion of the road where it sloped off, and I was really afraid if we got there we might not make it.
Q. When you say we get to the portion where it sloped off, what do you mean? A. The road sloped really sharply to the outside edge.
Q. Would that be the right or the left side as you were going up? A. The right side as you were going up.
Q. What was on the right side? A. A bank going down...
Q. Now just going back to before you made the fifth attempt, did you have any discussion with Mr. Hoglund about this particular place on the road that you would be coming to? A. Yes, we talked about it.
Q. What did he say about it? A. He said he realized it was a bad spot, and if it was slippery he would have to be real careful.

It must be mentioned that the appellant denied that this discussion took place. It is evident, however, that the learned trial judge accepted the respondent's evidence throughout and I see no reason to interfere with that finding. It should also be noted that the learned trial judge appears to have accepted the evidence of the respondent's husband over that of the appellant. Again I see no basis on which that finding should be disturbed.

That the appellant knew he was faced with a dangerous situation is, on his own testimony in cross-examination, beyond dispute.

• • •

Based upon his findings of fact the learned trial judge came to the conclusion that the appellant was grossly negligent. He said:

> Having regard to all of the circumstances, I have no hesitation in coming to the conclusion that the actions of the defendant amounted to gross negligence. He was aware of the clear danger that lay ahead and he nevertheless continued to drive. He departed from the standard of care that a responsible driver would have employed under the same circumstances and the result of his conduct was the accident complained of: see *Olgilvie v. Donkin*, [1949] 1 W.W.R. 439 (B.C. C.A.); *Brennan v. Sabatier* (1970), 75 W.W.R. 752, 16 D.L.R. (3d) 234 (Alta. C.A.); *Engler v. Rossignol* (1975), 10 O.R. (2d) 721, 64 D.L.R. (3d) 249 (C.A.); *McCulloch v. Murray*, [1942] S.C.R. 141, [1942] 2 D.L.R. 179, per Duff C.J.C. at p. 145; and *Walker v. Enders*, [1955] S.C.R. 103, [1955] 2 D.L.R. 66.

Counsel for the appellant argues that the learned trial judge used the wrong test in arriving at his conclusion that the appellant was grossly negligent. She points out that a mere *departure* from the standard of care is not the proper test. In the oft-repeated and universally accepted words of Duff C.J.C. in *McCulloch v. Murray, supra,*[1] at p. 145:

> All these phrases, gross negligence, wilful misconduct, wanton misconduct, imply conduct in which, if there is not conscious wrong doing, there is a *very marked departure* from the standards by which responsible and competent people in charge of motor cars habitually govern themselves. [The italics are mine.]

While it is true that the learned trial judge referred only to a *departure* from the standard of care, he did specifically cite cases in which the proper test is enunciated. I cannot come to any other conclusion than that he had in mind and applied the test set out in those cases.

It is further argued by counsel for the appellant that if the proper test is applied the conduct of the appellant does not fall within the ambit of "a very marked departure from the standards by which responsible and competent people in charge of motor cars habitually govern themselves."

That an appellate court is in as good a position as was the trial judge in deciding whether or not a driver was grossly negligent has been confirmed in *Walker v. Coates*, [1968] S.C.R. 599, 64 W.W.R. 449, 68 D.L.R. (2d) 436, and in *Brennan v. Sabatier, supra.* In *Walker v. Coates* Ritchie J. of the Supreme Court of Canada said at p. 456.

> I appreciate that this is an appeal in which neither the trial judge nor the appellate division of the supreme court of Alberta was prepared to draw an inference of gross negligence, but no question arises as to the veracity of the

witnesses and this is accordingly a case which is governed by the language used by Lord Halsbury in *Montgomerie & Co. v. Wallace-James,* [1904] A.C. 73 at 75, which was affirmed by the Privy Council in *Dom. Trust Co. v. New York Life Ins. Co.,* [1919] A.C. 254 at 257. Lord Halsbury said, in part: "where no question arises as to truthfulness, and where the question is as to the proper inference to be drawn from truthful evidence, then the original tribunal is in no better position to decide than the judges of an Appellate Court."

In my judgment the circumstances surrounding this accident, including the appellant's acknowledgment that he was aware of the dangerous situation and the warning he received from the respondent before he made the final attempt to ascend the hill, are such that a finding that the appellant was grossly negligent is justified.

The learned trial judge dealt with the question of *volenti non fit injuria*[2] and, relying upon the decision of the Supreme Court of Canada in *Lehnert v. Stein,* [1963] S.C.R. 38, 40 W.W.R. 616, 36 D.L.R. (2d) 159, said this:

> On the facts of the case at bar the plaintiff, although apprehensive, decided to stay in the vehicle during each attempt to go up the hill. In doing so she may have accepted some degree of physical risk but at no time did she communicate in any way, either expressly or by implication, to the defendant that she would not hold him responsible for the legal consequences that might flow from any accident that might be caused by his negligence.

The judgment in *Lehnert v. Stein, supra,* expressly approves of the principles governing the defence of *volenti non fit injuria* set forth by Mr. Glaville Williams in his work *Joint Torts and Contributory Negligence* (1951). In that text, at p. 296, the author points out that there is a distinction to be made between *physical* risk, which is the risk of damage in fact, and *legal* risk, which is the risk of damage in fact for which there will be no redress in law. He writes [p. 308]:

> To put this in general terms, the defence of *volens* does not apply where as a result of a mental process the plaintiff decides to take a chance but there is nothing in his conduct to show a waiver of the right of action communicated to the other party. To constitute a defence, there must have been an express or implied bargain between the parties whereby the plaintiff gave up his right of action for negligence.

• • •

In my respectful view the learned trial judge was correct, on the facts of the present case, to reject the defence of *volenti non fit injuria* for the reasons given in his judgment.

In finding that the respondent was not contributorily negligent the learned trial judge said:

> Shortly after the rainfall started, the plaintiff suggested that they leave because the hill would become slippery; she was assured by the defendant that his four-wheel drive Jeep would go anywhere. Later on, after the first attempt to climb the hill, she pointed out the fact that farther up, the road sloped off to the

right into a steep gully and suggested that they abandon the vehicle and walk home. Her advice was ignored by the defendant. Although she remained in the vehicle the circumstances do not necessarily lead to the conclusion that she voluntarily assumed the risk involved in the attempt to climb the hill. I do not find, on the part of the plaintiff, that she "did not, in her own interest, take reasonable care of herself and contributed, by this want of care, to her own injury", to use the language of Viscount Simon in *Nance v. B.C. Elec. Ry.*, [1951] A.C. 601, 2 W.W.R. (N.S.) 265, [1951] 3 D.L.R. 705, adopted by Kellock J. in *Car & Gen. Ins. Corpn. v. Seymour, supra*, at p. 332. The plaintiff found herself in a somewhat intimidating situation, seated between the defendant and her husband in the vehicle and realizing that her suggestions for the safety of all of them were being ignored.

This finding is, in my respectful view, inconsistent with that portion of his judgement wherein the learned trial judge deals with the defence of *volens* and says: "On the facts of the case at bar the plaintiff, although apprehensive, decided to stay in the vehicle during each attempt to go up the hill. In doing so she may have accepted some degree of physical risk."

The evidence makes it abundantly clear that the respondent was aware she was exposing herself to physical risk in continuing to ride in the appellant's motor vehicle. She had several opportunities to get out of the vehicle. She was within easy walking distance of her home and she knew the area well. Notwithstanding the assurances of the appellant that his vehicle would go anywhere and the conduct of her husband in continuing to ride in the vehicle, I am of the view that she did not, in the face of the risks known to her, take the precautions for her own safety that a reasonable person in those circumstances would have taken.

The question of the contributory negligence of a passenger in a motor vehicle is, of course, related to the defence of *volenti non fit injuria* in that the knowledge and the assumption of physical risk by the passenger is of paramount importance. The Supreme Court of Canada considered *volenti non fit injuria* and contributory negligence in *Car & Gen. Ins. Corpn. v. Seymour, supra*. In that case it was held that the defence of *volens* was not established but that the passenger was contributorily negligent to the extent of 25 per cent. In affirming the judgment of the Nova Scotia Court of Appeal Kellock J., after finding that the defence of *volens* had not been established, said at pp. 332-33:

> The result is, as was the view of the court below, that the present is a case of contributory negligence on the part of the plaintiff, who did not in her own interest take reasonable care of herself and contributed, by this want of care, to her own injury, to adopt the language of Viscount Simon delivering the judgment of the Judicial Committee in *Nance v. B.C. Elec. Ry. [supra]*. The plaintiff had full opportunity to leave the car while it was stopped at Ingramport and she then had the knowledge of the facts and an appreciation of the risk to herself in continuing, which the learned trial judge has above described.

In my judgment the above quotation describes a situation strikingly similar to the position and conduct of the respondent in the present case. The learned trial judge, in my respectful view, put too much emphasis upon the assurances given to the respondent by the appellant and upon the so-called "intimidation" of the circumstances. He ignored his previous findings that she "may have accepted some degree of physical risk". I find that the respondent was contributorily negligent and that such negligence was a cause of the injuries she suffered. I fix the degree of her negligence at 25 per cent.

[ed: The Court of Appeal then discussed the quantum of damages at some length and concluded that respondent should be awarded Special Damages of $14 400 and General Damages of $108 800 for a total of $123 200 less 25% for Contributory Negligence.]

NOTES

1.  Supra *means above: in other words, these cases were cited earlier in this decision.*

2.  *"Volenti non fit injuria"* is literally translated as "the willing cannot be harmed." In a legal sense, it means that those who consent cannot suffer damages which are recoverable in law.

# C. Occupational Liability

## Panko v. Simmonds et al.

*[1983] 3 W.W.R. 158*
*B.C. Supreme Court*
*December 2, 1982*

MCKAY J.: The plaintiff seeks damages against the defendant law firm and against the defendant Johnsen, an associate of that firm, for negligence in the handling of a real estate transaction.

[ed: The facts of this case can be summarized as follows: The plaintiff was 68 years of age, unschooled, unsophisticated and spoke with a pronounced accent. In an effort to give her daughter and son-in-law some financial help, she agreed to sign a transfer of her property to them so that they could arrange a small loan:

To accomplish this, the plaintiff attended at the office of the defendant solicitor who had been retained by the son-in-law to prepare the transfer documents. At the meeting with the plaintiff, the defendant did not explain the legal effect or significance of the document nor did he ask any questions of the plaintiff. Once the transfer had been effected the son-in-law and daughter mortgaged the property for $100 000 which ultimately resulted in foreclosure proceedings being started.]

Another matter of interest is with respect to the daughter Veronica. She had been examined prior to trial under R. 28[1] by counsel for the defendant. She said, in that examination, that she had no idea of why they had gone to Mr. Johnsen's office. She was called as a witness for the plaintiff and testified that she had lied on the R. 28 examination—that she was well aware that the object in going to Mr. Johnsen's office was to have the property transferred to her and her husband. She said that she could not bring herself to tell her mother how they had duped her. At trial she tried to maintain that she did not know that the document she signed on the 17th was a mortgage for $100 000. She was not telling the truth—she received independent legal advice prior to signing the mortgage. As already indicated I am satisfied that the plaintiff was vaguely aware that she was transferring her interest in the property to her daughter and son-in-law but expected to get it back after the "small loan" had been repaid.

The defendant Johnsen owned a duty of care to the plaintiff: see *Tracy v. Atkins* (1979), 16 B.C.L.R. 223, 11 C.C.L.T. 57, 105 D.L.R. (3d) 632, a decision of our Court of Appeal. Counsel for the defendant concedes that this was so. In that case the learned Chief Justice, who delivered the judgment of the court, had this to say [pp. 227-28]:

> The principal issue in this appeal is whether a duty of care was owed to the plaintiffs by the solicitor. In my opinion such a duty did arise. It arose in two ways:
>
> (1) As Lord Wilberforce put it in *Anns v. Merton London Borough Council*, [1978] A.C. 728 at 751-52, [1977] 2 All E.R. 492 (H.L.):
>
> "Through the trilogy of cases in this House—*Donoghue v. Stevenson*, [1932] A.C. 562 (H.L.), *Hedley Byrne & Co. v. Heller & Partners*, [1964] A.C. 465, [1963] 2 All E.R. 575 (H.L.), and *Dorset Yacht Co. v. Home Office*, [1970] A.C. 1004, [1970] 2 All E.R. 294, the position has now been reached that in order to establish that a duty of care arises in a particular situation, it is not necessary to bring the facts of that situation within those of previous situations in which a duty of care has been held to exist. Rather the question has to be approached in two stages. *First one has to ask whether, as between the alleged wrongdoer and the person who has suffered damage there is a sufficient relationship of proximity or neighbourhood such that, in the reasonable contemplation of the former, carelessness on his part may be likely to cause damage to the latter—in which case a prima facie duty$^2$ of care arises.*" [The italics are Nemetz C.J.B.C.'s].
>
> Not in every case will a solicitor be in a relationship of such proximity with an opposing party as was the case here. In the circumstances of this case, the solicitor undertook to carry out all the conveyancing including work that would ordinarily be done by the vendor's solicitor, such as registration of the mortgage back. By undertaking to do so, he placed himself in the position of dealing with the plaintiffs' interests at a time when he knew or ought to have known that the plaintiffs were or might by relying on him to protect those interests. In the circumstances of this case, he placed himself in "a sufficient relationship of proximity" that he incurred a duty of care towards the plaintiffs. He should have been alerted to the possibility of harm arising from various features of this transaction:...

Further on in the reasons he had this to say [p. 229]:

> I agree with the learned trial judge, who also found the duty of care to be imposed upon a solicitor who knows that he is acting for both parties, or is the only solicitor involved, in circumstances such as here. The defendant knew or should have known the effect of Ruling 1, "Acting for both sides", issued by the Law Society of British Columbia of which society he was a member. The ruling reads in part:
>
> "Where a solicitor is asked to act both for the vendor and the purchaser in a property transaction or in any other matter where a conflict of interest between two clients could arise, he should in all cases inform both parties that he is acting for both, obtain their consent to do so, and advise them that if a conflict of interest arises which cannot be resolved he cannot continue to act for both

parties in the matter nor will he be able to act for either.

"Where a solicitor acts for both parties with their consent, he should raise all issues which may be of importance to either of the parties and explain the legal effect of these issues. After giving such explanation, he may then take joint instructions from the parties as to the course to be followed.

"It is recommended, however, that in most cases the solicitor advise one of the parties to obtain independent legal advice."

It is the position of counsel for the defendant that the only duty cast on the solicitor was to ensure that the plaintiff appreciated that she was transferring the property to her daughter and son-in-law. He says further that even if she had been sent to another solicitor for independent advice the advising solicitor need only satisfy himself that she appreciated that title was passing. I do not agree that the duty is so limited.

The circumstances were such that warning lights should have been flashing.
1. The instructions for the transfer were given to the solicitor by the son-in-law. The plaintiff took no part in those instructions. That being so, the solicitor was unable to assess the plaintiff's appreciation of what was going on.
2. It should have been obvious to the solicitor that the plaintiff was an elderly, unschooled and unsophisticated person.
3. The property was valued at $160 000 but no money was to change hands.
4. The relationship of the parties was known to the solicitor. It is unfortunately not at all uncommon for sons and daughters to take advantage of elderly parents—particularly in the transferring of property.

The solicitor, faced with the above, should have immediately been alerted to the possibility that the plaintiff was either about to do something that was foolish and contrary to her best interests or that she was being defrauded by an unscrupulous daughter and son-in-law. Even the most rudimentary questioning would have elicited that the plaintiff merely wanted to assist her son-in-law in the arranging of a "small loan" and that she never contemplated the complete and final transferring of her home—at most the transferring, in her mind, was to have been for a limited period. She never contemplated the possibility of a mortgage of $100 000 on property which she still considered to be hers.

The solicitor undertook the responsibility of effecting the conveyance and he should have known that the plaintiff was relying on him to protect her interest. He failed to recognize the obvious danger signals. He failed to follow the ruling of the Law Society as to the responsibilities of a solicitor in a transaction such as this. He breached his duty to the plaintiff and liability must follow.

Counsel advised that, assuming liability, they were agreed as to the amount of damages. They asked for liberty to apply in the event of any problem. There will be judgment accordingly.

NOTES

1. *R. 28—refers to Rule 28 of the B.C. Supreme Court Rules which permits pre-trial examination of the parties to the case.*
2. Prima facie *duty—see General Explanatory Notes—Part 4.*

# Elliott et al. v. Ron Dawson and Associates (1972) Ltd. et al.

*(1982) 139 D.L.R. (3d) 323*
*B.C. Supreme Court*
*July 12, 1982*

HINDS J.: The plaintiffs sued the defendants in contract and in negligence for alleged incorrect advice given to the male plaintiff by the defendant Margaret DeCou, an employee of Ron Dawson & Associates, a division of Dawson & Dawson Consultants Ltd. (hereinafter called the defendants), in connection with luggage insurance included in a tenants' property insurance policy obtained by the plaintiffs from the defendants. Both counsel agreed that the action can be decided on the basis of the claim being founded in negligence rather than on breach of contract, and I shall therefore consider the claim on that basis. This action involves the determination of the standard of care to be exercised by an insurance agent in advising its client on coverage included in an insurance policy issued through such agent.

The male plaintiff had obtained insurance policies of various kinds from the defendants for some years prior to 1979. In August, 1979, he attended at the defendants' office and arranged through Mrs. DeCou to obtain a tenants' property insurance policy covering the furniture and furnishings owned by him and the female plaintiff, both of whom were shown as insureds on the policy issued by INA Insurance Company of Canada (hereinafter called INA). He obtained through Mrs. DeCou, at that time, or shortly thereafter, four other insurance policies insuring two boats, a trailer and furniture in storage.

In March 1980, the plaintiffs planned to get married and to take a honeymoon trip to Europe. The male plaintiff purchased airline tickets through the British Columbia Automobile Association and, at that office, was advised to purchase luggage insurance. Instead of purchasing luggage insurance from that organization the male plaintiff attended upon Mrs. DeCou and advised her of the planned trip and that he had been advised to get luggage insurance. I accept the evidence of Mr. Elliott that Mrs. DeCou told him that they did not need to purchase additional luggage insurance because they were covered to the full face value of their tenants' policy, namely, the sum of $15 000.

The plaintiffs were married and departed on their European trip. Whilst in Rome on April 19, 1980, the plaintiffs' luggage was stolen from the locked trunk of their rented car.

Immediately upon his return to Vancouver, the male plaintiff attended upon Mrs. DeCou on May 5, 1980, and reported the loss and gave her a list of the stolen items, having a value of $5257.40. According to the evidence of Mr. Elliott, which I accept, Mrs. DeCou told him that it was a good thing that they were insured through INA because other insurance companies had a limitation clause of 10% on the face value of the policy.

On May 8, 1980, Mr. Elliott read his policy and discovered a limitation clause which purported to limit the liability of the insurer to the sum of $1000 "on all personal property lost, damaged or destroyed by theft or attempt thereat while located at a locked vehicle while away from the described premises".

On May 9th Mr. Elliott telephoned Mrs. DeCou, and I accept his evidence that she seemed shocked and surprised and told him she would telephone INA. She did so and telephoned Mr. Elliott and told him that the $1000 limitation was in effect. On June 17th he received through the defendants a cheque from INA for $1000. The male plaintiff attempted, without success, to negotiate a settlement with the defendants for the balance of the claim, and eventually commenced these proceedings on August 21, 1980.

The evidence revealed that the plaintiffs could have purchased luggage insurance through the B.C. Automobile Association for $2,000 each, and that most insurance companies which issue tenants' property policies had a limitation in their policies of 10% of the face value of the policy, or $1500, whichever was the lesser, in connection with loss of personal property occurring away from the scheduled address of the tenant's abode.

In *Fine's Flowers Ltd. et al. v. General Accident Ass'ce Co. of Canada et al.* (1974), 49 D.L.R. (3d) 641 at p. 647, 50 O.R. (2d) 137, Frazer J. quoted from the decision in *Menna v. Guglietti et al.* (1969), 10 D.L.R. (3d) 132 at pp. 136-7, [1970] 2 O.R. 146, [1970] I.L.R. 1-308, where Grant J. had stated:

In *Halsbury's Laws of England*, 3rd ed., vol. 22, pp. 47-8, para. 80, it is stated:
"A person who, voluntarily and without any kind of consideration, promises to procure an insurance is not liable to an action for nonfeasance,[1] because there is no consideration for his promise; but if he in fact enters upon the performance of his undertaking, he is legally bound to use due care and skill. All agents, whether paid or unpaid, skilled or unskilled, are under a legal obligation to exercise due care and skill in performance of the duties which they have undertaken, a greater degree of care being required from a paid than from an unpaid, and from a skilled than from an unskilled, agent. The question in all such cases is whether the act or omission complained of is inconsistent with that reasonable degree of care and skill which persons of ordinary prudence and ability might be expected to show in the situation and profession of the agent."

At p. 648 it was stated by Fraser J. that the foregoing quotation from *Halsbury* appeared under the heading of marine insurance, but at p. 180, para. 347, of the same volume of *Halsbury* it was stated that the same basic principles were applicable to other insurance.

Later, on p. 647, Fraser J. continued to quote from the judgment of Grant J. in the *Menna* case. I find the following quotation to be apt in the circumstances of this case:

> Thus he was obliged to service the contract of insurance and if, during the lifetime of the policy, anything further was required to be done to retain it as a protection to the plaintiff, the defendant was duty bound to perform that service.

In the *Fine's Flowers Ltd.* case Fraser J. found the insurance agent Ault, Kinney, Campbell & Gallichan Limited liable to the plaintiff for failing to insure the plaintiff against loss arising out of a breakdown, in freezing weather, of a water pump which caused the heat in a large commercial greenhouse to be shut off, thereby damaging a valuable crop of commercial flowers. He found liability on the basis of breach of contract, on the basis of negligence and on the basis of breach of equitable duty. On appeal to the Ontario Court of Appeal (81 D.L.R. (3d) 139, 17 O.R. (2d) 529, [1978] I.L.R. 1-937) Estey C.J.O. (as he then was) upheld the decision of the trial court on the basis that the defendant was negligent and was in breach of equitable duty. Wilson J.A. (as she then was), with whom Blair J.A. concurred, upheld the decision of Fraser J. on the basis that the defendant was liable for breach of contract.

In considering whether or not Mrs. DeCou was negligent, I take into account a number of factors. The male plaintiff had acquired and paid for the tenants' policy through her. She was not an inexperienced agent. She is a mature person and had worked for the defendant for seven years selling general insurance. Since August 1981, she has been employed as school principal for Canadian Career Centre Ltd., a company which retrains people in particular fields. That suggests that she is a person of competence and her demeanour before me was that of a woman of sincerity and ability. Unfortunately, when Mr. Elliott inquired on her concerning the luggage coverage under his tenants' policy, she did not check the policy and, instead, gave him incorrect advice. If she had given him correct advice I am satisfied on the evidence of Mr. Elliott that he would have purchased additional insurance to cover the luggage of himself and his bride. In my view, the omission of Mrs. DeCou to give correct advice, or her act of giving incorrect advice, was inconsistent with the degree of care and skill which an experienced insurance agent of ordinary prudence and ability should have been expected to have rendered in the foregoing circumstances. Those factors lead me to conclude that she was negligent, and her employers (the defendants) are equally responsible for her negligence.

Counsel for the defendants submitted that, if the defendants were found liable in negligence, the male plaintiff was contributorily negligent in failing to read his own insurance policy before he left for Europe. In connection with that argument the following comment of Insley C.J.N.S. in *Reid v. Traders General Ins. Co. et al.* (1963), 41 D.L.R. (2d) 148 at p. 154, is noted: "I doubt that one assured in a hundred reads a policy on receiving it".

In *Okanagan Mainline Real Estate Board v. Canadian Indemnity Co. et al.* (1968), 70 D.L.R. (2d) 516 at p. 524, 66 W.W.R 257 at p. 265, [1969] I.L.R. 1-252 [reversed on other grounds 71 W.W.R 669, [1970] I.L.R. 1-316; affirmed 16 D.L.R. (3d) 715, [1971] S.C.R. 493, [1971] 1 W.W.R. 289], Brown J. referred to the foregoing comment of the former Chief Justice of the Nova Scotia Supreme Court and stated:

> With respect, I emphatically agree and I wish to add that people simply do not read things that they are asked to sign by those they have every right to trust, such as one's own lawyer, banker, or insurance agent. Otherwise business forms being what they are in prolixity[2] and obscurity, everyday commercial dealings would be intolerably impeded.

In my view, those comments are even more applicable to documents delivered for retention, such as insurance policies, than they are to documents submitted for signature.

 ˙ A perusal of the INA policy (ex. 1) issued to the plaintiffs through the defendants reveals that it has four additional pages stapled in a confusing manner to the original printed form of the contract. The original printed form of the contract sets out the statutory conditions and, in addition, there are numerous other sections dealing with coverage, exclusions, limitations, a tenants' coverage insert form, a replacement cost on contents form (which was not completed), a mandatory endorsement, a valuable personal articles endorsement coverage insert form, an additional provisions section, a section dealing with comprehensive personal liability and medical payments to others with various exclusions and conditions applicable thereto, a section dealing with general provisions applicable to the entire policy and, finally, a section headed "voluntary compensation for resident's employees". It was suggested by counsel for the defendants that it was a simple contract which should have been readily understandable to the male plaintiff. It may be readily under-standable to a person experienced in the insurance industry but I am not prepared to hold that it was a document which was readily understandable by an ordinary mortal citizen. Even if Mr. Elliott had read — or indeed had studied — the policy, it would be reasonable to assume that he would have contacted his agent for expert clarification and advice on the policy. It is apparent that he would have received from Mrs. DeCou the same advice she gave him in March, 1980. Consequently, his failure to read his policy before he contacted her would not have affected the advice he received. I am there-fore not persuaded that Mr. Elliott can be found responsible for contributory negligence in any degree.

Counsel for the defendants did not specifically agree with the correctness of the plaintiffs' estimate of the value of the lost articles in the sum of $5257.40. However, he did not specifically disagree with that estimate and in argument I gained the impression that he conceded that if liability was found against the defendants it should be in that amount less the $1000 received by the plaintiffs from INA and less any percentage of contributory negligence to which the plaintiffs could be found responsible.

The plaintiffs will have judgment in the sum of $4257.40 jointly and severally[3] against all the defendants except Ron Dawson & Associates (1972) Ltd. which, it became clear as the evidence unfolded, was not involved in the subject-matter of this litigation. The plaintiffs are entitled to interest under the *Court Order Interest Act,* R.S.B.C 1979, c. 76,[4] at the rate of 16% per annum from June 17, 1980, to the date hereof on the sum of $4257.40.

The plaintiffs are entitled to costs against all of the defendants except Ron Dawson and Associates (1972) Ltd. The action against that defendant is dismissed without costs.

NOTES

1. Nonfeasance *means inaction or a failure to do something.*
2. Prolix *means unduly long and verbose.*
3. Joint and several liability *means that each party is liable for the whole debt.*
4. *This Act permits the Court in its discretion to award interest from the time that the writ of summons was filed to begin the case up to the time that the judgment is issued. It serves to discourage defendants from contesting clearly losing cases in order to have use of the money during the lengthy period of the time the matter is before the courts.*

# Haig v. Bamford et al.

*(1976) 72 D.L.R. (3d) 68*
*Supreme Court of Canada (on appeal from Saskatchewan)*
*April 1, 1976*

DICKSON, J.: This appeal concerns the liability of an accountant to parties other than his employer for negligent statements. The Court is asked to decide whether there was in the relationship of the parties to the appeal such kind or degree of proximity as to give rise to a duty of care owed by the respondents to the appellant. The damages involved are not large but the question raised is of importance to the accounting profession and to the investing public.

# I

In October, 1961, Siegfried Scholler and his brother entered into partnership under the firm name of Scholler Brothers Millwork in the City of Moose Jaw. The firm made cabinets and other furniture and also undertook contracts for interior woodwork. The partnership was dissolved in December, 1962, and from then until February, 1964, Siegfried Scholler carried on the business as sole proprietor. In early 1964, following a fire, Saskatchewan Economic Development Corporation (Sedco) agreed to advance Scholler $34 000 for the purpose of establishing a plant to undertake millwork and the manufacture of furniture in Moose Jaw, conditional upon incorporation of the sole proprietorship. Scholler Furniture & Fixtures Ltd. (the Company) was incorporated and the sole proprietorship came to an end. Scholler was an excellent workman but poor financial planner. He evinced a compulsive urge to expand the business of the Company with the result that by January, 1965, a serious shortage of working capital became apparent. Scholler approached Sedco for a further loan of $20 000 which was approved, contingent upon (i) production of a satisfactory audited financial statement of the Company for the period from date of incorporation, February 10, 1964 to March 31, 1965, and (ii) the infusion of $20 000 of equity capital.

Instructions were issued to the firm of R. L. Bamford & Co. (the accountants), of whom the respondents (defendants) were partners, to prepare the required financial statement and Scholler began a search for an outside investor. He made it known to the accountants that he was seeking an investor. The trial Judge, MacPherson, J., made a crucial finding, not disturbed by the Court of Appeal for Saskatchewan, that the accountants knew, prior to completion of the financial statement, dated June 18, 1965, at the root of the present litigation, that the statement would be used by Sedco, by the bank with whom the Company was doing business, and by a potential investor in equity capital.

The manager of Sedco, a Mr. Wiltshire, helped Scholler in his search for a potential investor, and, with the consent of Scholler, showed a copy of the financial statement to his friend, the plaintiff Haig, who had been looking for a "likely opportunity". Haig discussed the statement with his bank manager and with a chartered accountant. The bottom line of the statement showed that the operations of the Company were profitable; the potential was promising; a $20 000 loan from Sedco and $20 000 of equity money would provide necessary working capital. Influenced by these considerations Haig, an experienced businessman, purchased in mid August, 1965, shares in the capital stock of the Company for $20 075 and guaranteed the bank loan to the extent of $20 000. He became president; Scholler became vice-president and operating head. All looked well: there was ample work for the Company as the Saskatchewan liquor laws had recently been altered to permit mixed drinking and the formerly all-male beer parlours were being upgraded. But something was wrong. Notwithstanding the addition of $40 000 in capital, which enabled trade creditors to be paid, within a very short time the Company was again troubled by serious cash shortage. The accountants were consulted and investigation soon disclosed the source of the trouble: a $28 000 prepayment received by the Company in March, 1965, on two contracts from the Robert Simpson Regina Limited, upon which work had not started, had been treated as if the work had been completed and the moneys earned. The $28 000 had been credited to revenue by the Company's book-keeper rather than shown as a liability. The accountants had failed to spot the error. On Haig's instructions a new financial statement, dated Stepternber 29, 1965, was prepared by the accountants for the period February 10, 1964 to March 31, 1965, in which the $28 000 prepayment was removed from revenue and shown under liabilities as "deferred revenue—progress advance". In the result, the position as certified by the accountants and the true position of the accounts were as follows:

|  | Position as certified by Accountants (June 18, 1965 statement) | True position (Sept. 29, 1965 statement) |
|---|---|---|
| Sales | $186 603.64 | $158 603.64 |
| Gross Profit | 80 896.50 | 52 896.50 |
| Net Profit before tax | 26 590.31 | (1994.25) |
| Net profit after tax | 20 717.04 | nil |
| Surplus | 21 321.04 | 600.00 |

Instead of making a profit in the period, as shown by the June statement, the Company had suffered a loss: instead of buying into a thriving business, as the financial statement of June 18, 1965, would have suggested, Haig bought into a distressed enterprise which never showed a profit. During the six months from March 31, 1965 to August 31, 1965, a net loss of $21 460.10 was sustained. By early December, the Company had reached the limit of its bank line of credit. To meet the payroll Haig made a further investment of $2500, matched by a like amount from Sedco. A meeting of creditors, held late in the month, decided against further support and at year-end, the Company ceased business. Haig lost the $20 075 paid for shares, the loan of $2500, and $6500 under the bank guarantee. He sued the accountants, the Company and Scholler to recover $20 075 and $2500 but later discontinued against Scholler and the Company.

## II

The trial Judge found negligence on the part of the accountants. I think the evidence amply supports that finding. From the expert testimony, it appears that the engagement of a chartered accountant can be on either an "audit" basis or a "non-audit" basis. If the engagement is for an audit, the accountant does what he considers necessary by way of auditing procedures, tests and verifications of internal controls, accounts, and records to permit him to give an opinion on the financial statements. In an engagement of the non-audit type, the accountant merely helps the client in the preparation of the financial statement on terms which permit him to accept the client's records and dispense with the checks and verifications expected in an audit. The product of an audit is a financial statement accompanied by an auditor's report expressing an opinion on the financial statement. At the end of a non-audit engagement, a financial statement is issued to which is appended a comment in which the auditor expressly disclaims responsibility.

The accountant had performed non-audit accounting services for the partnership, Scholler Brothers Millwork, in 1963, and at that time the financial statement was accompanied by a letter, the final paragraph of which disclaimed in these words:

> The attached financial statements have been prepared from the books and records and information furnished, without audit, and we are not able to express an opinion as to the financial position of the business.

In the present proceedings the accountants sought to maintain that their engagement in 1965 was of a non-audit nature and that they were performing for the Company a mere accounting function in preparing a financial statement from the client's financial records. This submission fails for two reasons: first, Sedco required audited financial statements as a condition of the further loan to the Company and the evidence is clear that the statements were prepared in satisfaction of that condition, as the accountants had been advised by Sedco and the Company; secondly, the auditor's report follows the format generally recognized as appropriate for audited financial statements.

●  ●  ●

In representing to have done an audit when they were aware that an audit had not been done, in my view the accountants were guilty of a serious dereliction of duty. This was more than honest blunder or error in judgment.[1]

### III

I come then to the question whether Haig, who received the defective financial statements, and relied on them to his loss, has a right of recovery from the accountants. Mr. Justice MacPherson at trial allowed recovery [32 D.L.R. (3d) 66, [1972] 6 W.W.R. 557]. He held that the accountants knew or ought to have known that the statements would be used by a potential investor in the Company; although Haig was not, in the Judge's words, "in the picture", when the statement was prepared, he must be included in the category of persons who could be foreseen by the accountants as relying on the statement and therefore the accountants owed a duty to Haig. The Judge applied a test of foreseeability.

The majority in the Court of Appeal for Saskatchewan (Hall, J.A., with Maguire, J.A., concurring) came to a different conclusion [53 D.L.R. (3d) 85, [1974] 6 W.W.R. 236]. The majority of the Court were satisfied that the accountants had been informed by Scholler that the statement would be used to induce persons to invest equity capital in the Company. Mr. Justice Hall noted that at that time there was no specific person or group in mind as a prospective investor or investors; Haig was not known to the accountants and they were not aware that he had been shown a copy of the statement or that he had been approached to invest in the Company. The learned Justice of Appeal observed that the financial statement had been given to Haig without the knowledge of Scholler or the Company. With respect, I think this observation is in error as Wiltshire testified that before giving a copy of the statement to Haig he had received Scholler's permission. The point is, however, of no great consequence for if the accountants, at the request of the Company prepared financial statements for distribution to, *inter alia,* potential investors, and furnished the Company with copies for that purpose, I fail to understand why the Company or anyone on its behalf would be expected to seek permission of the accountants before releasing a copy. The learned Justice of Appeal concluded that the accountants owed Haig the duty to be honest but that they were not liable to him for negligence and, since the misrepresentation contained in the financial statement was the result of an "honest blunder", the appeal should be allowed with costs. The dissenting Judge, Mr. Justice Woods, was of opinion that the accountants knew that the statement was intended for a special purpose, a purpose that would affect the economic interests of those from whom Scholler would attempt to secure funds and that Haig fell within this category. The outcome of this appeal rests, it would seem, on whether, to create a duty of care, it is sufficient that the accountants knew that the information was intended to be disseminated among a specific group or class, as Mr. Justice MacPherson and Mr. Justice Woods would have it, or whether the accountants also needed to be apprised of the plaintiff's identity, as Mr. Justice Hall and Mr. Justice Maguire would have it.

## IV

The increasing growth and changing role of corporations in modern society has been attended by a new perception of the societal role of the profession of accounting. The day when the accountant served only the owner-manager of a company and was answerable to him alone has passed. The complexities of modern industry combined with the effects of specialization, the impact of taxation, urbanization, the separation of ownership from management, the rise of professional corporate managers, and a host of other factors, have led to marked changes in the role and responsibilities of the accountant, and in the reliance which the public must place upon his work. The financial statements of the corporations upon which he reports can affect the economic interest of the general public as well as of shareholders and potential shareholders.

With the added prestige and value of his services has come, as the leaders of the profession have recognized, a concomitant and commensurately increased responsibility to the public. It seems unrealistic to be oblivious to these developments. It does not necessarily follow that the doors must be thrown open and recovery permitted whenever someone's economic interest suffers as the result of a negligent act on the part of an accountant. Compensation to the injured party is a relevant consideration but it may not be the only relevant consideration. Fear of unlimited liability for the accountant, "liability in an indeterminate amount for an indeterminate time to an indeterminate class", was considered a relevant factor by Mr. Justice Cardozo in *Ultramares Corp. v. Touche et al.* (1931), 255 N.Y. 170. From the authorities, it appears that several possible tests could be applied to invoke a duty of care on the part of accountants vis-à-vis third parties: (i) foreseeability of the use of the financial statement and the auditor's report thereon by the plaintiff and reliance thereon; (ii) actual knowledge of the limited class that will use and rely on the statement; (iii) actual knowledge of the specific plaintiff who will use and rely on the statement. It is unnecessary for the purposes of the present case to decide whether test (i), the test of foreseeability, is or is not a proper test to apply in determining the full extent of the duty owed by accountants to third parties. The choice in the present case, it seems to me, is between test (ii) and test (iii), actual knowledge of the limited class or actual knowledge of the specific plaintiff. I have concluded on the authorities that test (iii) is too narrow and that test (ii), actual knowledge of the limited class, is the proper test to apply in this case.

THE ENGLISH AUTHORITIES

I do not think one can do better than begin with Lord Denning's dissent in *Candler v. Crane Christmas & Co.*, [1951] 1 All E.R. 426 (C.A.), which later found favour in *Hedley Byrne & Col., Ltd. v. Heller & Partners, Ltd.*, [1963] 2 All E.R. 575 (H.L.). After identifying accountants as among those under a duty to use care, Lord Denning, in answer to the question "To whom do these professional people owe this duty?" said, at p. 434:

> They owe the duty, of course, to their employer or client, and also, I think to any third person to whom they themselves show the accounts, or to whom they know their employer is going to show the accounts so as to induce him to invest money or take some other action on them. I do not think, however, the duty can be extended still further so as to include strangers of whom they have heard nothing and to whom their employer without their knowledge may choose to show their accounts.

and

> The test of proximity in these cases is: Did the accountants know that the accounts were required for submission to the plaintiff and use by him?

One can find some support in these words for the position taken by the majority in the Saskatchewan Court of Appeal but their effect is tempered by what appears later in the judgment, at p. 435:

> It will be noticed that I have confined the duty to cases where the accountant prepares his accounts and makes his report for the guidance of the very person in the very transaction in question. That is sufficient for the decision of this case. I can well understand that it would be going too far to make an accountant liable to any person in the land who chooses to rely on the accounts in matters of business, for that would expose him, in the words of Cardozo, C.J., in *Ultramares Corpn. v. Touche* (174 N.E. 444), to
> "...liability in an indeterminate amount for an indeterminate time to an indeterminate class."
> Whether he would be liable if he prepared his accounts for the guidance of a specific class of persons in a specific class of transactions, I do not say. I should have thought he might be, just as the analyst and lift inspector would be liable in the instances I have given earlier.

In the case at bar, the accounts were prepared for the guidance of a "specific class of persons", potential investors, in a "specific class of transactions", the investment of $20 000 of equity capital. The number of potential investors would, of necessity, be limited because the Company, as a private company, was prohibited by s. 3(1)(o)(iii) of the *Companies Act* of Saskatchewan, R.S.S. 1965, c. 131, from extending any invitation to the public to subscribe for shares or debentures of the Company.

One comes then to the *Hedley Byrne* case. The argument was raised in that case that the relationship between the parties was not sufficiently close to give rise to any duty. Lord Reid dealt with that argument in these words, at p. 580:

> It is said that the respondents did not know the precise purpose of the inquiries and did not even know whether National Provincial Bank, Ltd. wanted the information for its own use or for the use of a customer: they knew nothing of the appellants. I would reject that argument. They knew that the inquiry was in connection with an advertising contract, and it was at least probable that the information was wanted by the advertising contractors. It seems to me quite immaterial that they did not know who these contractors were: there is no suggestion of any speciality which could have influenced them in deciding whether to give information or in what form to give it. I shall therefore treat this as if it were a case where a negligent misrepresentation is made directly to the person seeking information, opinion or advice, and I shall not attempt to decide what kind or degree of proximity is necessary before there can be a duty owed by the defendant to the plaintiff.

In the present case the accountants knew that the financial statements were being prepared for the very purpose of influencing, in addition to the bank and Sedco, a limited number of potential investors. The names of the potential investors were not material to the accountants. What was important was the nature of the transaction or transactions for which the statements were intended, for that is what delineated the limits of potential liability. The speech of Lord Morris of Borth-y-Gest in *Hedley Byrne* included this observation, at p. 588:

> It is, I think, a reasonable and proper inference that the bank must have known that the National Provincial were making their inquiry because some customer of theirs was or might be entering into some advertising contract in respect of which Easipower, Ltd., might become under a liability to such customer to the extent of the figures mentioned. The inquiries were from one bank to another. The name of the customer (Hedleys) was not mentioned by the inquiring bank (National Provincial) to the answering bank (the bank); nor did the inquiring bank (National Provincial) give to the customer (Hedleys) the name of the answering bank (the bank). These circumstances do not seem to me to be material. The bank must have known that the inquiry was being made by someone who was contemplating doing business with Easipower Ltd. and that their answer or the substance of it would in fact be passed on to such person.

● ● ●

In summary, Haig placed justifiable reliance upon a financial statement which the accountants stated presented fairly the financial position of the Company as at March 31, 1965. The accountants prepared such statements for reward in the course of their professional duties. The statements were for benefit and guidance in a business transaction, the nature of which was known to the accountants. The accountants were aware that the Company intended to supply the statements to members of a very limited class. Haig was a member of the class. It is true the accountants did not know his name but, as I have indicated earlier, I do not think that is of importance. I can see no good reason for distinguishing between the case in which a defendant accountant delivers information directly to the plaintiff at the request of his employer (*Candler's* case and *Glanzer's* case), and the case in which the information is handed to the employer who, to the knowledge of the accountant, passes it to the employer who, to the knowledge of the accountant, passes it to members of a limited class (whose identity is unknown to the accountant) in furtherance of a transaction the nature of which is known to the accountant. I would accordingly hold that the accountants owed Haig a duty to use reasonable care in the preparation of the accounts.

I am of the view, however, that Haig cannot recover from the accountants the sum of $2500 which he advanced to the Company in December, 1965, because by that time he was fully cognizant of the true state of affairs. It cannot be said that the sum was advanced in reliance upon false statements. Haig had the choice of advancing additional money in the hope of saving his original investment. He chose to make a further advance, but the choice was his and not one for which the accountants are liable.

I would allow the appeal, set aside the judgment of the Court of Appeal for Saskatchewan and reinstate the judgment of MacPherson, J., subject only to disallowance of the claim of $2500, the whole with costs in this Court and in the Courts below.

NOTES

1. *The mistake apparently arose because the student who did the work had left the firm before the opinion of the senior partner was given. This work admittedly fell well short of an audit, and was insufficient to enable the opinion to be given. The trial judge felt that had the student not left, the senior partner would have discovered these facts.*

# PART TWO

# Contracts

# A. Offer and Acceptance

## Re Viscount Supply Co. Ltd.

*[1963] 1 O.R. 640*
*Ontario Supreme Court in Bankruptcy*
*March 4, 1963*

[ed: The offer occurred when an official of Viscount Supply Co. Ltd. telephoned from Ontario to Montreal and requested Atwater Lumber to supply a quantity of redwood. Later, this offer was accepted when Atwater Lumber telephoned from Montreal to Ontario to inform Viscount that the wood was available. The chief issue in this case was whether the contract was made in the Province of Quebec or in Ontario, in order to determine the law which would govern. Viscount Supply had gone bankrupt. If the claim were to be settled by Quebec law, Atwater could recover the two cars of lumber which had been sold to it; if, however, Ontario law applied, Atwater could not obtain the cars but would merely be a general creditor for the price of the lumber.]

SMILY J.: The learned Registrar relying on the judgment in the case of *Re Hudson Fashion Shoppe Ltd., Ex p. Royal Dress Co., [1926] 1 D.L.R. 199, 58 O.L.R. 130, 7 C.B.R. 68,* found that the contract was a Quebec contract and that the law of Quebec applied. It would appear that the learned Registrar was of the view that the contract was made in the Province of Quebec because he denied to follow the case of *Entores Ld. v. Miles Far East Corp., [1955] 2 Q.B. 327.* He does not expressly say so but says, in his opinion, the decision in the case of *Re Hudson Fashion Shoppe Ltd.* is applicable and should be followed. However, the facts in the case of *Re Hudson Fashion Shoppe Ltd.* are somewhat different from those in the case at the bar. In the former, as stated by Riddell J.A., at p. 200 D.L.R., p. 132 O.L.R., p. 70 C.B.R., the facts were:

> An order is taken in Ontario for certain goods at a certain price, deliverable at a time mentioned, on terms f.o.b.[1] at Montreal, price payable at Montreal, the

order "subject to approval of the firm" at Montreal, a card sent by the firm acknowledging the receipt of the order and saying, "Same will receive our usual prompt attention," the goods shipped and accepted as though received without further communication under the order, what must necessarily follow as to the place of making the contract, the *locus contractus.*[2]

After discussing some of the authorities as to whether the card was a sufficient acceptance of the contract, Riddell J.A., at p. 201 D.L.R., p. 133 O.L.R., p. 71 C.B.R., went on to say:

> It is wholly unnecessary in the present case to decide whether, had the card stood alone, a contract was concluded; it might mean only that the Royal Dress Co. (the appellants) would think it over and decide, but it must certainly mean that they would make up their mind before delivery, and that delivery would show that their mind had been made up approving the order. There is no pretence that they did not fulfill their contract. The delivery f.o.b. at Montreal was a completion of the contract on their part, and there can be no doubt that the contract was a Quebec contract.

It will be noted that the contracts in the case at bar are f.o.b. Toronto and delivery was made in Toronto. If the judgment in the *Entores Ld. v. Miles Far East Corp.* case is followed, I think it must be said the contracts in the instant case were made in Ontario.

This case held that [headnote and at p. 335]: "...although where a contract made by post acceptance is complete as soon as the letter of acceptance is put into the post box, where a contract is made by instantaneous communication, e.g., by telephone, the contract is complete only when the acceptance is received by the offeror, since the ordinary rule of law is, that the acceptance must be communicated to the offeror and the place where the contract is made is the place where the offeror receives the notification of acceptance by the offeree."

The judgment is that of the English Court of Appeal composed of Lord Justices Denning, Birkett and Parker. I think it would be useful to quote from the reasons for judgment of their Lordships. Denning L.J., says at pp. 332-3:

> The question for our determination is where was the contract made?
>
> When a contract is made by post it is clear law throughout the common law countries that the acceptance is complete as soon as the letter is put into the post box, and that is the place where the contract is made. But there is no clear rule about contracts made by telephone or by Telex. Communications by these means are virtually instantaneous and stand on a different footing.
>
> The problem can only be solved by going in stages. Let me first consider a case where two people make a contract by word of mouth in the presence of one another. Suppose, for instance, that I shout an offer to a man across a river or a courtyard but I do not hear his reply because it is drowned by an aircraft flying overhead. There is no contract at that moment. If he wishes to make a contract, he must wait till the aircraft is gone and then shout back his acceptance so that I can hear what he says. Not until I have his answer am I bound. I do not agree with the observations of Hill J. in *Newcombe v. De Roos* (1859), 2 E. & E.271.

Now take a case where two people make a contract by telephone. Suppose, for instance, that I make an offer to a man by telephone and, in the middle of his reply, the line goes "dead" so that I do not hear his words of acceptance. There is no contract at that moment. The other man may not know the precise moment when the line failed. But he will know that the telephone conversation was abruptly broken off; because people usually say something to signify the end of the conversation. If he wishes to make a contract, he must therefore get through again so as to make sure that I heard. Suppose next, that the line does not go dead, but it is nevertheless so indistinct that I do not catch what he says and I ask him to repeat it. He then repeats it and I hear his acceptance. The contract is made, not on the first time when I do not hear, but only the second time when I do hear. If he does not repeat it, there is no contract. The contract is only complete when I have his answer accepting the offer.

And Birkett L.J., at p. 335 says: "The ordinary rule of law, to which the special considerations governing contracts by post are exceptions, is that the acceptance of an offer must be communicated to the offeror, and the place where the contract is made is the place where the offeror receives the notification of the acceptance by the offeree."

At p. 336, Parker L.J., says:
As was said by Lindley L.J. in *Carlill v. Carbolic Smoke Ball Co.*, [1893] 1 Q.B. 256, 262; 9 T.L.R. 124: "Unquestionably, as a general proposition, when an offer is made, it is necessary in order to make a binding contract, not only that it should be accepted, but that the acceptance should be notified." In the same case Browen L.J., said, [1893] 1 Q.B. 256, 269: "One cannot doubt that, as an ordinary rule of law, an acceptance of an offer made ought to be notified to the person who makes the offer, in order that the two minds may come together. Unless this is done the two minds may be apart, and there is not that consensus which is necessary according to English law—I say nothing about the laws of other countries—to make a contract." Accordingly, as a general rule, a binding contract is made at the place where the offeror receives notification of the acceptance, that is where the offeror is.

Williston in his *Selections from Williston's Treatise on the Law of Contracts, 1938, pp. 97-8, §82,* had this to say:

By analogy to the law governing contracts by mail, it is held that a contract by telegraph may be completed by delivering a telegram dispatch of acceptance for transmission at the receiving office of the telegraph company. The same analogy has been suggested in case of contracts by telephone. The analogy between the telegraph and mail is by no means perfect, and the telephone presents still greater differences from the mail...In neither case is anything tangible sent by the offeree and received by the offeror. In the use of the telegraph the risks of error are also vastly greater than in the case of mail. Nevertheless if the assumption is sound that the offeror has impliedly assented to the starting of a telegram on its way, as the only necessary manifestation of acceptance, the result of the cases is unquestionably right. The difficulty is because of the probability that such an assumption is based on a legal fiction. So far as the telegraph is concerned, however, the law is doubtless settled; but a contract by telephone presents quite as great an analogy to a contract made where the parties are orally addressing one another in each other's presence. It has not been suggested in the latter case that the offeror takes the risk of hearing an acceptance addressed to him. The contrary has been held. If then it is essential that the offeror shall hear what is said to him, or at least be guilty of some fault in not hearing, the time and place of the formation of the contract is not when and where the offeree speaks, but when and where the offeror hears, or ought to hear, and it is to be hoped that the principles applicable to contracts between parties in the presence of each offer will be applied to negotiations by telephone. This view has been adopted by the Restatement of Contracts.

• • •

Therefore, in my opinion, the contracts are Ontario contracts and the Ontario law is the proper law thereof, particularly, and with respect, as Riddell J.A., said "so far as the ownership of property and its results are concerned." Having come to this conclusion, I do not think any useful purpose would be served by considering the law of Quebec with respect to the rights and obligations of the parties thereunder so as to determine the other branches of the respondent claimant's case. In fact it might be presumptuous to rule on a point of Quebec law where it is unnecessary to do so to decide the matter.

The appeal should be allowed with costs and the appeal of the claimant from the disallowance of its claim should be dismissed. As…the question of the *locus contractus* in the circumstances such as existed here seems not to have been previously considered by the Ontario Courts, there will be no costs of the appeal to the Registrar excepting as directed by him in the order appealed from.

*Appeal allowed.*

NOTES

1. *F.o.b. is the abbreviation for "free on board", signifying that the seller will pay for shipping the goods to the point named. From that point on, the buyer is responsible for the costs of freight, insurance, etc.*
2. *"Locus contractus" means the "place of the contracting".*

# Livingstone v. Evans

*[1925] 4 D.L.R. 769*
*Alberta Supreme Court*
*October 30, 1925*

WALSH J.: The defendant, Thomas J. Evans, through his agent, wrote to the plaintiff offering to sell him the land in question for $1800 on terms. On the day that he received this offer the plaintiff wired his agent as follows: "Send lowest cash price. Will give $1600 cash. Wire." The agent replied to this by telegram as follows: "Cannot reduce price." Immediately upon the receipt of this telegram the plaintiff wrote accepting the offer. It is admitted by the defendants that this offer and the plaintiff's acceptance of it constitute a contract for the sale of this land to the plaintiff by which he is bound unless the intervening telegrams above set out put an end to his offer so that the plaintiff could not thereafter bind him to it by his acceptance of it.

It is quite clear that when an offer has been rejected it is thereby ended and it cannot be afterwards accepted without the consent of him who made it. The simple question and the only one argued before me is whether the plaintiff's counter-offer was in law a rejection of the defendant's offer which freed him from it.

*Hyde v. Wrench,* 3 Beav. 334 (49 E.R. 132) a judgment of Lord Langdale M.R. pronounced in 1840 is the authority for the contention that it was. The defendant offered to sell for £1000. The plaintiff met that with an offer to pay £950 and (to quote from the judgment) "he thereby rejected the offer previously made by the Defendant. I think that it was not afterwards competent for him to revive the proposal of the Defendant, by tendering an acceptance of it."

*Stevenson v. McLean,* 5 Q.B.D. 346, 49 L.J.Q.B. 701, 42 L.T. 897, 28 W.R. 916, a later case relied upon by Mr. Grant is easily distinguishable from *Hyde v. Wrench* as it is in fact distinguished by Lush J. who decided it. He held that the letter there relied upon as constituting a rejection of the offer was not a new proposal but a mere enquiry which should have been answered and not treated as a rejection but the learned Judge said that if it had contained an offer it would have likened the case to *Hyde v. Wrench.*

*Hyde v. Wrench* has stood without question for 85 years. It is adopted by the text writers as a correct exposition of the law and is generally accepted and recognized as such. I think it not too much to say that it has firmly established it as a part of the law of contracts that the making of a counter-offer is a rejection of the original offer.

The plaintiff's telegram was undoubtedly a counter-offer. True, it contained an inquiry as well but that clearly was one which called for an answer only if the counter-offer was rejected. In substance is said, "I will give you $1600 cash. If you won't take that wire your lowest cash price." In my opinion it put an end to the defendant's liability under his offer unless it was revived by his telegram in reply to it.

The real difficulty in the case, to my mind, arises out of the defendant's telegram "cannot reduce price." If this was simply a rejection of the plaintiff's counter-offer it amounts to nothing. If, however, it was a renewal of the original offer it gave the plaintiff the right to bind the defendant to it by his subsequent acceptance of it.

With some doubt I think that it was a renewal of the original offer or at any rate an intimation to the plaintiff that he was still willing to treat on the basis of it. It was, of course, a reply to the counter-offer and to the enquiry in the plaintiff's telegram. But it was more than that. The price referred to in it was unquestionably that mentioned in his letter. His statement that he could not reduce that price strikes me as having but one meaning, namely, that he was still standing by it and, therefore, still open to accept it.

There is support for this view in a judgment of the Ontario Appellate Division which I have found, *In re Cowan and Boyd,* 49 O.L.R. 335, 61 D.L.R. 497. That was a landlord and tenant matter. The landlord wrote the tenant offering a renewal lease at an increased rent. The tenant replied that he was paying as high a rent as he should and if the landlord would not renew at the present rental he would like an early reply as he purposed buying a house. To this the landlord replied simply saying that he would call on the tenant between two certain named dates. Before he called and without any further communication between them the tenant wrote accepting the landlord's original offer. The county Court Judge before whom the matter first came held that the tenant's reply to the landlord's offer was not a counter-offer but a mere request to modify its terms. The Appellate Division did not decide that question though from the ground on which it put its judgment it must have disagreed with the Judge below. It sustained his judgment, however, on the ground that the landlord's letter promising to call on the tenant left open the original offer for further discussion so that the tenant had the right thereafter to accept it as he did.

The landlord's letter in that case was, to my mind, much more unconvincing evidence of his willingness to stand by his original offer in the face of the tenant's rejection of it than is the telegram of the defendant in this case. That is the judgment of a very strong Court, the reasons for which were written by the late Chief Justice Meredith. If it is sound, and it is not for me to question it, *a fortiori*[1] must I be right in the conclusion to which I have come.

I am, therefore, of the opinion that there was a binding contract for the sale of this land to the plaintiff of which he is entitled to specific performance. It was admitted by his counsel that if I reached this conclusion his subsequent agreement to sell the land to the defendant Williams[2] would be of no avail as against the plaintiff's contract.

There will, therefore, be judgment for specific performance[3] with a declaration that the plaintiff's rights under his contract have priority over those of the defendant Williams under his. The plaintiff will have his costs as agreed by the case.

NOTES

1. *"A fortiori" means "even more so". As used here the judge is saying that if the decision in* Cowan and Boyd *is correct then with stronger reason his present conclusion is right.*

2. *Williams was the person to whom Evans had subsequently sold the property that he had already sold to Livingstone.*

3. *Specific performance is an order made by a court requiring a party to carry out the terms of the contract, in this instance convey the land to the purchaser.*

# Williams and Wilson Ltd. v. OK Parking Stations Ltd.

*(1970) 17 D.L.R. (3rd) 243*
*County Court of York, Ontario*
*December 8, 1970*

GROSSBERG CO.CT.J. (orally): On the evening of March 9, 1968, between 8:00 and 9:00 o'clock, Alec Churchman left or parked a motor vehicle, owned by the plaintiff,[1] in the parking lot of the defendant, situated on the north side of Front St. in the City of Toronto near the Royal York Hotel. Churchman and his wife and two friends had proceeded in the motor vehicle on the Gardiner Expressway. After making an exit from the expressway, Churchman proceeded northerly and then westerly on Front St. He turned right at the entrance to the parking lot and entered the parking lot. He was requested by an attendant, who was the defendant's employee, to leave the keys in the motor vehicle so the attendant could park or move the vehicle. He was given a ticket, in the form of ex.5, which he placed in his pocket. Churchman testified he did not read the ticket.

Exhibits 1, 2 and 3 demonstrate the location of the only sign on the premises. There was no sign on the attendant's hut or office. The sign did not directly face one as he entered the lot, but is on a north-south direction as shown on a photograph. There was no sign on any wall. Churchman testified he did not observe or read the sign. This was the first occasion that he parked a motor vehicle on this lot.

When Churchman returned between 1:00 [and] 1:30 a.m. the following morning, the motor vehicle could not be found. The attendant said to him, "I thought you drove out two hours ago."

The president of the defendant company testified that there was only one entrance to the lot, which was also the only exit. He said that a vehicle should not be permitted to make an exit without a parking ticket being produced or surrendered. It was necessary to pass the attendant's hut on entering or on leaving the parking lot. The plaintiff's vehicle was found by the police about two weeks later in a damaged condition.

I believe Churchman. I find he was an entirely credible witness, notwithstanding his interest in the litigation. I find he did not read the ticket or the sign, nor was his attention called to the printing on the ticket or to the sign.

I find as a fact that the defendant did not do what was reasonable, or take reasonable steps or measures, to bring to the attention of Churchman the notice purporting to limit its liability as a custodian for hire. The location of the only sign on the premises was not designed to meet the eyes of one entering the lot from Front St. There was no sign on the hut to meet one's eye when one approached the hut. There were no signs on the walls. The portion of the sign purporting to restrict liability is at the bottom of five or six portions of the sign shown on the photographs. The portion purporting to restrict liability was not in a position which would attract attention. It was dark when Churchman entered the lot. There was apparently only one attendant on the lot upon the entry.

I find, in the circumstances of this case, that it was not reasonable for Churchman to have seen the alleged limiting condition either on the sign or on the ticket.

In *Samuel Smith & Sons Ltd. v. Silverman,* [1961] O.R. 648, 29 D.L.R. (2d) 98, the parking-lot owner was held not liable for damage to a motor vehicle which had been parked. In that case, the ticket was printed in bold black type. In the *Smith v. Silverman* case there were four lighted signs on the premises.

I have made a study of many of the authorities, commencing with *Spooner v. Starkman,* [1937] O.R. 542, [1937] 2 D.L.R. 582, to the present, in Ontario and in other Provinces and in England. Each case depends on its own facts. I, of course, yield complete obedience to the law in *Smith v. Silverman,* but, in my opinion, the facts in the case which I have to decide are different.

Counsel for the plaintiff further submitted that the defendant could not rely on the alleged exclusion of liability because there was a breach of, or deviation from, a fundamental term of the contract of bailment.

I have already stated that the evidence of the defendant was that there was an obligation on the defendant's employee not to permit a vehicle to make an exit from the lot unless the appropriate ticket was produced or surrendered. In my opinion, permitting the vehicle to leave the lot without the production or surrender of the appropriate ticket was a breach of a fundamental term of the bailment. A breach of this term of the contract of bailment was a breach going to the root of the contract. Accordingly, I hold that the defendant cannot take refuge behind the alleged exclusion of liability.

Counsel for the defendant sought to answer the submission of counsel for the plaintiff by contending that, if the attendant actually or personally delivered the vehicle to someone without surrender or production of the ticket, there might be a breach of fundamental term. He argued, however, that, where the vehicle is otherwise removed, there was not a fundamental breach. I disagree. The fundamental breach or deviation from the contract of bailment in this case is permitting the vehicle to exit through the only exit without obtaining production of or surrender of the ticket. I do not accept that there must be an actual delivery of the vehicle by the attendant to an unauthorized person as contended by counsel for the defendant. The pendulum in the cases has begun to swing to a denial of protection by an alleged exclusionary clause where there has been a fundamental breach or deviation from the contract of bailment.

I mention some of the authorities on this point which I have considered. In *Bontex Knitting Works, Ltd. v. St. Johns Garage*, [1943] 2 All E.R. 690, affirmed in the Court of Appeal, [1944] 1 All E.R. 381, it was held that the defendant could not invoke an exclusionary clause in the contract of bailment where there was a breach of time for delivery. The note of the decision of the Court of Appeal refers to breach of an implied term. In *Alexander v. Railway Executive*, [1951] 2 All E.R. 442, a cloak-room official permitted an unauthorized person to have access to goods. It was held that the defendant could not rely on an exclusionary clause in the ticket.

I also refer to *Mendelssohn v. Normand, Ltd.*, [1969] 2 All E.R. 1215. The parking ticket in that case contained a term that the garage proprietors would not accept responsibility for any loss sustained by the vehicle, its accessories or contents, however caused. The bailor was requested to leave his keys in the vehicle. The attendant promised to lock the car, but he failed to do so. Luggage was stolen from the car. It was held that the garage was liable. The Court held that the deviation from the contract of bailment prevented the bailee from relying upon the exclusionary clause.

I also refer to *Anson's Law of Contract, 22nd ed.*, p. 156 and following, particularly p. 158, which was cited by counsel for the plaintiff.

I hold, in the circumstances of this case, that the contract of bailment included the term, which I earlier mentioned, and that deviation from such term was a breach of a fundamental term which went to the root of the contract of bailment.

It would have been a simple matter to have checked any vehicle making an exit to ensure that a ticket was surrendered or produced. I also comment that the parking-lot attendant was not called as a witness.[2]    The plaintiff is entitled to succeed on either of the two points I have referred to.

The parties have agreed that the damages be assessed at $508.58. for the reasons given, the plaintiff will have judgment for $508.58 and costs.

I thank both counsel who submitted their arguments with conspicuous clarity and brevity.

*Judgment for plaintiff.*

NOTES

1. *This is why the company, and not Mr. Churchman, was the plaintiff: the loss through damage to the car (the amount of which was not in issue) was that of the company.*

2. *A judge is entitled to draw conclusions from the unexplained failure of a party to call an obvious witness. Here the suggestion is that the evidence of the parking-lot attendant would not have been favourable to the arguments put forward by the defendant.*

# 296349 Ontario Ltd. v. Halton Board of Education

*(1980) 126 D.L.R. (3d) 439*
*Ontario High Court of Justice*
*September 10, 1980*
*Upheld on Appeal*

O'LEARY J. (orally): In this action the plaintiff claims for the return of a $30 000 deposit and the defendant counterclaims for its alleged loss because of the refusal of the plaintiff to complete a real estate transaction, both claims being related to a tender submitted by the plaintiff to buy property from the defendant.

On July 12, 1977, Gary Walker, the president of and sole shareholder of the plaintiff, learned from a real estate agent that the defendant was offering to sell by way of tender a vacant parcel of land that it had acquired as a school site in the Town of Oakville. The agent told Mr. Walker that there was a registered plan of subdivision for the parcel of land containing approximately 32 lots.

The defendant had advertised that it would accept sealed tenders to buy the property up until 3:00 p.m., July 12, 1977. It never held out to anyone that there was a plan of subdivision for the property.

Mr. Walker somehow acquired a tender to purchase form and an offer to purchase form prepared by the defendant, completed them on behalf of the plaintiff and had them delivered to the defendant at 2:33 p.m. on July 12, 1977. The offer to purchase stipulated that the plaintiff was prepared to buy the land for $600 000....

It is to be noted that there is nothing in the tender to purchase or the offer to purchase which expressly says that the offer to purchase is irrevocable until a certain date or event.

The various tenders received by the defendant were opened in public by

one of its servants on July 12, 1977, commencing about 3:05 p.m. The various
tenders received were as follows:

| | |
|---|---|
| Manley, Grant & Camisso | $600 000[1] |
| Angleo A. Serafini | 381 000 |
| The Fox Group | 365 684 |
| Bot Holdings Limited | 357 000 |
| Ticino Building Corporation | 350 000 |
| Morris Rosen Construction Limited | 316 500 |
| Tonewood Construction Limited | 304 912 |
| Abraham Nerenberg | 201 000 |

On the morning of July 13, 1977, Mr. Walker found out that his company's
bid was the highest bid and that is bid exceeded that of the next highest
bidder by $219 000. After making some investigation he discovered that the
parcel of land in question had not been subdivided by a plan of survey but
rather, that it was a parcel of undivided land. He instructed his solicitor to
withdraw the offer to purchase that had been made by the plaintiff.

After witnessing the opening of the various tenders on the afternoon of
July 12, 1977, Mr. Bruce Lindley, the superintendent of business and finance
for the Halton Board of Education, recommended in writing to the members
of the board that the board accept the tender of the plaintiff company.

On the evening of July 14, 1977, the board met in private in committee of
the whole between 7:00 p.m. and 8:15 p.m. Mr. Lindley placed before the
board both a list of those who tendered on the property and the amount of
each offer made and his recommendation that the plaintiff's offer be accepted.
No member of the board commented adversely on Mr. Lindley's recommendation.

Commencing at 8:15 p.m. on July 14, 1977, the board held a formal open
meeting. While that meeting was in progress, but before the board dealt with
the sale of the land in question, at approximately 8:30 p.m., a letter from the
plaintiff's solicitors was delivered to Mr. Lindley. That letter reads:

> We are solicitors for 296349 Ontario Limited and in accordance with our said
> client's instructions we do hereby deliver to you a formal rescission of our
> client's Tender Offer to Purchase dated July 12,
>    It is our opinion that the Offer to Purchase made by our client was clearly
> not irrevocable and accordingly is capable of revocation at any time prior to
> formal acceptance in accordance with the provisions of Clause 2 of the "Tender
> to Purchase".
>    We accordingly request immediate return of our client's deposit in the
> amount of $30 000.00.

Attached to the solicitor's letter was a document under the seal of the
plaintiff company which stated:

> We refer you to that Tender to Purchase dated July 12, 1977 and the Offer to
> Purchase attached thereto also dated July 12, 1977 whereunder we offered to

purchase part of Lots 28 and 29, Concession 3, S.D.S., Town of Oakville, Regional Municipality of Halton.
We do hereby revoke and rescind the said Tender and Offer to Purchase and accordingly same shall hereafter be of no further force or effect.
DATED at Toronto this 13th day of July, 1977.

The person who delivered the letter of revocation asked for, but was denied by the board, permission to speak to the board.

The contents of the letter and the notice of revocation attached were, however, brought to the attention of the board. The board thereafter considered Mr. Lindley's recommendation and passed a resolution accepting the plaintiff's offer.

The next day the board executed its acceptance of the offer and a copy of the accepted offer was mailed with a covering letter to the plaintiff's solicitors.

The plaintiff refused to complete the purchase of the property and the defendant sold the property to the second highest bidder for $381 000; that is to say, $219 000 less the amount the plaintiff had offered to pay for it.

The plaintiff takes the position that on any of three grounds it was entitled to refuse to complete the transaction. Firstly, it is submitted that the offer to buy the land could be revoked at any time prior to its acceptance by the defendant.

As mentioned earlier, neither the tender to purchase, the offer to purchase nor any other document states expressly that the offer to purchase is irrevocable until a certain date or event.

The defendant submits that bearing in mind that the defendant had advertised that it would accept offers to buy the property by way of sealed tenders up until 3:00 p.m. on July 12, 1977, and that the tender to purchase document provides, in part, "We understand that...we shall be notified of acceptance or rejection by registered mail not later than 30 days after the last date for receiving tenders...", the Court should conclude that the offer to purchase could not be revoked by the plaintiff for 30 days after July 12, 1977. It is the defendant's position that any other interpretation of these words just quoted would make nonsense of the whole tendering process and would permit anyone who found out after the tenders were opened that his bid was too high to withdraw his bid.

The argument seems to be founded on the premise that some special obligation attaches to one who submits a tender, not to withdraw that tender after the tenders have been opened and have become public. In this case the defendant argues that since the plaintiff has stated in the tender to purchase document that the defendant shall notify it of acceptance or rejection of the offer within 30 days of July 12, 1977, that therefore the plaintiff has agreed to keep the offer open for acceptance for that period.

I am not aware that special rules apply when offers are submitted by way of tender. I consider the words of Stewart J. in *Hamilton Bd. Ed. v. U.S.F. & G.*, [1960] O.R. 594, apt on this point. He said at p. 599:

Counsel further submits that such a tender cannot be withdrawn or, in the alternative, that it cannot be withdrawn for a reasonable time. In my view, the advertisement to tender cannot be regarded as anything more than an offer to treat and the tender itself must be regarded as the offer. There is nothing in the documents, which have been filed, nor any evidence of trade custom to the contrary, and therefore I am of opinion that the ordinary principle applies, namely, that any offer may be withdrawn prior to acceptance in the absence of a provision to the contrary.

The plaintiff was then entitled to withdraw its offer before acceptance unless it agreed otherwise.

In my view the words, "We understand that...we shall be notified of acceptance or rejection by registered mail not later than 30 days after the last day for receiving tenders", do no more than stipulate how notice of acceptance is to be sent to the plaintiff and that the offer to buy will terminate after 30 days without the plaintiff taking any steps to terminate it. The clause is silent as to whether the plaintiff can terminate the offer at any earlier date, and in my view then the ordinary rule applies that it can be terminated at any time before it is accepted.

To take away the ordinary right to revoke an offer prior to acceptance of it, requires clear and unequivocal language.

In *Fraser et al. v. Morrison et al.* (1958), 12 D.L.R. (2d) 612, 25 W.W.R. 326, the plaintiffs made an offer to purchase in writing which contained these words: "...should this offer not be accepted within ten days, this deposit is to be refunded to me". The offer was withdrawn before acceptance and the plaintiffs brought an action to recover the deposit. The learned trial judge dismissed the action.

On appeal, Schultz J.A. of the Manitoba Court of Appeal stated, at p. 615:

> Unless there was an acceptance by the owner (the defendants), and that acceptance had been communicated to the plaintiffs, there could be no contract. The 10-day clause did not make the offer to purchase binding on the plaintiffs for that period because the offer in terms did not so provide and in any case there was no consideration given on which such a contract could be founded. The plaintiffs, therefore, had the right to cancel their offer to purchase any time before acceptance by the defendants had been communicated to them. Their right to cancel under such circumstances is thus stated by Pollock in his work on Contract, 13th ed., p. 20:
>
> "An offer may be revoked at any time before acceptance, but not afterwards.
>
> "For before acceptance there is no agreement, and therefore the proposer cannot be bound to anything. So that even if he purports to give a definite time for acceptance, he is free to withdraw his proposal before that time has elapsed. He is not bound to keep it open unless there is a distinct contract to that effect, founded on a distinct consideration."

I should say that in the case before me the plaintiff executed[2] the tender to purchase document and affixed its seal thereto and so if it had agreed that the offer to purchase was irrevocable it would have been bound to that agreement even though the defendant had given no consideration for it. However, I conclude that the plaintiff did not agree or state that its offer could not be revoked. The plaintiff was then entitled to and did withdraw its offer to buy on July 14, 1977, before its offer was accepted and no contract could thereafter come into existence based on that offer.

Interestingly, counsel for the defendant conceded that the plaintiff could have withdrawn its tendered offer at any time before the tenders were opened on the basis there would have been no communication of the offer to the defendant until the tender was actually opened. In my view the plaintiff submitted its offer to purchase when it delivered its tender to the defendant on July 12, 1977, and though the defendant did not know what the offer was it had, in fact, been made. If the plaintiff was entitled, as the defendant concedes, to withdraw its offer up to the moment tenders were opened, then it seems to me the defendant is conceding that at least for that period the plaintiff was entitled to revoke an offer it had made. Quite apart from any apparent concession by the defendant I have already concluded that the plaintiff could withdraw its offer not only prior to the tenders being opened but up until its offer had been accepted.

[ed: The Court then dismissed the arguments of the plaintiff relating to mistake and to the existence of a condition precedent.]

I have already concluded that no agreement of purchase and sale came into existence. It follows, then, that the plaintiff's $30 000 deposit should have been refunded. There will be judgment for the plaintiff in the amount of $30 000 and the counterclaim will be dismissed...

[ed: The plaintiff was awarded costs.]

NOTES

1. *A reasonable explanation is that Manley, Grant & Camisso were representing the plaintiff corporation either as agents or as legal counsel.*

2. *A contract is executed or completed by being signed.*

# B. Consideration

## Gilbert Steel Ltd. v. University Construction Ltd.

*(1976) 67 D.L.R. (3d) 606*
*Ontario Court of Appeal*
*April 6, 1976*

WILSON J.A.: This is an appeal from the order of Mr. Justice Pennell dismissing the plaintiff's action for damages for breach of an oral agreement for the supply of fabricated steel bars to be incorporated into apartment buildings being constructed by the defendant. The case raises some fundamental principles of contract law.

The circumstances giving rise to the action are as follows: On September 4, 1968, the plaintiff entered into a written contract to deliver to the defendant fabricated steel for apartment buildings to be erected at three separate sites referred to in the contract as the "Flavin, Tectate and University projects". The price fixed by that contract was $153 per ton for "Hard grade" and $159 per ton for "Grade 60 000". Deliveries for the Flavin and Tectate projects were completed in August, 1969, and October, 1969, respectively, and paid for at the agreed-upon prices.

Two apartment buildings calling for the supply of 3000 tons of fabricated steel were to be erected at the University site. However, prior to the defendant's notifying the plaintiff of its intention to commence construction on the first of these two buildings, the owners of the steel mill announced an increase in the price of unfabricated [sic][1] steel. They also gave warning of a further increase to come. The plaintiff approached the defendant about a new contract for the University project and a written contract dated October 22, 1969, was entered into for the supply of fabricated steel for the first building. The new price was $156 per ton for "Hard grade" and $165 per ton for "Grade 60 000". In fact this increase in price did not reflect the full amount of the initial increase, announced by the mill owners.

On March 1, 1970, while the building under construction was still far from completion, the mill owners announced the second increase in price and a further discussion took place between John Gilbert and his brother Harry representing the plaintiff and Mendel Tenenbaum and Hersz Tenenbaum representing the defendant with respect to the price to be paid for the steel required to continue the first building. It is this discussion which the plaintiff alleges resulted in a binding oral agreement that the defendant would pay $166 per ton for "Hard grade" and $178 per ton for "Grade 60 000". Although the plaintiff submitted to the defendant a written contract embodying these revised prices following their meeting, the contract was not executed. It contained, in addition to the increased prices, two new clauses which the trial Judge found had not been the subject of any discussion with the defendant but were unilaterally imported into the document by the plaintiff. The trial Judge also found, however, that the defendant agreed at the meeting to pay the increased price.

From March 12, 1970, until the completion of the first building the defendant accepted deliveries of the steel against invoices which reflected the revised prices but, in making payments on account, it remitted cheques in rounded amounts which at the date of the issuance of the writ resulted in a balance owing to the plaintiff in accordance with the invoices.

Having found on the evidence that the defendant had orally agreed to pay the increased prices, the legal issues confronting Mr. Justice Pennell was whether the agreement was legally binding upon the defendant or whether it failed for want of consideration. Counsel for the defendant submitted at the trial that past consideration is not consideration and that the plaintiff was already obliged before the alleged oral agreement was entered into to deliver the steel at the original prices agreed to in the written contract of October 22, 1969. When then was the *quid pro quo*[2] for the defendant's promise to pay more?

Counsel for the plaintiff sought to supply this omission from the evidence of Hersz Tenenbaum who, during the course of discussion which took place in September, 1970, with a view to a contract for the supply of steel for the second building at the University site, asked whether the plaintiff would give him "a good price" on steel for this building. Plaintiff's counsel argued that the promise of a good price on the second building was the consideration the defendant received for agreeing to pay the increased price on the first. The trial Judge rejected this submission and found the oral agreement unenforceable for want of consideration. In the course of his reasons for judgment the trial Judge adverted briefly to an alternate submission made by the plaintiff's counsel. He said:

> I should, in conclusion, mention a further point which was argued with ingenuity by Mr. Morphy. His contention was that the consideration for the oral agreement was the mutual abandonment of right under the prior agreement in writing. I must say, with respect, that this argument is not without its attraction for me.

On the appeal Mr. Morphy picked up and elaborated upon this submission which had intrigued the trial Judge. In launching his main attack on the trial Judge's finding that the oral agreement was unenforceable for want of consideration, he submitted that the facts of this case evidenced not a purported oral variation of a written contract which failed for want of consideration but an implied rescission of the written contract and the creation of a whole new contract, albeit oral, which was subsequently reneged on by the defendant. The consideration for this new oral agreement, submitted Mr. Morphy, was the mutual agreement to abandon the previous written contract and to assume the obligations under the new oral one. Mr. Morphy submitted to the Court for its consideration two lines of authority, the first line illustrated by the leading case of *Stilk v. Myrick* (1809), 2 Camp. 317, 170 E.R. 1168, in which the subsequent agreement was held to be merely a variation of the earlier agreement and accordingly failed for want of consideration, and the other line illustrated by *Morris v. Baron & Co.,* [1918] A.C. 1, in which the subsequent agreement was held to have rescinded the former one and was therefore supported by the mutual agreement to abandon the old obligations and substitute the new. Mr. Morphy invited us to find that the oral agreement to pay the increased price for steel fell into the second category. There was, he acknowledged, no express rescission of the written contract but price is such a fundamental term of a contract for the supply of goods that the substitution of a new price must connote a new contract and impliedly rescind the old.

It is impossible to accept Mr. Morphy's submission in face of the evidence adduced at the trial. It is clear that the sole reason for the discussions between the parties in March, 1970, concerning the supply for steel to complete the first building at the University site was the increase in the price of steel by the mill owners. No changes other than the change in price were discussed. The trial Judge found that the other two changes sought to be introduced into the written document submitted by the plaintiff to the defendant for signature following the discussions had not even been mentioned at the meeting. Moreover, although repeated references were made at trial by the Gilbert brothers to the fact that the parties had made a "new contract" in March, 1970, it seems fairly clear from the evidence when read as a whole that the "new contract" referred to was the agreement to pay the increased price for the steel, *i.e.,* the agreement which effected the variation of the written contract and not a new contract in the sense of a contract replacing *in toto*[3] the original contract of October 22, 1969.

I am not persuaded that either of the parties intended by their discussions in March 1970, to rescind their original contract and replace it with a new one. Indeed, it is significant that no such plea was made in the statement of claim which confirmed itself to an allegation that "it was orally agreed in March 1970 that the prices as set forth in the said contract [*i.e.,* of October 22, 1969] would be varied...". Accordingly, consideration for the oral agreement is not to be found in a mutual agreement to abandon the earlier written contract and assume the obligations under the new oral one.

Nor can I find consideration in the vague references in the evidence to the possibility that the plaintiff would give the defendant "a good price" on the steel for the second building if it went along with the increased prices on the first. The plaintiff, in my opinion, fell far short of making any commitment in this regard.

Counsel for the appellant put before us as an alternate source of consideration for the agreement to pay the increased price, the increased credit afforded by the plaintiff to the defendant as a result of the increased price. The argument went something like this. Whereas previously the defendant had credit outstanding for 60 days in the amount owed on the original prices, after the oral agreement was made he had credit outstanding for 60 days in the amount owed on the higher prices. Therefore, there was consideration flowing from the promise and the law does not inquire into its sufficiency. Reliance was placed by counsel on the decision of Chief Justice Meredith in *Kilbuck Coal Co. v. Turner & Robinson* (1915), 7 O.W.N. 673. This case, however, is clearly distinguishable from the case at bar, as Mr. Justice Pennell pointed out in his reasons, on the basis of the *force majeure*[4] clause which had relieved the plaintiff of its obligations under the original contract. In undertaking to supply coal despite the strike the plaintiff was unquestionably providing consideration of real substance in that case. I cannot accept counsel's contention, ingenious as it is, that the increased credit inherent in the increased price constituted consideration flowing from the promise for the promisor's agreement to pay the increased price.

The final submission put forward by counsel by the appellant was that the defendant, by his conduct in not repudiating the invoices reflecting the increase in price when and as they were received, had in effect acquiesced in such increase and should not subsequently be permitted to repudiate it. There would appear to be two answers to this submission. The first is summed up in the maxim that estoppel can never be used as a sword but only as a shield.[5] A plaintiff cannot found his claim in estoppel. Secondarily, however, it should perhaps be pointed out that in order to found an estoppel the plaintiff must show, not only that the conduct of the defendant was clearly referable to the defendant's having given up its right to insist on the original prices, but also that the plaintiff relied on the defendant's conduct to its detriment. I do not think the plaintiff can discharge either of these burdens on the facts of the case.

In summary, I concur in the findings of the trial Judge that the oral agreement made by the parties in March, 1970, was an agreement to vary the written contract of October 22, 1969, and that it must fail for want of consideration.

Argument was directed on the appeal to the question of interest, a matter not dealt with by the trial Judge. The written contract of October 22, 1969, is silent on the subject of interest although it specifies in the terms of payment "net 60 days from date of invoice." I have considered whether it is to be implied from these words that interest will be exigible if the amount owing is not paid within the 60-day period. Such meagre authority as exists on the meaning of "net" in different contexts does not appear to be helpful. Generally it has reference to the amount established after all proper expenses or deductions have been allowed for. However, it is also commonly used to mean the "rock-bottom price" from which no discount will be given. "Net" may not be an apt word to use in connection with an extension of credit but I have concluded that this is what the parties had in mind in this case. Payment could be deferred by the defendant for the 60-day period free of any sanction but after the expiry of that period, interest would be exigible. Since no rate is specified I find that interest is payable on overdue amounts at the statutory rate of 5% per annum. I attach no significance to the notation "1% per month interest on overdue accounts" on the invoices received by the defendant at the increased prices on the basis that interest cannot be imposed unilaterally in this manner.

The judgment of Pennell, J., should be varied to provide that the plaintiff shall have judgment for interest at the rate of 5% on the payments which were overdue for more than 60 days under the contract dated October 22, 1969. Subject to this variation the appeal should be dismissed with costs.

• • •

NOTES

1. *Presumably this is a slip of either tongue or pen: the context calls for "fabricated."*
2. *"Quid pro quo"—"something for something"—relates to consideration and refers here to the price paid for the promise that was obtained.*
3. *"In toto" means "in the whole" or better, "completely".*
4. *"Force majeure" means literally "superior force". As used here it refers to a clause in a contract excusing one or both of the parties from performing its promise in the event of something outside of the parties' control rendering performance difficult or impossible. In the* Kilbuck *case this was the occurrence of a strike.*
5. *That is, estoppel cannot be used as the basis to make a claim (sword) when consideration is not present, but is available as a defence (shield).*

# C. Capacity

## Wong v. Kim Yee

*(1961) 34 W.W.R. 506*
*Saskatchewan District Court*
*March 14, 1961*

POPE. D.C.J.: During the years 1957 and 1958 the plaintiff and the defendant were both attending school at Gravelbourg. They became great friends and their friendship gradually became one of romance, and they could definitely be regarded as school-day sweethearts. The defendant's home was in Moose Jaw and his father had sent him to school at Gravelbourg and gave him an allowance to pay his expenses. He says that the allowance which he received was $100 per month. Apparently he was rather extravagant and found it difficult to get along on the amount of his allowance and so from time to time he borrowed moneys from the plaintiff for various purposes.

In the fall of 1958 he enrolled at the University of Saskatchewan. He was a student at the University of Saskatchewan until Christmas, 1959, and because of his poor standing he discontinued his further studies. In the fall of 1959 he telephoned the plaintiff asking her for a loan of $1000 to purchase a car. This apparently upset her considerably and, as she says, from then on she did not have the same regard for the defendant. Their romance faded and withered and they are both now married to other individuals.

The defendant denied that he borrowed any money at all from the plaintiff. He says that any money that he did receive was given to him as a gift and he contends that he has no legal obligation to repay the various amounts which he received. The plaintiff on the other hand says that all the money which she paid to the defendant was give to him as loans and it was understood that they were such at the time the loans were made. The defendant denies, too, that he received all the payments that the plaintiff alleges were made to him; but he does admit that he received the sum of $50 to cover the cost of repairing his car, the sum of $148 to cover the cost of paying his life insurance, and the sum of $40 which the plaintiff forwarded to him while he was at the university to enable him to come to Gravelbourg to visit her; a total of $238.

The defendant also has definitely established, through the evidence of his mother, that he was under age when most of the payments were received by him, and his counsel contends that he is under no legal obligation to repay the amounts received during the time he was in his minority. He was not 21 until December 14, 1958, and all the money received by him from the plaintiff, with the exception of one payment of $15, was paid prior to that date.

The law is very definite that an infant is not bound to pay for anything other than the necessaries of life for himself and members of his family. He is not liable to repay a loan unless such loan was made to provide him with these necessaries. I am satisfied that the plaintiff did loan to the defendant all the moneys she said that she loaned him. I am satisfied, too, that he understood that the payments made to him were loans and that if there was not a definite promise to repay on each occasion, there certainly was an implied understanding between them that the amounts which the plaintiff gave to the defendant from time to time for the various things would be repaid by him when he was in a position to do so. If the defendant were as honourable as he would wish the court to believe him to be, then certainly he would have repaid some of the moneys which he admits he did receive from the plaintiff. He certainly would have done something about the first loan of $50 which was paid by the plaintiff for repair to the car. It was an obligation that certainly should have been satisfied and paid for by him. He should, too, have done something about repayment of the insurance which was paid on his life-insurance policy. He says, of course, the plaintiff talked him into paying this insurance and that he has since dropped the insurance and, accordingly, received no benefit from such payment. Certainly the plaintiff showed good judgment in advising the defendant that this insurance should be retained when he had already paid two premiums on it. If the payment that was made was the third payment, it would appear that the policy itself would have then possessed some cash surrender value.

Actually, I am of the opinion that all the moneys which were advanced by the plaintiff, amounting to $433, should have been repaid by the defendant but, unfortunately, the law does not permit an infant to bind himself legally to repay a loan unless such a loan is given for necessaries. What are necessaries? They are things which the infant requires for his living, for his health, for his education, and they must be things which a person who is an infant would be expected to require at the time such things are secured. We must, therefore, determine as to why these various loans were made by the plaintiff to the defendant, and as to whether any of them were for necessaries.

I am listing them, setting forth the purpose for which each was secured: May 28, 1958, $50 obtained for repairs to car; June 13, 1958, $20 to cover cost of a trip to Morse; June 24, 1958, $148 to cover payment of insurance premium; June 26, 1958, $10 for daily use; June 28, 1958, $10 to pay for school transfer; September 7, 1958, $110 to cover part of the cost of school books for the university; October 2, 1958, $40 to cover expenses [of] coming from Saskatoon for a visit; October 11, 1958, $30 to purchase a jacket; March 28, 1959, $15, a cash loan.

When you examine these items it would appear that there are only a few of them that could be considered as loans to cover necessaries. The repairs for the car could not be considered necessaries and, certainly, the various items covering daily use and expenses for trips of one kind or another cannot be considered necessaries either. I have given very careful consideration to the item in regard to insurance but I do not believe that any insurance which is being carried by a single man can be considered to be a necessary requirement of an infant. Even though *The Insurance Act* definitely empowers an infant to contract for life insurance, I still do not think that an insurance premium on that policy is an item that can be considered a necessary expenditure for which an infant can bind himself by way of loan, unless the infant has some obligations that make it necessary for him to have insurance.

There are, however, three items which definitely are necessaries. Any item that is properly made in connection with the education of an infant comes within the class of an expenditure for which an infant can be held liable. There are two such items, one amounting to $10 to cover the transfer fee at the Gravelbourg school, and the other amounting to $110 covering the amounts expended for school books. The third item is the amount of $30 which was loaned by the plaintiff to the defendant to pay for the jacket. And there is one other item for which the defendant is responsible, and that is the last loan made on March 18, 1959, amounting to $15, which was made at a time when the defendant had reached the age of 21 years.

In the result, therefore, I find that the defendant is responsible to the plaintiff for the following items, namely: June 28, 1958, for school transfer, $10; September 7, 1959, for school books, $110; October 11, 1958, for jacket, $30; March 28, 1959, for personal use $15; total, $165.

The defendant, of course denies that he has made any of these loans. The letter which he wrote to the plaintiff, however, on September 9, 1958, is rather significant. In the last paragraph he says in part:

> Darling, I registered yesterday morning and got nearly all my books today, mine and your hard earned money are spent like hay these days. My tuition and incidental and books alone cost me in the neighbourhood of $300.00

It will be noticed that he refers to "mine and your hard earned money" in the same paragraph dealing with the purchase of his books and other incidentals. There is no doubt in my mind but that $110 of the money which he spent buying books represented the loan made by the plaintiff to him for this purpose. I am satisfied, too, that in view of his attitude concerning the entire transaction between himself and the plaintiff, he received the other items for which I find him liable as well.

For these reasons there will, accordingly, be judgment for the plaintiff for $165 and the costs of this action.

• • •

# D. Legality of Object

## Wong et al. v. Cook

*(1979) 48 C.P.R. (2d) 78*[1]
*B.C. Supreme Court*
*June 27, 1979*

LOCKE, J.: The plaintiff Wong and the defendant Cook were once equal partners in a pick-up and delivery service which they commenced in 1973, and later incorporated so that they each held an equal number of shares. In 1975, as a result of certain personal problems, Cook sold his 50% interest in the company to the plaintiff, Gordon Wong, in an agreement in which two of the clauses were numbered 4 and 5 as follows:

> 4. The Vendor, shall not for a period of five (5) years from the date of this Agreement, directly or indirectly, in any capacity whatsoever, alone or in association with any other person, firm or corporation, or as employees, shareholders or directors of any other person, firm or corporation, complete with or engage or be financially concerned or interested in, any business similar to the business presently carried on the Company in any place in the Province of British Columbia, without the express permission in writing of the Purchaser.
> 5. The Vendor will do all reasonable acts and things to assist the Purchaser and the officers and directors of the Company in continuing and furthering the business and goodwill of the Company.

At the time of signing the agreement Cook laid it down as a condition that he be permitted to go into business at least in the City of Kamloops and, in the result, on the same day, a written consent was annexed to the agreement giving him the right to operate a bus pick-up or courier service in Kamloops, Prince George, Kelowna, Vernon, Penticton and throughout the northern interior of British Columbia.[2] The practical effect of this was to permit him to operate anywhere except the lower mainland.

After signing the agreement the defendant went to Kamloops and attempted to operate a delivery service but the business failed and he returned to Vancouver. He was rehired as a servant of the corporate plaintiff some months later and assigned to his old area, a route styled "No. 2" in the False Creek area. Twice Cook renegotiated a raise in his salary; in April of 1978, he left for good to operate a rival firm. The evidence of Wong is that within two weeks route No. 2 was decimated and the corporate plaintiff was left with only about 25% of its former business and has never really recovered. This action is for damages for breach of contract, for inducing breaches of contracts with customers, and for a permanent injunction to restrain breaches.

The pick-up and delivery business especially from buses in the lower mainland, which is where the plaintiff's business is principally carried on, is volatile in nature, and appears to depend much upon the personality and reliability of the driver of the vehicle who calls at the customer's premises, receives a bill of lading and delivers it to its appropriate destination. Personal loyalty to the driver plays a great part in building up business and customers can and do switch their business quite rapidly. There are no signed contracts with the carrier, but only an authorization given by the customer to a certain company to pick up and deliver parcels for it. From the beginning Wong was the inside or accounting man and the salesman was Cook and there is no conflict that probably 75% of the business in route No. 2 and perhaps elsewhere was built up by Cook, with the concurrence of both of them.

As stated, when Cook left for the first time after selling his interest, the business of the company was principally in the lower mainland but there were plans for expansion and indeed agencies were set up later, in Victoria, Nanaimo, Kelowna, Penticton, 100 Mile House, Williams Lake, Prince George and apparently Kamloops. It was to the most money making of all the routes handled by the company, however, that Cook was reassigned and on his return in late 1975 or early 1976, he was greeted by many of his former customers and reacquired most of them and also some new ones. He continued to service them all until he left and set up business on his own account in July of 1978, when he became what is known as an owner-driver: that is, one who under the banner of another company—in this case A-1 Bus-Lines—operates a truck he himself owns, certain bookkeeping and other expenses being paid by the employer, with the owner-driver receiving an agreed percentage of each bill of lading that he picks up. On at least two occasions prior to leaving, Cook had told Wong that he had been offered employment by A-1 at more favourable terms and threatened to leave and this resulted in his negotiating upward what he was paid by Metropolitan. Cook said he had been offered 85¢ per bill by A-1 about a year before he left but he did not take the offer because he did not believe one could make such a good deal; but after watching similar arrangements apparently being happily effectuated by two other drivers, he decided it was a valid offer and took the jump and in answer to a question in cross-examination, said that he thought he had done very well for himself.

Shortly after he returned from Kamloops, Cook apparently consulted a lawyer who, according to him, gave him a written opinion that the restrictive covenant, cl. 4, was unenforceable. He did not tell Wong this and it is apparent to me he conceived the idea that he could continue to operate in his former territory and leave when he wanted. After he left he did in fact approach substantially all Metropolitan's customers and his influence was such that 75% of them followed him to A-1.

There were either one or two conversations with Wong at the time the A-1 offers were discussed in which Wong said that Cook was bound by the clauses of the agreement. I accept Wong's testimony on this where it conflicts with Cook's, and on any other material points.

There is, however, little dispute as to the fact: Cook is apparently a devastatingly effective salesman and because of what is pleaded as breaches of the agreement, the plaintiffs have substantially lost the revenue which came from route No. 2.

The real argument in this case is legal. The Court is assigned by the recent judgment of the Supreme Court of Canada in *Elsley et al. v. J.G. Collins Ins. Agencies Ltd.* (1978), 36 C.P.R. (2d) 65, 83 D.L.R. (3d) 1, [1978] 2 S.C.R. 916, in particular at pp. 70-4 C.P.R., pp. 5-9 D.L.R., of the unanimous judgment of a seven-man Court given by Mr. Justice Dickson. I can do no better than quote a portion from pp. 70-1 C.P.R., pp. 5-6 D.L.R.,

> The principles to be applied in considering restrictive covenants of employment are well-established. They are found in the cases above-mentioned and in such familiar authorities as the *Nordenfelt* case, *Nordenfelt v. Maxim Nordenfelt Guns & Ammunition Co., Ltd.*, [1894] A.C. 535; *Mason v. Provident Clothing & Supply Co., Ltd.*, [1913] A.C. 724, and *Attwood v. Lamont*, [1920] 3 K.B. 571. Of more recent vintage: *Scorer v. Seymour-John*, [1966] 3 All E.R. 347, and *Gledhow Autoparts Ltd. v. Delaney*, [1965] 1 W.L.R. 1366. A covenant in restraint of trade is enforceable only if it is reasonable between the parties and with reference to the public interest. As in many of the cases which come before the Courts, competing demands must be weighed. There is an important public interest in discouraging restraints on trade, and maintaining free and open competition unencumbered by the fetters of restrictive covenants. On the other hand, the Courts have been disinclined to restrict the right to contract, particularly when the right has been exercised by knowledgeable persons of equal bargaining power. In assessing the opposing interests the word one finds repeated throughout the cases is the word "reasonable". The test of reasonableness can be applied, however, only in the peculiar circumstances of the particular case. Circumstances are of infinite variety. Other cases may help in enunciating broad general principles but are otherwise of little assistance.
>
> It is important, I think, to resist the inclination to lift a restrictive covenant out of an employment agreement and examine it in a disembodied manner, as if it were some strange scientific specimen under microscopic scrutiny. The validity, or otherwise, of a restrictive covenant can be determined only upon an overall assessment, of the clause, the agreement within which it is found, and all of the surrounding circumstances.
>
> The distinction made in the cases between a restrictive covenant contained in an agreement for the sale of a business and one contained in a contract of employment is well-conceived and responsive to practical considerations. A person seeking to sell his business might find himself with an unsaleable com-

modity if denied the right to assure the purchaser that he, the vendor, would not later enter into competition. Difficulty lies in definition of the time during which, and the area within which, the non-competitive covenant is to operate, but if these are reasonable, the Courts will normally give effect to the covenant.

A different situation, at least in theory, obtains in the negotiation of a contract of employment where an imbalance of bargaining power may lead to oppression and a denial of the right of the employee to exploit, following termination of employment, in the public interest and in his own interest, knowledge and skills obtained during employment. Again, a distinction is made. Although blanket restraints on freedom to compete are generally held unenforceable, the Courts have recognized and afforded reasonable protection to trade secrets, confidential information, and trade connections of the employer.

In the case of *Mason v. Provident Clothing & Supply Co., Ltd.,* [1913] A.C. 724, Lord Shaw of Dunfermline says at pp. 737-38:

> It is necessary, my Lords, to look, in the first place, at the nature of the contract itself. As to that, the diversities may be wide and the view of the law may be different as to the upholding or the scope of a covenant in restraint of personal or industrial freedom. If the contract, for instance, be for the sale of a business to another for full consideration or price, there may be elements going in the strongest degree to shew that such a contract—in so far as it restrains the vendor from becoming a rival of a business whose goodwill he has sold and which he has bargained he shall not oppose—there may be elements showing that such a contract is enforceable, and, indeed, that a declinature by the law to enforce it would amount to a denial of justice. It may clearly appear that the express view of the bargain may have been the elimination from the sphere of competition of the powerful personality of a possible rival who by the very terms of the contract had been paid for disappearing into retirement, carrying his sheaves with him. In such cases a restraint is enforced by the law.
>
> But, to use Lord Macnaghten's language in the *Nordenfelt Case* [*Nordenfelt v. Maxim Nordenfelt Guns & Ammunition Co., Ltd.* [1894] A.C. 535 at p. 565], "There is obviously more freedom of contract between buyer and seller than between master and servant or between an employer and a person seeking employment." And in my opinion there is much greater room for allowing, as between buyer and seller, a larger scope for freedom of contract and a correspondingly large restraint in freedom of trade, than there is for allowing a restraint of the opportunity for labour in a contract between master and servant or an employer and an applicant for work.

I deal immediately with the question as to whether the covenant is reasonable with reference to the public interest. There are about 50 or 60 different trucking companies in the lower mainland and about 40 of them apparently are combination pick-up and courier services, relying on accounts with the buses for varying parts of their revenue. About a dozen depend on bus traffic for a good portion of their profit margin. The Supreme Court of Canada disposed of this matter in its reasoning at p. 9 of the *Elsley* case, *supra,* by saying:

> Unless it can be said that any and every restraint upon competition is bad, I do not think that enforcement of the clause could be considered inimical to the public interest. There were twenty to twenty-two general agents in Niagara

Falls according to the evidence, as of the date of trial, employing eighty to ninety employees. There was nothing to suggest that the people of Niagara Falls would suffer through the loss, for a limited period, of the services of Elsley in the general insurance business.

That reasoning is valid here when applied to these facts.

The real question is whether the clause is reasonable between the parties: *i.e.*, has the purchaser overreached himself attempting to obtain a protection to which he was not legally entitled?

As in the *Elsley* case, the *first question* to ask is: was there a proprietary interest? The answer is yes: Wong paid $8000 for the goodwill that Cook left behind him: both parties agreed that the payment was for goodwill and not for physical assets. He therefore had a proprietary interest to be protected. *Second,* were the temporal or spatial features of the clause too broad? In a business where personal connections apparently run so strong, I see no reason to say that the five-year period is unreasonable for the protection of the purchaser. Again, I find an astonishing similarity between this and the *Elsley* case. As to space, the evidence on this was somewhat sparse though, as indicated, most of the business seems to have been in the lower mainland. Nevertheless, expansion was contemplated and did in fact take place. But it is significant that the written consent executed at the same time as the agreement, limited the area of prohibition only to the lower mainland of British Columbia. This is the area in which the plaintiffs conceived they had a proprietary interest and I think that the net effect of the province-wide prohibition in cl. 4, cut down by the consents in the annexure, gave a not unreasonable protection to ensure Wong got what he had paid for: a goodwill not to be assaulted by the formidable sales talents of Cook.

It was argued that cl. 4 was the governing clause and that the Province of British Columbia was too large an area and therefore the clause was bad *per se,* and could not be "fixed up" by consents which limited the area. It was argued that even if cl. 4 remained the same and a consent was given which permitted Cook to operate in everything but False Creek area No. 2, then this part of the contract would still be bad. I do not agree with this; businessmen make writings to construct workable contracts, and Courts should uphold them where possible. In my opinion the net effect of contract and consents makes a workable document, legal under the authorities, and should be enforced.

In considering this I have noted the point mentioned in the *Elsley* case as to the distinction between sales of business and master and servant relationship and have quoted from Lord Shaw at p. 737 of *Mason v. Provident Clothing & Supply Co. Ltd., supra.*

In the result, and for the above reasons, it is my opinion that the clause is valid and I grant a permanent injunction with damages, with which I will deal later.

There is in this case, in addition, an element of plain breach of contract, *i.e.*, of cl. 5. Even if there were no such specific clause, it expresses nothing but the common law. The 20th edition of *Chitty on Contracts* (1974), states that a former vendor may be restrained by injunction from soliciting any person who was a customer of the old firm prior to the sale; the ground of this may be either that a man may not derogate from his own grant or that the vendor has impliedly contracted not to service his former customers as it would be a fraud on the contract to do so.

> It is not right to profess and to purport to sell that which you do not mean the purchaser to have; it is not an honest thing to pocket the price and then to recapture the subject of the sale, to decoy it away or call it back before the purchaser has had time to attach it to himself and make it his very own. (*Trego v. Hunt*, [1896] A.C. 7 at p. 25, *per* Lord Macnaghten.)

That has happened in this case. The rehiring of Cook was perhaps a good deal to the advantage of the plaintiffs but Cook was hired *as a employee of the company*. As such he was bound to loyally exert his influences in favour of his employer Metropolitan, and not in his own interests. I find it inconceivable that within two weeks of the time of Cook's departure 75% of the trade of route No. 2 would vanish if Cook had not been, throughout at least the last part of his re-employment, working basically in his own interests and not that of his employer. Cook, with the secret knowledge of what the lawyer had told him in his head, was deliberately feathering his own nest, secure he thought in the fact that he was legally invulnerable.

It was argued that the re-employment of Cook in his old route with Wong's personal knowledge of Cook's power over the customer, amounted to an act of waiver. There is not the slightest legal justification for this plea. It may have been unwise of Wong: he may have thought he could make a deal with Cook when the five-year period was over; there may have been a number of other reasons but, whatever they were, I accept Wong's evidence that he was always relying upon the contract and find there was no waiver, either expressly or by necessary implication. Nor do I accept Mr. Culhane's able and ingenious argument that to "impose" on Cook as an employee the obligations of cl. 4 was unreasonable in itself. Clause 4 was and remained a subsisting obligation.

As to damages, the evidence is that the gross revenue loss over a period of a year would be approximately $50 000 to $60 000. The period of time elapsed since Cook's departure is almost exactly a year, and I will take the lower of the two figures. Wong testified that the profit margin was about 30% within 5% or 10% on a general average and considering all the evidence, I award the sum of $15 000 damages against the defendant who shall also pay the costs of this action.

NOTES

*1. C.P.R. means "Canadian Patent Reporter"*

*2. These cities are all 400 kilometres (250 miles) or more to the north and/or east of Vancouver.*

# E. Mistake

## Staiman Steel Ltd. v. Commercial & Home Builders Ltd.

*(1976) 71 D.L.R. (3d) 17*
*Ontario High Court of Justice*
*July 14, 1976*

SOUTHEY, J.: This is an action for damages for breach of alleged contract for the sale of goods from the defendant Commercial and Home Builders Limited ("Commercial") to the plaintiff. The contract was alleged to have been made by the defendant F. Caldarone Auctions Limited ("Caldarone Auctions") as agent for Commercial at an auction sale conducted by Caldarone Auctions on the premises of Commercial on June 15, 1972.

Commercial had been in the business of steel fabricating and erecting, specializing in the assembly of overhead cranes. A decision had been made to terminate the active business operations of Commercial and the auction sale was advertised in a mailing piece sent out by Caldarone Auctions as a complete liquidation of all construction equipment and 273-ton steel inventory of Commercial.

The goods to be sold included many items of equipment, including motors, cranes, welders, truck and parts, as well as an inventory of pieces of steel. Prior to the sale, Caldarone Auctions, working closely with Stephen Szillard, president of Commercial, separated the items to be sold into 383 numbered lots, which were listed in a catalogue that was made available to persons attending the sale. Each lot was tagged with a conspicuous tag or sticker bearing the lot number. Any goods that were added to the group to be sold after the lots had been made up were inserted into the selling programme at the appropriate place and designated by a lot number prefixed with the letter A.

More than 100 persons attended the sale. After Lots 1 to 192 had been sold, consisting of supplies and mechanical equipment, the auctioneer commenced to dispose of the inventory of steel in the yard. The first three lots (Lots 193, 194 and 195) were the only items of new steel offered for sale and the plaintiff successfully bid for them at $135 per ton. All other items in the inventory of steel were used steel and they had been divided into a number of small lots in the catalogue (Lots 196 to 232).

When the auctioneer started to offer the lots of used steel, one or two of the buyers suggested that the items of used steel be sold in bulk, instead of by individual lot. This procedure would save time and would eliminate any disputes as to the precise contents of each lot. Having satisfied himself that the buyers generally preferred to have such bulk sale, the auctioneer called a short break to enable the buyers to walk around the yard and inspect the lots which would be put up together.

Before the bidding commenced, there was specific agreement that a number of items in the yard would not be included in the bulk sale, because they were not structural steel. Most of the items thus excluded were mechanical items. The auctioneer excluded them by referring to their lot numbers. Some lots after Lot 232 were included in the bulk sale, because they also were items of used structural steel, or could be conveniently treated as such. Any such items to be included in the bulk lot, were referred to specifically by reference to their lot numbers.

At one point, according to some of the witnesses, the auctioneer described the bulk lot in general terms as being all the steel in the yard except mechanical items. When this general description was given. Bernard Staiman, president of the plaintiff, picked up a piece of scrap steel from the ground and asked "Even this?". The auctioneer replied "Yes".

The plaintiff was the successful bidder for the bulk lot at a unit price of $32 per ton.

The action relates to a pile of steel beams, doors and other members, which were the component members of a prefabricated steel building with craneway. This steel had been sold by Commercial several weeks before the auction sale, but was still piled in the yard of Commercial on the day of the sale. The plaintiff contended that this pile of steel was included in the bulk lot, whereas the defendants asserted that it was never their intention to include this steel in the sale, because it did not belong to Commercial.

The difference between the parties became apparent soon after the bulk lot was knocked down to the plaintiff and the auction sale was disrupted for a substantial time by a heated dispute between Staiman and the auctioneer as to the contents of the bulk lot. Staiman asserted that the steel he had purchased included the steel for the prefabricated building (hereinafter called the "building steel"). Commercial and the auctioneer both took the position that the steel purchased by the plaintiff in bulk did not include the building steel.

After consulting its solicitor, the plaintiff agreed on the day of the sale to take the lot without the building steel, but gave notice that it might bring legal procee 'ings to establish that the building steel should have been included in the lot. The auctioneer, acting on instructions from Commercial, required the plaintiff to sign a waiver to the effect that the lot purchased by it did not include the building steel. When the plaintiff refused to sign such waiver, the defendants refused to deliver any of the bulk lot to the plaintiff. The defendants' position was that if the plaintiff intended to bid for the building steel as part of the bulk lot, when the defendant had not intended that the bulk lot include such sale, then there was no *consensus ad idem*[1] as to the subject of the sale and, therefore, no contract of sale. The position thus taken by the parties remained substantially unchanged at trial.

The first question to be decided is whether the building steel was included in the bulk lot offered for sale at the auction. There is some conflict in the evidence bearing on this question and I must first make findings as to the credibility of some of the witnesses.

It is apparent from the evidence that Staiman behaved in a hot-tempered, quarrelsome and difficult manner throughout the incident in question. He refused to make the deposits on his purchases in the amounts and at the times required by the condition of sale and he created a disturbance at the sale which threatened to disrupt it beyond repair. I find that Staiman became involved emotionally in the dispute that occurred and that I cannot accept as accurate his recollection of the matters in dispute.

I was not impressed by Staiman's reliance on the question he put to the auctioneer as to whether the bulk lot included a piece of scrap steel and the answer received thereto as being of critical significance. I think the question may well have been intended to trap the auctioneer and set the stage for the dispute that occurred, but it is unnecessary for me to decide that point. If Staiman had any question that he genuinely wanted answered as to whether the building steel was included in the bulk lot, he should have made specific inquiries, as did Frank Clark and Irving Greenspoon, who were present at the auction and also gave evidence at trial.

• • •

Returning then to the first question, as to whether the building steel was part of the bulk lot, I have concluded that it was never the intention of Commercial or Caldarone Auctions to offer the building steel for sale at the auction. That steel had already been sold. Furthermore, in my view, the defendants at no time manifested an intention to offer the building steel for sale. When the auctioneer agreed to sell the remaining inventory of steel in bulk, he was agreeing, in my view, to include in one bulk lot the items that had previously been offered for sale in separate lots. Even if he said that the bulk lot included all the steel in the yard except mechanical items, as some witnesses said he did, I think it should have been apparent to Staiman and the others at the sale that the auctioneer was offering only the steel belonging to Commercial that had been included in the auction sale. It should have been obvious that the auctioneer was not including the building steel in the bulk lot because that steel was separately piled from the rest; was not tagged; and was not listed in the catalogue. It was new steel, painted grey, that had obviously been fabricated for a particular purpose, whereas the other steel in the yard was all used.

For the foregoing reasons, I find that the bulk lot for which the plaintiff was the successful bidder, did not include the building steel.

The defendants were thoroughly fed up with Staiman's conduct at the sale. Someone, probably Staiman, had shouted the words "I'll see you in Court" during the argument that arose during the sale. No doubt in the forlorn hope of avoiding this litigation, Frank Caldarone, the auctioneer, acting on the instructions of Commercial, refused to recognize the plaintiff as the buyer of any of the steel in the bulk lot, unless Staiman would execute an acknowledgement that the building steel was not included in the bulk lot.

Counsel for Commercial sought to justify the position thus taken by Commercial on the ground that if the plaintiff intended to buy a bulk lot containing the building steel, whereas Commercial intended to sell a lot without that steel, then there was no *consensus ad idem* and, therefore, no contract for the sale of any steel.

Counsel for Commercial relied on *Raffles v. Wichelhaus et al.* (1864), 2 H. & C. 906, 159 E.R. 375, involving two ships named "Peerless" which sailed from Bombay, one in October and one in December, and *Scriven Brothers & Co. v. Hindley & Co.*, [1913] 3 K.B. 564, where the purchaser at an auction bid an extravagant price for the bales of tow in the mistaken belief that they were bales of hemp. In both cases the Courts held that there was no contract, apparently because there was no *consensus ad idem*.

Counsel for the plaintiff, on the other hand, relied on the basic rule of contract law that it is not a party's actual intention that determines contractual relationships, but rather the intention manifested by the words and actions of the parties. Mr. Catzman referred to the following passage in the judgment of Middleton, J.A., in *Lindsey v. Heron & Co.* (1921), 50 O.L.R. 1 at p. 8, 64 D.L.R. 92 at pp. 98-9:

> The apparent mutual assent of the parties essential to the formation of a contract, must be gathered from the language employed by them, and the law imputes to a person an intention corresponding to the reasonable meaning of his words and acts. It judges of his intention by his outward expressions and excludes all questions in regard to his unexpressed intention. If his words or acts, judged by a reasonable standard, manifest an intention to agree in regard to the matter in question, that agreement is established, and it is immaterial what may be the real but unexpressed state of his mind on the subject." [*Corpus Juris*, vol. 13, p. 265]
> "If, whatever a man's real intention may be, he so conducts himself that a reasonable man would believe that he was assenting to the terms proposed by the other party, and that other party upon that belief enters into the contract with him, the man thus conducting himself would be equally bound as if he had intended to agree to the other party's terms." Blackburn, J., in *Smith v. Hughes*, L.R. 6 Q.B. at p. 607.

Mr. Catzman submitted that if the Court found that the building steel was not a part of the bulk lot, then the result should not be a finding that there was no contract. He contended that there should then be a finding that there was a contract for the sale of the lot without the building steel, even though it was not the plaintiff's intention to bid for a lot with the building steel.

In my judgment the plaintiff must succeed on this secondary point. The basis of the successful defence by Commercial on the first point is that the circumstances were such that a reasonable man would infer that the auctioneer, despite his words, was manifesting an intention to offer for sale the bulk lot without the building steel. By making the highest bid, Staiman so conducted himself that a reasonable man would believe that he was assenting to the purchase of that lot. A contract for the sale of that lot to the plaintiff thereupon came into existence. That contract was never subsequently repudiated by Staiman. The plaintiff was at all times willing to take delivery of and to pay for the bulk lot without the building steel, which was what Commercial and Caldarone Auctions said was the subject of the contract of sale, although the plaintiff made it quite clear that it might still commence proceedings to establish that the bulk lot should have included the building steel.

Commercial had the right to insist that the plaintiff take delivery and pay for the bulk lot excluding the building steel, but Commercial had no right, in my judgment, to require the plaintiff to give up its claim that the contract included the building steel as well as the remainder of the bulk lot. By insisting on such waiver or acknowledgement, Commercial was attempting to introduce unilaterally a new term into the contract of sale.

If, as appears to have been the case, the plaintiff thought the bulk lot he was purchasing included the building steel and the defendants thought that the bulk lot they were selling did not include the building steel, then the case was one of mutual mistake, as that expression is used in Cheshire and Fifoot's *Law of Contract,* 8th ed. (1972), p. 221. In such a case, the Court must decide what reasonable third parties would infer to be the contract from the words and conduct of the parties who entered into it. It is only in a case where the circumstances are so ambiguous that a reasonable bystander could not infer a common intention that the Court will hold that no contract was created. As pointed out in Cheshire and Fifoot at p. 212:

> If the evidence is so conflicting that there is nothing sufficiently solid from which to infer a contract in any final form without indulging in mere speculation, the court must of necessity declare that no contract whatsoever has been created.

In this case, in my judgment, a reasonable man would infer the existence of a contract to buy and sell the bulk lot without the building steel and therefore I have held that there was a contract to that effect binding on both parties, notwithstanding such mutual mistake.

The case is quite unlike *Raffles v. Wichelhaus* and *Scriven Brothers & Co. v. Hindley & Co.,* because, in those cases, it was impossible for the Court to impute any definite agreements to the parties.

In *Raffles v. Wichelhaus,* the Court had no more reason to find out both parties had manifested an intention to deal in cotton shipped on the "Peerless" sailing in October than to deal with cotton shipped in the "Peerless" sailing in December. In *Scriven Brothers & Co., v. Hindley & Co.,* there was no reason to find that both parties had manifested an intention to buy and sell tow. The purchaser had manifested an intention to buy hemp, whereas the auctioneer had put tow up for sale.

By refusing to deliver any steel from the bulk lot to the plaintiff, Commercial has clearly breached its contract for the sale of such bulk lot to the plaintiff. It remains to assess the damages suffered by the plaintiff because of such breach of contract.

The evidence of the witness Clark and Greenspoon was that steel of the type contained in the bulk lot could have been purchased elsewhere in Toronto at the time of the auction sale. The measure of the damages sustained by the plaintiff for non-delivery of the steel in question, in my judgment, is the difference between the price contained in the contract between the plaintiff and Commercial and the price at which such steel could have been purchased elsewhere.

It appears from the evidence of witnesses whom I accept that about 30% of the steel in the bulk lot was scrap, having a market price of about $20 per ton; and that 70% was useable, used steel, available at a price of about $80 per ton. It was agreed at trial that the bulk lot, apart from the building steel, contained 547.89 tons. Applying the price of $20 per ton for scrap and $80 per ton for useable, used steel, the bulk lot could have been purchased elsewhere for $33 968.

Commercial agreed to sell the lot to the plaintiff at $32 per ton, giving a total price of $17 532. The damages suffered by the plaintiff, therefore, amounted to $16 436.

There will be judgment for the plaintiff against Commercial for $16 436. The plaintiff is also entitled to recover its costs of the action from Commercial.

Caldarone Auctions acted throughout within the scope of its authority as agent for Commercial. The action against Caldarone Auctions will be dismissed with costs, but the costs recovered by Caldarone Auctions from the plaintiff will be added to the costs to be recovered by the plaintiff from Commercial.

The third party proceedings[2] by Commercial against Caldarone Auctions and by Caldarone Auctions against Commercial will be dismissed without costs.

NOTES

1. *"Consensus ad idem" is usually freely translated to mean a "meeting of the minds" and refers to the requirement of agreement for the proper formation of a contract.*

2. *See General Explanatory Notes, Part 6.*

# Commercial Credit Corporation Ltd. v. Newall Agencies Ltd.

*[1981]* 6 W.W.R. 281
British Columbia Supreme Court
July 29, 1981

HYDE L.J.S.C.: This is an application.... based on the following statement of facts:

1. That on August 19, 1977 the Defendant, Newall Agencies Ltd., signed a contract with Westerham Leasing Ltd. for the lease of a 1974 Mercedes Benz motor vehicle, Model 450, Serial Number 107024-12-004226.
2. That for good and valuable consideration the said contract was executed by the Defendant, Alan Newman, as guarantor of Newall Agencies Ltd.
3. That pursuant to the terms of the said contract the Defendant took delivery of the said motor vehicle and made monthly rent payments as scheduled.
4. That the intent of Westerham Leasing Ltd. under the terms of the said contract was assigned to Commercial Credit Corporation Limited on December 20, 1978.
5. That on or about July 16, 1979, the Defendants desired to purchase the said motor vehicle from the Plaintiff and requested a pay out statement from the Plaintiff.
6. That on July 16, 1,979, the Plaintiff advised the Defendants in writing that the pay out figure for the purchase of the said motor vehicle was $13 513.67.
7. That on July 18, 1979, the Plaintiff confirmed in writing to the Canadian Imperial Bank of Commerce Branch at 6151 No. 3 Road, Richmond, B.C. that the pay out figure was $13 513.67 and that in return for same the said motor vehicle would belong with clear title to the Defendant, Alan Newman.
8. That on or about July 18, 1979, the Plaintiff released the Defendants from any obligations under the contract and transferred title in the said motor vehicle to the Defendant, Alan Newman, in exchange for payment in the amount of $13 513.67.
9. That title in the said motor vehicle was transferred to the Defendant, Alan Newman, on July 18, 1979.
10. That when title in the said motor vehicle was transferred to the Defendant by the Plaintiff, the amount owing under the terms of the said contract was $19 827.61.

POINT OF LAW:

Whether the Plaintiff is entitled to rely on the doctrine of mistake of fact to claim the amount of $6313.94 pursuant to the said contract despite the fact that on or about July 18, 1979, the Plaintiff released the Defendants from any obligations under the said contract and despite the fact that the alleged error in determining the amount owing under the contract was that of the plaintiff.

CONCLUSION

The plaintiff is not entitled to rely on the doctrine of mistake of fact in these circumstances.

REASONS

One of the broadest statements of the equitable doctrine of mistake appears in the judgment of Denning L.J. in *Solle v. Butcher*, [1950] 1 K.B. 671 at 692, [1949] 2 All E.R. 1107 (C.A.):

> Whilst presupposing that a contract was good at law, or at any rate not void, the court of equity would often relieve a party from the consequences of his own mistake, so long as it could do so without injustice to third parties. The court, it was said, had power to set aside the contract whenever it was of opinion that it was unconscientious for the other party to avail himself of the legal advantage which he had obtained...
> The court had, of course, to define what it considered to be unconscientious, but in this respect equity has shown a progressive development. It is now clear that a contract will be set aside if the mistake of the one party has been induced by a material misrepresentation of the other, even though it was not fraudulent or fundamental; or if one party, knowing that the other is mistaken about the terms of an offer, or the identity of the person by whom it is made, lets him remain under his delusion and concludes a contract on the mistaken terms instead of pointing out the mistake.

The facts in this case do not support an inference that the defendant either knew or ought to have known that the plaintiff had made a mistake in calculating the payout figure. The issue is whether the plaintiff ought to be relieved of the consequences of his own error in these circumstances even though the facts as presented disclose no trace of unfair dealing on the part of the defendant.

In *Riverlate Properties Ltd., v. Paul*, [1975] Ch. 133, [1974] 2 All E.R. 656, the English Court of Appeal considered a similar problem. In that case, a lessor had made a mistake in drafting the lease agreement. He had intended to make the lessee title for certain repairs, and instead made himself liable. The lessee believed all along that the lessor was to be liable for those repairs, and was unaware of the lessor's mistake. The lessor claimed that he was entitled to rectification of the lease with an option in the lessee to rescind. Russell L.J., speaking for the court, declined to give the lessor a remedy. He said this at p. 661:

> Is the plaintiff [the lessor] entitled to rescission of the lease on the mere ground that it made a serious mistake in the drafting of the lease which it put forward and subsequently executed, when (a) the defendant did not share the mistake, (b) the defendant did not know that the document did not give effect to the plaintiff's intention, and (c) the mistake of the plaintiff was in no way attributable to anything said or done by the defendant? What is there in principle, or in authority binding on this court, which requires a person who has acquired a leasehold interest on terms on which he intended to obtain it, and who thought when he obtained it that the lessor intended him to obtain it on those terms, either to lose the leasehold interest, or, if he wish to keep it, to submit to keep it only on the terms which the lessor meant to impose but did not? In point of principle, we cannot find that this should be so. If reference is made to principles of equity, it operates on conscience. If conscience is clear at the time of the transaction, why should equity disrupt the transaction? If a man may be said to

have been fortunate in obtaining a property at a bargain price, or on terms that make it a good bargain, because the other party unknown to him has made a miscalculation or other mistake, some high-minded men might consider it appropriate that he should agree to a fresh bargain to cure the miscalculation or mistake, abandoning his good fortune. But if equity were to enforce the views of those high-minded men, we have no doubt that if would run counter to the attitudes of much the greater part of ordinary mankind (not least the world of commerce), and would soon be venturing on the field of moral philosophy in which it would soon be in difficulties.

The *Riverdale* case was criticized by S.M. Waddams in a comment appearing in (1975), 53 Can. Bar Rev. 339, but he did not disagree with the actual outcome of the case. His criticism was that the case might be taken to mean that the plaintiff must prove that the defendant had actual knowledge of the mistake. Professor Waddams said that it should be sufficient for the plaintiff to prove that a reasonable man in the defendant's position would have realized that the plaintiff had made a mistake. I note that these criticisms were accepted and given effect to by Grange J. in *Stepps Invts. Ltd. v. Security Capital Corp. Ltd.* (1976), 14 O.R. (2d) 259, 73 D.L.R. (3d) 351 (H.C.). In the case at bar, however, there is not actual or constructive knowledge on the part of the defendant. In my view, the facts, insofar as they are relevant to a consideration of the doctrine of mistake, are very similar to the facts in the *Riverlate* case, *supra*.

Of the cases referred to by counsel, only one has come close on its facts to this case, though the subject matter of the contract is an annuity rather than an automobile. *Sykes v. R.,* [1939] Ex. C.R. 77, [1939] 3 D.L.R. 585, affirmed [1945] 4 D.L.R. 807 (S.C.C.), involved a plaintiff who applied to the federal government to purchase an annuity. The appropriate federal officials quoted him a price. The plaintiff commenced paying the necessary instalments. Some time later they government officials discovered that they had erred in their annuity calculations, and demanded more money. The plaintiff sued to enforce the contract on its original terms. Maclean J. held that the federal government was not entitled to be relieved of its obligations under the original terms of the contract. He said this at pp. 592-93.

> But generally, where a party is seeking to enforce a contract which he has entered into in good faith, and unaware of a mistake of fact made by the other party, such lack of knowledge will as a rule operate to make the contract enforceable, notwithstanding the unilateral mistake.

The court found that there was no error as to the subject matter or terms of the contract. The only error was in the underlying calculations, of which the plaintiff knew nothing and of which he could be expected to know nothing. The government was required to bear the loss ensuing from its own error.

Most of the other cases cited involved a mistake on the part of one party of which the other party was aware or ought to have been aware.

In *Imperial Glass Ltd. v. Consol. Supplies Ltd.* (1960), 22 D.L.R. (2d) 759, the British Columbia Court of Appeal held that, even where a purchaser knows that a calculation error underlies an offer made by a seller, the seller is not entitled to rescind the contract. The case has been much criticized, but has not yet been overruled. If actual knowledge of an underlying error does not entitle the seller to rescission, then the plaintiff in the case at bar has a very weak case indeed, because here there is no knowledge of the error.

In *McMaster Univ. v. Wilchar Const. Ltd.,* [1971] 3 O.R. 801, 22 D.L.R. (3d) 9, affirmed 12 O.R. (2d) 512n, 69 D.L.R. (3d) 400n (C.A.), Thompson J. held that, where a purchaser purported to accept an offer which he knew was made on the basis of an error by the offeror, there was no binding contract between the parties. He said this at p. 808: "To me this is patently a case where the offeree, for its own advantage, snapped at the offeror's offer well knowing that the offer as made was made by mistake." The learned judge distinguished the *Imperial Glass* case, *supra* (albeit unconvincingly) and declined to follow it. But the facts of the case at bar disclose no unfair "snapping up" of a mistaken offer. In my opinion, the statements of the law in the *McMaster Univ.* case are correct but are not applicable to this case.

• • •

[ed: The judge went on to consider several other authorities which he held did not apply to to the facts of the present case. He concluded by saying:]

Fridman, *The Law of Contract* (1976), recognizes that a party who is completely ignorant of the mistake of another is in a different position than a party who is not so ignorant (p. 84). He approves the statement of principle set out by Thompson J. in the *McMaster Univ.* case, *supra* (p. 87), but does not go so far as to contend that a purchaser who is entirely ignorant of the underlying mistake of the defendant can be forced to suffer the imposition of new contractual terms.

In my judgment this case is governed by *Sykes v. R., supra,* and *Riverlate Properties, supra.* It is not unconscientious for the defendant in these circumstances to avail himself of the legal advantage he has obtained, and the plaintiff is therefore not entitled to be relieved from the consequences of his own mistake. Accordingly, the point of law should be determined in favour of the defendant.

The defendant will have one set of costs of the action, on a party-and-party basis.[1]

*Judgment in defendant's favour.*

NOTES

1. *Although there were two defendants (see paragraphs 1 and 2 of the agreed facts) they were both represented by one counsel and their defences would have been almost identical so the judge only awarded one set of costs.*

# Bomek v. Bomek

*[1983] 3 W.W.R. 635*
*Manitoba Court of Appeal*
*March 21, 1983*

MATAS J.A. (FREEDMAN C.J.M. concurring): This is an appeal by one of the defendants, Dauphin Plains Credit Union Limited (the "credit union") from a judgment of Hamilton J. delivered on 28th April 1982, and entered on 24th August 1982. Hamilton J. set aside a real property mortgage from Mr. and Mrs. Bomek to the credit union. Hamilton J. also ordered damages of $3600 and solicitor-client costs to be paid by both defendants. However, with respect to damages, the court order refers to the credit union alone.

The individual defendant, James Michael Bomek, is the plaintiff's son. To avoid confusion with the male plaintiff, I will refer to the defendant by his first name. At the time of the trial Mrs. Bomek was 54 years of age; Mr. Bomek was 64. He had obtained a Grade III education and could barely read. Mrs. Bomek had obtained a Grade IX education. Mr. Bomek was a labourer and was to retire in 1982 from his job with the city of Brandon.

James was the registered owner of 1498 common shares out of 1500 issued and outstanding in Bomek Investments Ltd. (Investments Ltd.). Investments Ltd. was the registered owner of 2000 common shares out of 2003 issued and outstanding in Dynamic Foods Limited (Dynamic). Dynamic carried on a restaurant business. James was the president and manager of both companies. The companies and James had had banking accounts with the credit union since 1975.

In March 1977 a loan was arranged by the credit union for James and his companies for $395 000, to cover an existing obligation with the credit union and to finish construction of a restaurant at Clear Lake. The 395 000 was to be carried as a term loan of $365 000 and as an operating line of credit of $30 000. The loan was payable on demand. The credit union received several security documents to cover the loan from Investments Ltd., Dynamic and James. The operating account was in Dynamic's name as a matter of convenience to James.

On 12th August 1977 the term loan stood at $338 684.60. The operating account stood at $70 235.94. The amount which was in excess of the operating line of credit of $30 000, namely $40 235.94, was designated as an overdraft. On 12th August 1977 the credit union, which has financial problems of its one, wrote to James to advise that the credit union required the overdraft to be reduced at the rate of $5000 per week. Although James had reservations about the proposed schedule of payments, the overdraft [sic][1] was reduced to about $51 000 by 23rd September 1977.

In the latter part of September 1977, James approached Mr. W. C. T. Wyborn, an officer of the credit union, to advise that he had made arrangements with his parents to borrow $25 000. The money was to be used to reduce the overdraft. James promised to make monthly payments of $1000 on the mortgage.

James' evidence about his arrangements with the credit union were different from this account but his version was rejected by the learned trial judge.

James, in discussing the loan with his parents, did not tell them that he was in financial difficulty nor did he tell them the truth about the purpose of the loan. Mr. and Mrs. Bomek had a notion from what James had told them that the money was to be used for an expansion of their son's business in Saskatchewan. When Mr. and Mrs. Bomek said they did not have the cash to help him, James suggested they could mortgage their home.

The marital home was the Bomeks' only substantial asset. Its value was $50 000. In addition, the Bomeks owned personal property worth about $16 000.

The learned trial judge, in his reasons for judgment, described the parents' feelings in this way: "They were prepared to lend [the $25 000] to their son and as far as they were concerned, he was entitled to use the money as he saw fit. Nevertheless, the plaintiffs thought they were making a personal loan to their son. They were led by their son to believe that he had a lot of money but couldn't put his hands on it."

Mr. J. D. Deans, solicitor for the credit union, confirmed the financial difficulties of James and his companies. He referred to the cash flow problems James had in meeting his weekly commitments and he referred to the mortgage by James' parents as being given to "shore up" the credit union's security. He said timing was important and that the credit union and James were anxious to have the transaction completed as soon as possible.

The credit union processed the loan application in a cursory way. An appraisal of the property was obtained by Mr. M. Edwards, an official of the credit union, who phoned an official of another credit union in Brandon for information. Mr. Edwards thought that may be a "check" was done with the Canadian Imperial Bank of Commerce. No formal credit check was made. Mr. Edwards said that the loan was approved by the credit committee after the loan had gone through his hands. He expressed surprise that the loan had been approved because the credit union was dealing with someone from outside the credit union's area. Mr. Edwards, as the official of the credit union who monitored the Dynamic and Investments Ltd. account, was aware that the companies were having trouble meeting their financial commitments.

Mr. Edwards prepared part of the documentation for the loan. He filled out as much of the loan application as he could in the absence of any direct contact with the Bomeks. In addition, a promissory note, membership cards and signature cards were prepared. The documents were to be taken by James to his parents.

According to Mr. Edwards, the discussions he had with James was to the effect that the proceeds of the loan were to be applied to the overdraft in the Dynamic account. Nevertheless, the purpose of the loan was shown on the application, disingenuously in my view, to be an "Investment loan to James Bomek". The explanation given by Mr. Edwards for categorizing the purpose of the loan in this way without any reference to the two companies was that he did not know how James intended to treat the loan on his "company books". Neither Mr. Edwards, nor anyone else in the credit union, asked the Bomeks anything about the loan then, nor did anyone discuss it with the Bomeks later when the documents were returned to the credit union. With respect to the idea of the Bomeks obtaining independent legal advice. Mr. Edwards was "under the assumption that the lawyers would be looking after that during their proceedings with the mortgage documentation".

Mr. Edwards sent instructions for preparation of the mortgage to the solicitors for the credit union. They had been solicitors for James, but had never acted for Mr. and Mrs. Bomek. The solicitors prepared the mortgage and also prepared an authorization, or order to pay. The payment clause in the mortgage called for repayment on demand. This provision was exactly the same as the payment clause in the promissory note signed by the Bomeks, and was the same as in the other documentation executed by the two companies and James in favour of the credit union. The order to pay was in line with the expressed purpose of the loan in the application form, and was in line with what James told his parents. It reads:

> Consider this your full and sufficient authority to deposit Twenty-Five Thousand Dollars ($25 000.00) standing in my Account at Dauphin Plains Credit Union Limited to the credit of James Michael Bomek.

James was given all the documents. He paid a hurried visit to his parents and had them sign. Mr. and Mrs. Bomek did not read the papers. Mrs Bomek said, "It was Jim we were signing for and he was our son and we had no reason to discuss with him, so we just didn't bother." James did not go through the documents with his parents. He told them they were "the mortgage papers, etc., etc.", and showed them where to sign. James witnessed their signatures and as a commissioner for oaths swore their respective dower[2] affidavits. Mr. and Mrs. Bomek understood they were signing mortgage documents to secure a loan for $25 000. But, as I mentioned earlier, they thought the money was to go to James. They expected from what James told them that he would make any payments due under the mortgage.

The mortgage was registered against the Bomek property on 3rd October 1977 by the solicitors, and in due course all the documents were returned to the credit union. The solicitors did not have any contact with Mr. and Mrs. Bomek at any time.

The credit union went through the motions of setting up an account in the plaintiffs' name as new members and credited $25 000 to that account on 13 October 1977. Contrary to the authorization prepared by the solicitors for the credit union, the money was transferred from the Bomeks' account into the Dynamic account. The transfer was made on 13th October 1977 in this way on the oral authority which the credit union believed it had received from James. The result of the internal entries was that the Dynamic overdraft [sic][1] was brought down close to the $30 000 limit. No new money was actually involved.

Eventually, in October 1978, the credit union put Investments Ltd. and Dynamic in receivership.

Aside from two payments of $250 each, James did not keep his promise to see that the mortgage was paid. Mr. and Mrs. Bomek paid $3600 over a period of time in order to stave off foreclosure proceedings....

In my view, the facts in the case before us engage the equitable jurisdiction of the court to relieve against an unconscionable transaction. Statutory recognition of that jurisdiction is found in s. 3 of the *Unconscionable Transactions Relief Act,* C.C.S.M., c. U20, which reads:

> 3.  Where, in respect of money lent, the court finds that, having regard to the risk and to all the circumstances at the time the loan was made, the cost of the loan is excessive or that the transaction is harsh or unconscionable the court may,
> (a)  re-open the transaction and take an account between the creditor and the debtor;
> (b)  notwithstanding any statement or settlement of account or any agreement purporting to close previous dealings and create a new obligation, re-open any account already taken and relieve the debtor from payment of any sum in excess of the sum adjudged by the court to be fairly due in respect of the principal and the cost of the loan;
> (c)  order the creditor to repay any such excess if it has been paid or allowed on account by the debtor;
> (d)  set aside either wholly or in part, or revise or alter, any security given or agreement made in respect of the money lent, and, if the creditor has parted with the security, order him to indemnify the debtor.

Professor Bradley E. Crawford in (1966), 44 *Canadian Bar Review* 142, discussed the kind of cases in which the courts have demanded a "peculiarly exacting duty of fairness and disinterestedness" of "persons who transact business with others dealing with them on less than an equal footing". The inequality may exist "through a disparity of commercial experience or native intelligence or otherwise". At p. 143, Professor Crawford discusses the circumstances which may give rise to the court's intervention:

> In the cases now under discussion the courts intervene to rescind the contract whenever it appears that one of the parties was incapable of adequately protecting his interest and the other has made some immoderate gain at his expense. If the bargain is fair the fact that the parties were not equally vigilant of their interest is immaterial. Likewise if one was not preyed upon by the other, an improvident or even grossly inadequate consideration is no ground upon which to set aside a contract freely entered into. It is the combination of inequality and improvidence which alone may invoke this jurisdiction. Then the onus is placed upon the party seeking to uphold the contract to show that his conduct throughout was scrupulously considerate of the other's interests. (Footnotes omitted)....

The difference between the business knowledge and experience of the Bomeks and the credit union is obvious.

The casual procedure followed by the credit union in processing the loan indicates that it regarded the transaction as a means of obtaining additional security for a shaky loan with James and his companies. The credit union had a community of interest with James in having the additional security in place as quickly and smoothly as possible. The credit union was an active participant in the transaction. It had the documentation drawn to indicate an advance to James when everyone except the Bomeks knew that what was intended was to get more security for the credit union. The disbursement of the loan was consistent with this objective and was in accord with the misleading nature of the documentation.

The credit union compounded its involvement by distancing itself from any contact with its new members who were to become the mortgagors, and by handing the misleading documents to James for obtaining the necessary signatures. The credit union made no effort to ensure that the mortgagors understood the implications of what they were doing.

The circumstance that the Bomeks did not read the documents is of no help to the credit union in its resistance to a claim for equitable relief. The documents were consistent with what James had told the Bomeks. If the Bomeks had read the papers they would not have been enlightened. No doubt when the documents were drawn it was assumed that the mortgagors would read them. That they did not does not justify the actions of the credit union. In my view, the plaintiffs' omission to read the documents is irrelevant.

Any reasonable competent legal adviser would have taken the age and financial position of the Bomeks into account and would wonder about the $25 000 mortgage payable on demand to be registered against the mortgagors' only substantial asset, the efficacy of an oral promise to pay the mortgage and about the financial ability of the promissor to make good on his promise. The documentation would have been examined to see if it expressed the understanding of the mortgagors about the purpose of the loan and what was to happen to the proceeds. I am satisfied that no reasonably competent legal adviser would have advised the Bomeks to enter into the transaction. In light of its self-interest and its knowledge of James' self-interest, the credit union had a duty to see that the Bomeks had independent legal advice. In my view, the absence of independent legal advice in the circumstances of this case is fatal to the defence of the credit union: Lord Denning M.R. in *Bundy, supra,* at p. 765.

I respectfully agree with the conclusion of the learned trial judge that the mortgage is unconscionable and with his conclusion to set it aside and to order damages payable by the credit union.

I would dismiss the appeal with costs.

[ed: The dissenting opinion of Huband J.A. is omitted.]

NOTES

1. *In both these cases, it appears that the judge should have referred to the operating line of credit rather than to "overdraft."*

2. *Dower or homestead rights are those rights that a spouse acquires as a result of marriage, in the property that both are using as a home. In some provinces they accrue to both spouses, in others only to the wife. Should one spouse die, the other will become entitled to a life interest in the land; the land cannot be disposed of or mortgaged without the consent of the other.*

# Marvco Colour Research Ltd. v. Harris et al.[1]

*(1983) 141 D.L.R. (3 cl) 577*
*Supreme Court of Canada*
*December 6, 1982*

This case arose when the defendant husband and wife, Mr. and Mrs. Harris (respondents), were induced to sign a mortgage on their property, by the representations of a friend of their daughter that it was an entirely different document. Neither, however, read what they signed, because they thought they were helping their daughter by financing the friend's purchase of a business. The monies were not repaid by the friend and Marvco Colour Research Ltd. The mortgagee commenced foreclosure proceedings to recover the money from the land. Mr. and Mrs. Harris defended on the ground of *non est factum.*

[This defence was successful at the Trial and in the Ontario Court of Appeal. Marvco Colour then appealed to the Supreme Court of Canada with Mr. and Mrs. Smith as respondents. The defence was rejected because of their failure to read what they signed. Mr. Justice Estey, delivering the judgment of the court said, in part:]

In my view, with all due respect to those who have expressed views to the contrary, the dissenting view of Cartwright J. (as he then was) in *Prudential, supra,* correctly enunciated the principles of the law of *non est factum.* In the result the defendants-respondents are barred by reason of their carelessness from pleading that their minds did not follow their hands when executing the mortgage so as to be able to plead that the mortgage is not binding upon them. The rationale of the rule is simple and clear. As between an innocent party (the appellant) and the respondents, the law must take into account the fact that the appellant was completely innocent of any negligence, carlessness or wrongdoing, whereas the respondents by their careless conduct have made it possible for the wrongdoers to inflict a loss. As between the appellant and the respondents, simple justice requires that the party, who by the application of reasonable care was in a position to avoid a loss to any of the parties, should bear any loss that results when the only alternative available to the courts would be to place the loss upon the innocent appellant. In the final analysis, therefore, the question raised cannot be put more aptly than in the words of Cartwright J. in *Prudential, supra,* at p. 5 D.L.R., p. 929 S.C.R.: "...which of two innocent parties is to suffer for the fraud of a third". The two parties are innocent in the sense that they were not guilty of wrongdoing as against any other person, but as between the two innocent parties there remains a distinction significant in the law, namely, that the respondents, by their carelessness, have exposed the innocent appellant to risk of loss, and even though no duty in law was owed by the respondents to the appellant to safeguard the appellant from such loss, nonetheless the law must take this discarded opportunity into account.

In my view, this is so for the compelling reason that in this case, and no doubt generally in similar cases, the respondents' carelessness is but another description of a state of mind into which the respondents have fallen because of their determination to assist themselves and/or a third party for whom the transaction has been entered into in the first place. Here the respondents apparently sought to attain some advantage indirectly for their daughter by assisting Johnston in his commercial venture. In the *Saunders* case, *supra,* the aunt set out to apply her property for the benefit of her nephew. In both cases the carelessness took the form of a failure to determine the nature of the document the respective defendants were executing. Whether the carelessness stemmed from an enthusiasm for their immediate purpose or from a confidence in the intended beneficiary to save them harmless matters not. This may explain the origin of the careless state of mind but is not a factor limiting the operation of the principle of *non est factum* and its application. The defendants, in executing the security without the simple precaution of ascertaining its nature in fact and in law, have nonetheless, taken an intended and deliberate step in signing the document and have caused it to be legally binding upon themselves. In the words of *Foster v. Mackinnon* this negligence, even though it may have sprung from good intentions, precludes the defendants in this circumstance from disowning the document, that is to say, from pleading that their minds did not follow their respective hands when signing the document and hence that no document in law was executed by them.

This principle of law is based not only upon the principle of placing the loss on the person guilty of carelessness, but also upon a recognition of the need for certainty and security in commerce. This has been recognized since the earliest days of the plea of *non est factum.* In *Waberley v. Cockerel* (1542), 1 Dyer 51a, 73 E.R. 112, for example, it was said that:

...although the truth be, that the plaintiff is paid his money, still it is better to suffer a mischief to one man that an inconvenience to many, which would subvert a law; for if matter in writing may be so easily defeated, and avoided by such surmise and naked breath, a matter in writing would be of no greater authority than a matter of fact...

More recently in *Muskham Finance Ltd. v. Howard, supra,* at p. 912, Donovan L.J. stated:

Much confusion and uncertainty would result in the field of contract and elsewhere if a man were permitted to try to disown his signature simply by asserting that he did not understand that which he had signed.

The appellant, as it was entitled to do, accepted the mortgage as valid, and adjusted its affairs accordingly. For example, the appellant released Suwald from the chattel mortgage held by the appellant.

I wish only to add that the application of the principle that carelessness will disentitle a party to the document of the right to disown the document in law must depend upon the circumstances of each case. This has been said throughout the judgments written on the principle of *non est factum* from the earliest times. The magnitude and extent of the carelessness, the circumstances which may have contributed to such carelessness, and all other circumstances must be taken into account in each case before a court may determine whether estoppel shall arise in the defendant so as to prevent the raising of this defence. The policy considerations inherent in the plea of *non est factum* were well stated by Lord Wilberforce in his judgment in *Saunders, supra,* at pp. 1023-4.

...the law...has two conflicting objectives: relief to a signer whose consent is genuinely lacking...protection to innocent third parties who have acted upon an apparently regular and properly executed document. Because each of these factors may involve questions of degree or shading any rule of law must represent a compromise and must allow to the court some flexibility in application.

The result in this case has depended upon the intervention by this court in the development of the principle of *non est factum* and its invocation in a way inconsistent with that applied many years ago in the *Prudential* case, *supra.* The respondents have pleaded their case in the courts below and in this court consistent with the result in the *Prudential* judgment. In these circumstances consideration can and should be given to the application of the general principle that costs follow the event. The appellant, of course, was required to persevere to the level of this court in order to bring about a review of the reasoning which led to the determination in the *Prudential* case. The respondents, on the other hand, acted reasonably in founding their position upon that decision notwithstanding the revision of the law of England consequent upon the judgments in *Saunders.* In all these circumstances, therefore,I would award to the appellant costs only before the court of first instance with no costs being awarded either party in the Court of Appeal or in this court.[2]

*Appeal allowed.*

NOTES

1. *This case is a good example of the court changing the law. Here the Supreme Court of Canada overruled its decision in* Prudential Trust Co. Ltd. v. Cugnet *[1956] S.C.R. 914 (referred to in Smyth and Soberman,* The Law and Business Administration in Canada, *4th ed., p. 216) which had held that the careless conduct of an individual would not prevent his raising the defence of non est factum. Thus from December 6, 1982, the law was just the opposite to what it had previously been.*

2. *The disposition of costs is interesting. The Supreme Court felt that both parties had been reasonable in what they had done. The respondents defended on the law as it had been and were successful as far as the Supreme Court. The appellants had had to continue to that court in order to get the law changed. Hence the plaintiff was given the costs in the court of first instance where, by this decision, it had now been successful. Since neither party was at fault in the two appeals, neither party was awarded costs.*

# F. Misrepresentation; Undue Influence

## F. and B. Transport Ltd. v. White Truck Sales Manitoba Ltd.

*(1965) 51 W.W.R. 124*
*Manitoba Court of Appeal*
*January 13, 1965*

MILLER, C.J.M.: This is an appeal from a judgment in favour of the plaintiff by Dickson, J. (1965) 47 D.L.R. (2d) 419, who allowed the plaintiff's claim for a rescission of a contract for sale of a truck and for judgment in the amount involved.

In any important feature the facts are not in dispute.

The defendant sold to the plaintiff a 1956 model transport tractor truck as a 1958 model. A short time earlier the defendant had accepted this same truck on a trade-in as a 1957 model, although it was subsequently found to be a 1956 model. However, the salesman for the defendant company did not dispute that he had represented the vehicle to the plaintiff as a 1958 model and that the plaintiff purchased it as such. The defendant agreed to recondition the equipment and did spend almost $3000 on reconditioning; it also spent $1000 on supplying an extra which plaintiff had requisitioned. The cab of the vehicle was a 1958 model, even though the vehicle itself was, as above stated, a 1956 model. The plaintiff maintained the defendant was guilty of fraud; also that it was a condition of the contract that the truck should be a 1958 model.

The evidence discloses the representation to have been that the vehicle was a 1958 model and that plaintiff thought it was purchasing a 1958 truck when, in fact, the vehicle delivered was a 1956 truck with a 1958 cab. As soon as the plaintiff discovered the misrepresentation it promptly repudiated the contract and notified the defendant that it rejected the truck. This, the defendant concedes. The plaintiff contends that it did not obtain what it had bargained for. All the employees and officers of the defendant company who gave evidence admitted that the plaintiff did not receive what it bargained for.

The defendant maintains that the representation as to the year was neither a term nor a condition of the contract.

In my opinion, the plaintiff was entitled to repudiate and reject the truck, even though the misrepresentation was innocent, and this notwithstanding the fact that the sales documents had been executed and completed. This is so because there was a difference in substance between what was contracted for and what was delivered; indeed, as above admitted, the plaintiff did not get what it had bargained for.

Counsel for the defendant argued at some length to the effect that the admitted representation was not fraudulent, but, in my view of the matter, this is unimportant as the article delivered was not the article contracted for: See *Wallis, Son & Wells v. Pratt & Haynes* [1910] 2 K.B. 1003, at 1008, 79 L.J.K.B. 1013, reversed [1911] A.C. 394, 80 L.J.K.B. 1058; *Alabastine Co., Paris Ltd. v. Canada Producer & Gas Engine Co.* (1914) 30 O.L.R. 394, affirming 8 D.L.R. 405 (C.A.); *Rafuse Motors Ltd. v. Mardo Construction Ltd.* (1963) 48 M.P.R. 296 (N.S.C.A.); *Cushman Motor Works of Canada v. Laing* [1921] 2 W.W.R. 206, [1920] S.C.R. 649, affirming [1919] 3 W.W.R. 494, 15 Alta. L.R. 53; *O'Flaherty v. McKinley* (1951) 30 M.P.R. 172 (Nfld.); *White v. Munn Motors Ltd.* (1960) 45 M.P.R. 253 (Nfld.); *Freear v. Gilders* (1921) 50 O.L.R. 217; *Thurston v. Streilen* (1950) 59 Man. R. 55; *Comeller v. Billinkoff* (1954) 11 W.W.R. (N.S.)279, 62 Man. R. 35.

The defendant also sought to rely on an escape clause in the conditional-sale contract which reads as follows:

> 8. Purchaser acknowledges that this agreement constitutes the entire contract and that there are no representations, warranties, or conditions, expressed or implied, statutory or otherwise, other than as contained herein. Without limiting the generality of the foregoing Purchaser agrees that there is no warranty as to the "year model" even if stated herein.

This argument cannot prevail as the purchaser did not receive what he bargained for: See *Schofield v. Emerson-Brantingham Implement Co.* [1918] 3 W.W.R. 434, 57 S.C.R. 203, reversing [1918] 1 W.W.R. 306, 11 Sask. L.R. 11, *Hayes Mfg. Co. v. Perdue & Cope* (1931) 43 B.C.R. 545; *Hart-Parr Co. v. Jones* (1917) 2 W.W.R. 888 (Sask.). On this branch of the case *Karsales (Harrow) Ltd. v. Wallis* [1956] 1 W.W.R. 936, [1956] 2 All E.R. 866, and the cases discussed therein commencing at p. 868 are also helpful.

I doubt that the misrepresentations were fraudulent, even though made carelessly but, in my opinion, it was not necessary to decide the question of fraud in the court below, nor is it necessary for us in deciding this appeal to make any finding with respect to fraud.

I hold that the plaintiff was entitled to rescind and to recover a judgment in the amount allowed by the learned trial judge, namely, $7940, with costs in this court and in the court below as stipulated by the learned trial judge.

The truck shall be delivered by the plaintiff to the defendant.

The appeal is accordingly dismissed.

# Canadian Imperial Bank of Commerce v. Larsen

*[1983] 5 W.W.R. 179*
*British Columbia Court of Appeal*
*May 17, 1983*

ANDERSON J.A.: This is an appeal from the judgment of Cooper Co. Ct. J. holding the appellant liable to the respondent on a guarantee executed by the appellant.

At the beginning of January 1980, the defendant herein, Margaret Jean Merton, and her husband, the defendant John Merton, began operation of a cabaret business in Castlegar, British Columbia. They had incorporated Devil's Den Cabaret Ltd. ("the company") for that purpose and had opened a corporate bank account at the Castleaird Plaza Branch of the respondent bank.

On 10th April 1980 the defendant, John Merton, attended the home of the appellant and asked him to sign a personal guarantee to a maximum limit of $10 000 for the indebtedness of the company to the respondent. The appellant is the stepfather of the defendant Margaret Jean Merton.

The appellant had already signed one personal guarantee for this company in January 1980 and was reluctant to become more heavily responsible. As a result, he telephoned the manager of the Castleaird Plaza Branch, one John Craven, and inquired as to the financial status of the company:

Q. But the gist of his inquiry was that he wanted to know what the status of the company was; is that correct? A. Yes, I would say that, yes.

Q. And the reason he was inquiring was because he was possibly going to be on the hook for $10 000 with this company; is that correct? A. Yes, it is.

At the time of this telephone conversation, Mr. Craven knew that the appellant had been asked to sign the personal guarantee and he also knew that the appellant, if he did sign, would be the only major source of security for these funds.

In answering the appellant's inquiry, Mr. Craven stated that he was fairly satisfied with the way the business was going, "that things were going to go", that the deposits were up over the last few weeks, and that the appellant had nothing to worry about. He also mentioned that he had been informed by Merton that the Federal Business Development Bank was now in position to provide its funds and he disclosed that there was an outstanding loan of $1000 with his bank. Mr. Craven stated that "what the company needed was capital".

At the time of the telephone conversation, Mr. Craven knew that in addition to the small outstanding loan of $1000 which he had disclosed, the company was also overdrawn at the respondent's branch by approximately $7000. Mr. Craven also knew that there was a trend in the overdraft of the company which had been doubling every month from the date of its commencement of operations:

| | |
|---|---|
| January 30, 1980 | — overdraft $1392.25, |
| February 29, 1980 | — overdraft $3502.23, |
| March 27, 1980 | — overdraft $7140.11, |
| April 7, 1980 | — overdraft $7056.27. |

Mr. Craven was also aware that in March 1980 he had returned as "N.S.F." a cheque of the company in the amount of $5000 to a company called Millwood Components.

On 11th April 1980, after the further advance of $10 000 was made, the bank balance of the company was $72.60.

There was no further communication from Mr. Craven to the appellant until 4th June 1980, when Mr. Craven forwarded a letter to the appellant demanding immediate payment in full of the $10 000 which had been guaranteed, plus interest from that date. Mr. Craven's reason for making this demand was that he had received notice that the Federal Business Development Bank was about to do the same thing. The Federal Business Development Bank ultimately appointed a receiver.

The appellant testified that he would not have signed the guarantee if he had known of the true state of affairs of the company.

The appellant also testified that he was told that the loan would be a term loan and not a demand loan. The learned trial judge held that such a representation had not been made. This finding is binding upon the appellant.

• • •

[ed: Mr. Justice Anderson quoted from the reasons for judgment in the court below and its reliance on *Lloyds Bank Ltd. v. Bundy* [1975] Q.B. 326 which was decided on the basis of undue influence and not misrepresentation. He continued:]

• • •

Counsel for the appellant contends:

1. That as the appellant was induced as the result of misleading statements made to the appellant by Craven, to sign the guarantee that he should not be held liable on the guarantee.

2. That Craven owed a duty to take reasonable care to advise the appellant of the true financial status of the company and failed in carrying out that duty.

As I purpose to resolve this matter on the basis of the first issue, it is not necessary for the purpose of this appeal to deal with the second issue.

As to the first issue, although the learned trial judge clearly stated the question to be determined: "Were these misrepresentations which induced Larsen to enter into the guarantee?" by endeavouring to apply the principles enunciated in *Lloyds Bank v. Bundy, supra,* he failed to come to grips with the real issue in the case.

The *Bundy* case was not a case involving misrepresentation. In that case the guarantor was fully aware of all relevant facts. The ratio relates to the doctrine of "undue influence" as can be seen by reference to the judgment of Lord Denning M.R., where he clearly excluded established categories of discharge, including misrepresentation, as follows [at p. 763]:

> Now let me say at once that in the vast majority of cases a customer who signs a bank guarantee or a charge cannot get out of it. No bargain will be upset which is the result of the ordinary interplay of forces. There are many hard cases which are caught by this rule. Take the case of a poor man who is homeless. He agrees to pay a high rent to a landlord just to get a roof over his head. The common law will not interfere. It is left to Parliament. Next take the case of a borrower in urgent need of money. He borrows it from the bank at high interest and it is guaranteed by a friend. The guarantor gives his bond and gets nothing in return. The common law will not interfere. Parliament has intervened to prevent moneylenders charging excessive interest. But it has never interfered with banks.
>
> Yet there are exceptions to this general rule. There are cases in our books in which the courts will set aside a contract, or a transfer of property, when the parties have not met on equal terms, when the one is so strong in bargaining power and other so weak that, as a matter of common fairness, it is not right that the strong should be allowed to push the weak to the wall. Hitherto those exceptional cases have been treated each as a separate category in itself. But I think the time has come when we should seek to find a principle to unite them. *I put on one side contracts or transactions which are voidable for fraud or misrepresentation or mistake. All those are governed by settled principles.* I go only to those where there has been inequality of bargaining power, such as to merit the intervention of the court. (The italics are mine.)

In my opinion, the learned trial judge in searching for a special relationship, as outlined in *Bundy,* approached his consideration of the evidence on a misconceived legal basis and as a result found that there was no misrepresentation which induced the appellant to sign the guarantee. He should have approached the issue on "settled principles", as stated in *Anson, Law of Contract,* 24th ed. (1975), at p. 242: "The remedy of rescission is common to all classes of operative misrepresentation. When a person has been induced to enter into a contract by a misrepresentation of any description, the effect on the contract is not to make it void, but to give the party misled an option, either to avoid it, or, alternatively, to affirm it.

Any material misrepresentation, even though made innocently, entitles the guarantor to rescission of the guarantee if it results in inducing the guarantor to enter into the contract.

I have perused the evidence of both Craven and the appellant and it seems to me that Craven misrepresented the financial status of the company and thereby induced the appellant to sign the guarantee. The material innocent misrepresentation made by Craven was his failure, in all the circumstances, to advise the appellant that the company's bank account was overdrawn in the amount of approximately $7000. The failure to advise the appellant of the overdraft would lead any reasonable person to believe that if an advance of $10 000 was made by the respondent to the company that there would be a true "infusion of capital" and that after the $1000 already owing to the respondent was repaid the company would have working capital available in the amount of $9000. I point out, as well, that Craven had advised the appellant that the sum of $1000 was owing to the respondent. Such a statement would cause the appellant to believe that the sum of $1000 was the only indebtedness of the company to the respondent and that nothing was owing by overdraft.

The learned trial judge in his reasons for judgment suggested that the appellant should have made inquires of his step-daughter and son-in-law. One of the major reasons for seeking information from Craven was because he did not trust his son-in-law. He wanted to obtain advice as to the financial status of the company from a reliable source.

As the appellant was indeed to sign the guarantee by the innocent misrepresentation made by Craven he is not liable on the guarantee.

For the above reasons, I would allow the appeal.

*Appeal allowed.*

# Public Trustee v. Skoretz[1]

*(1972) 32 D.L.R. (3d) 749*
*British Columbia Supreme Court*
*December 12, 1972*

ANDERSON, J.: In this case the plaintiff sues for the return of moneys and securities received by the defendant from one David L. M. Roberts, during his lifetime. The plaintiff alleges that the defendant acquired the moneys and securities as a trustee. The defendant says that he received the moneys and securities as a gift.

The deceased who died at the age of 71, on June 13, 1971, had resided in a lodging house at 1036 E. Hastings St., Vancouver, B.C., from October, 1958 to September 21, 1970. He lived alone, kept to himself and had few friends. His room was kept in a filthy condition and, in addition he was in an unkempt and dirty physical condition. His clothes smelt of urine. He was blind in one eye and have very little sight in the other. He had to read with the aid of a magnifying glass. He was quite deaf.

He was able to look after his financial affairs as follows:
a) he deposited his pension cheques at the bank,
b) he paid his rent each month,
c) he purchased bonds from time to time, redeemed the same and purchased new bonds in substitution.

As a result of the circumstances outlined above, the owner of the lodging-house got in touch with a social worker who visited Mr. Roberts and convinced him that he should be in a rest-home. She ascertained that he had a income of $3500 to $4000 per annum. It was difficult for her to converse with Mr. Roberts because he was quite deaf. She had to shout into his ear to make herself understood. She got in touch with the defendant, the operator of "Kay's Rest Home" and made arrangements for Mr. Roberts to go to the rest-home. She told the defendant the approximate amount of Mr. Roberts' annual income and also requested that the defendant make arrangements to have Mr. Roberts examined by a doctor as soon as possible. The defendant does not recall this conversation with the social worker and says that he was not aware of the financial situation of Mr. Roberts prior to his arrival at the rest-home. I accept the evidence of the social worker with respect to the aforesaid conversation and find that the defendant was aware of the annual income of Mr. Roberts.

On September 21, 1970, the defendant picked up Mr. Roberts and brought him to the rest-home. While the rate payable by Mr. Roberts was $175 per month, there is no evidence that any payment was made by Mr. Roberts on his arrival.

On September 23, 1970, Mr. Roberts approached the defendant and asked him to take him to a bank near the vicinity of the rest-home. The defendant told Mr. Roberts that there was a bank close at hand at the corner of Broadway and MacKenzie. Mr. Roberts went with the defendant to the bank where he arranged for transfers of certain bank accounts. He also signed a power of attorney form appointing the defendant his attorney. Mr. Roberts told the defendant he wanted the defendant to have access to the accounts and to handle the same. The employees at the bank explained to Mr. Roberts the effect of the appointment of an attorney.

On September 24, 1970, Mr. Roberts asked the defendant to drive him to the Bank of Montreal, Main and Hastings Branch, so that he could arrange for a transfer of more bank accounts. On the way to the bank, Mr. Roberts told the defendant that he was very happy and that the care he had received at the rest-home was the best he had received during his life. He said: "You and your wife are very friendly—very good to me—I should have been here long before this."

At the Bank of Montreal, Mr. Roberts said: "I want Mr. Skoretz to have my money." The bank employer said: "What do you mean?" The defendant said: "I think he means power of attorney." Mr. Roberts said: "Yes, the same as yesterday." Mr. Roberts again signed a power of attorney form.

After signing the power of attorney form, Mr. Roberts said to the defendant: "I want you to have what's in the box." As a result a form was signed enabling the defendant to gain access to the safety deposit box of Mr. Roberts.

Later in the day (September 24th), the defendant said to Mr. Roberts: "What do you have in your box that you want me to have?" Mr. Roberts pulled a safety deposit key out of his pocket and said: "Take it. It's all yours. You are giving me good care and looking after me. No one visits me. I have no friends here. I'm happy that you are looking after me so well. All the money I have is yours."

In the evening (September 24th) Mr. Roberts said to the defendant: "Go to the box tomorrow and take everything out. It is all yours." The defendant said: "What do you have there?" Mr. Roberts replied. "You'll see when you open the box."

In the late afternoon of September 25, 1970, the defendant went to the bank, opened the safety deposit box and returned home with bonds having a face value of $25 000, registered in the name of Mr. Roberts. The defendant went to Mr. Robert's room where Mr. Roberts was lying on the bed, and said to Mr. Roberts: "Here are your bonds." Mr. Roberts said: "Do you have a pen?" The defendant got a pen and gave it to Mr. Roberts who was looking through the bonds. Mr. Roberts said: "It's all yours. You're giving me good care and I'm glad to be able to give this to you as a gift." Mr. Roberts also said: "All the money I have in the bank is yours. You look after me as long as I live." The defendant assured Mr. Roberts that he would give him the best care he could.

On September 26, 1970, Mr. Roberts fell and fractured his hip and was taken to the Vancouver General Hospital, where he was operated on. During he stay at the hospital he was always confused and disoriented and it was impossible to get any information from him. He was hostile and belligerent.

On March 10, 1971, Mr. Roberts was taken to Valleyview Hospital, at which time the plaintiff became the statutory committee of Mr. Roberts. Mr. Roberts died on June 13, 1971.

Within one week of Mr. Robert's departure to the Vancouver General Hospital, the defendant had transferred all the bank accounts into his own name and had cashed the bonds, the proceeds of which he deposited in his own name. The total amount received by the defendants, including the bonds, was $49 160.

The defendant was aware at all material times that Mr. Roberts had a sister living in the United Kingdom.

During his stay in hospital, Mr. Roberts was in a public ward. The defendant paid small sums of money (approximately $60) to the hospital for the use of Mr. Roberts and also paid $369 by cheque to the hospital. The defendant did not pay Mr. Roberts' funeral expenses.

The defendant did not disclose to anyone that he had received these large "gifts".

The plaintiff submits that:

a) there never were any gifts,

b) there was no corroboration of any gifts,

c) the defendant owed a fiduciary duty to the deceased which was not discharged,

d) the relationship between the defendant and the deceased was such that there was presumption of undue influence which placed an onus on the defendant to show the gift made by the deceased "only after full, free and informed thought about it",

e) the "gifts" were void by virtue of s. 21 of the *Patients' Estates Act*, 1962 (B.C.), C44[2]

The defendant submits that:

a) the gifts were made by the deceased spontaneously and of his own free will,

b) there was evidence of corroboration,

c) the relationship between the defendant and the deceased was such that it was necessary for the plaintiff to prove that the defendant exercised a "dominating influence" over the deceased,

d) s. 21 of the *Patients' Estates Act* was not applicable in the circumstances.

I deal first with the question of corroboration. The evidence relied upon by way of corroboration is as follows:

a) the testimony of Mrs. Skoretz that on September 24, 1970, Mr. Roberts came into the kitchen and stated that he wanted to transfer the rest of his money to the defendant and

b) the endorsement of the bonds by Mr. Roberts.

The evidence of Mrs. Skoretz is corroborative of the desire of Mr. Roberts to transfer the rest of his money to the defendant but not as a gift. After the conversation which Mrs. Skoretz heard, the defendant went with Mr. Roberts to the Bank of Montreal and, when the defendant said to the bank employee that he thought Mr. Roberts wanted to sign a power of attorney, Mr. Roberts said: "Yes, the same as yesterday." It appears to me, therefore, that the conversation overheard by Mrs. Skoretz was not referable to a gift but to an agency relationship.

The endorsement of the bonds is not corroborative because the making of the endorsement does not point only to a gift. In other words, the endorsement of the bonds is equally referable to the relationship of principal and agent as it is to the relationship of donor and donee.

I have examined the evidence of the defendant with great care and while I am not prepared to say that I entirely disbelieve the defendant, I am unable to say that I am so convinced of the truth of the story told by the defendant that I can accept his evidence without some corroboration.

If I am wrong on the question of corroboration, I am of the opinion that the plaintiff should succeed on the ground that the relationship between the defendant and the deceased was such that undue influence is to be presumed and the defendant has not met the onus upon him of proving "that in fact the gift was the spontaneous act of the donor acting under circumstances which enabled him to exercise an independent will" after "full, free and informed thought" about the "gift": see *Inche Noriah v. Shaik Allie Bin Omar*, [1929] A.C. 127 at p. 133, [1928] 3 W.W.R. 608, and *Zamet v. Hyman*, [1961] 1 W.L.R. 1442 at p. 1444.

Some of the circumstances which I have considered in dealing with the question of undue influence are as follows:

a) deceased almost blind,

b) deceased very deaf,

c) undue haste,

d) no independent advice,

e) deceased physically dependent on defendant,

f) no full discussion with deceased,

g) radical change of circumstances of deceased which may have caused deceased to believe that he owed a debt of gratitude to the defendant,

h) size of "gifts",

i) the defendant had become the agent of the deceased when the "gifts" were made,

j) the income from the fund (without impairing capital) far exceeded the cost of care ($175 per month),

k) no logical reason for making a "gift" of this size to defendant.

The surrounding circumstances are such that a clear inference can and should be drawn from the facts that the relationship between the parties was such that the defendant did, on the balance of probabilities, exert a "dominating influence" over the deceased. While there was not, as could be expected, any evidence of express undue influence, the surrounding circumstances provided ample evidence from which, by implication, an inference could and should be drawn that there was in fact, a "dominating influence" exerted by the defendant over the deceased....

Counsel for the defendant submits the case of *Shaw v. Jancowski* is authority for the proposition that unless the relationship is one of the "protected" classes (solicitor and client, physician and patient, trustee and *cestui que trust*, etc.) the plaintiff must adduce positive evidence that a "dominating influence" was, in fact, exerted or that the defendant donee had gained "complete ascendancy" over the donor.

I cannot accept this submission and I do not think the judgment of Robertson, J., in *Shaw v. Jancowski, supra*, supports this contention. If, however, the submissions of counsel for the defendant are supported by the judgment in *Shaw v. Jancowski, supra,* I refuse to follow the said judgment. The judgment of the Judicial Committee in the *Inche Noriah* case, *supra,* is quite to the contrary. In that case Lord Hailsham, L.C., said at pp. 132-3:

> The appellant's evidence at the trial was disregarded, because it was recognized by both sides that her mind was then in such a state as to render her evidence quite valueless. The respondent gave evidence, but the learned trial judge did not believe his testimony. The learned trial judge found that from the death of her daughter onwards the appellant was a feeble old woman, unable to leave the house, relying entirely upon the respondent for everything—even for her food and clothes—leaving the management of her affairs to him, so that she had no knowledge of her own affairs or as to the value of her properties, and so that she was totally and completely in the respondent's hands. He held that when the deed was executed by the appellant her relationship with the respondent was such that he had gained complete ascendancy over her, and that the presumption arose that the deed was procured by his undue influence. He held further that the appellant had had no independent legal advice, and that the circumstances were not such as to rebut the presumption. At the hearing before this Board the respondent contended that there was no confidential relationship between the parties giving rise to any presumption; that if there was any such relationship, the gift was not referable to the relationship; and that in any event the evidence called by the respondent was sufficient to rebut the presumption, if it ever arose.
>
> The principles upon which this case falls to be decided have been the subject of a series of decisions in the English Court of Chancery; and it was not disputed between the parties that the principles of English law must be applied. The question to be decided is stated in the judgment of Cotton L.J. in the well known case of *Allcard v. Skinner,* 36 Ch. D 145, 171, as follows: "The question is: Does the case fall within the principles laid down by the decisions of the Court of Chancery in setting aside voluntary gifts executed by parties who at the time were under such influence as, in the opinion of the Court, enabled the donor afterwards to set the gift aside? These decisions may be divided into two classes: first, where the Court has been satisfied that the gift was the result of influence expressly used by the donee for the purpose; secondly, where the relations between the donor and donee have at or shortly before the execution of the gift been such as to raise a presumption that the donee had influence over the donor. In such a case the Court sets aside the voluntary gift, unless it is proved that in fact the gift was the spontaneous act of the donor acting under circumstances which enable him to exercise an independent will and which justify the Court in holding that the gift was the result of a free exercise of the donor's will. The first class of cases may be considered as depending on the principle that no one shall be allowed to retain any benefit arising from his own fraud or wrongful act. *In the second class of cases the Court interferes, not on the ground that any wrongful act has in fact been committed by the donee, but on the ground of public policy, and to prevent the relations which existed between the parties and the influence arising therefrom being abused.*"
>
> In their Lordships' view the relations between the appellant and respondent are correctly summarized in the judgment of the trial judge, and they are amply sufficient to raise the presumption of the influence of the respondent over the appellant and to render it incumbent upon him to prove that the gift was the spontaneous act of the appellant, acting under circumstances which enabled

her to exercise an independent will, and which justified the Court in holding that the gift was the result of the free exercise of her will.

(Emphasis mine.)

In the *Inche Noriah case, supra,* there was no positive evidence adduced to prove "complete ascendancy" or a "dominating influence", but the presumption of "complete ascendancy" or a "dominating influence" was inferred from the surrounding circumstances.

If I am wrong in refusing to accede to the above submission, I am of the view that the relationship was within the "protected classes." The categories of "protected classes" are not closed. The law does not stand still but moves in accord with social change. I am quite unable to accept the contention that the relationship between rest-home operators and elderly patients is different (to any substantial degree) from the relationship between parent and child, solicitor and client, etc. In fact, elderly patients in rest-homes probably need more protection than the above "protected classes". As a matter of policy, the Courts should protect these elderly and friendless persons by bringing them within the "protected classes". While I do not suggest that the defendant was guilty of fraud or anything of that nature, it is not difficult to imagine how an unscrupulous operator could garner unto himself the assets of many of his patients. It is my view, therefore, that in cases of this kind there must be at least some evidence of independent advice to the donor within the meaning of the judgment of Fletcher Moulton, L.J., in *Re Coomber,* [1911] 1 Ch. 723 at p. 730, where he said:

> All that is necessary is that some independent person, free from any taint of the relationship, or of the consideration of interest which would affect the act, should put clearly before the person what are the nature and the consequences of the act. It is for adult persons of competent mind to decide whether they will do an act, and I do not think that independent and competent advice means independent and competent approval. It simply means that the advice shall be removed entirely from the suspected atmosphere; and that from the clear language of an independent mind, they should know precisely what they are doing.

In the result I find that the defendant was a trustee of the monies and bonds. The defendant must pay to the plaintiff the sums converted by him together with interest at the rate of 7% per annum. If there is any difficulty in ascertaining the proper amount, this matter may be spoken to by counsel.

Judgment accordingly. The plaintiff is entitled to costs.

NOTES

1. *This case does not involve a contract but the effect on a gift made by one individual to another, when the two are not of equal bargaining capacity and there is no adequate consideration to the weaker person. The principles outlined herein are equally applicable to the situation where the two parties enter a contract which is unduly beneficial to the stronger.*

2. *Section 21 of the* Patients' Estate Act (B.C) *provides that every gift made by any person who is or becomes unable to manage his affairs is void as against a committee (legal representation) if the gift is not made for a full and valuable consideration or if the donee had notice of the mental condition of the donor at the time the gift was made.*

   *Having set the transaction aside on the ground of undue influence, the judge did not need to deal with this argument.*

# G. Requirement of Writing

## Chapman v. Kopitoski

*[1972] 6 W.W.R. 525*
*Saskatchewan Queen's Bench*
*October 19, 1972*

DISBERY J.: In this action the plaintiff asks, *inter alia*,[1] for certain declarations and for specific performance of an oral contract for the sale to him by the defendant of the parcel of land hereinafter described.

The plaintiff pleads the alleged contract in paras. 2 and 3 of his statement of claim as follows:

> 2. On the 27th day of March, A.D.1971, the Defendant, Albert Henry Kopitoski, agreed to sell to the plaintiff who agreed to purchase from the said Defendant the land and premises composed of the North-west Quarter of Section 31, in Township 57, in Range 23, West of the Third Meridian, at and for the price or sum of $300.00, with the Plaintiff to pay the taxes outstanding on said land. Pursuant thereto, the Plaintiff did thereupon pay to the Defendant the sum of $25.00 and being a partial payment for the said land and did receive a document in writing from the Defendant evidencing said agreement.
>
> 3. The land and premises referred to in paragraph 2 hereof, of which the Defendant is the registered owner, is more particularly described as follows:
>  "Legal subdivision Eleven (11), Thirteen (13), and the North Half and the South East Quarter of Legal subdivision Fourteen (14), in Section Thirty-One (31), in Township Fifty-seven (57), in Range Twenty-three (23), West of the Third Meridian, in the Province of Saskatchewan, according to a plan of survey of said Township dated at Ottawa on the 7th day of August A.D.1913, containing One Hundred and Forty-nine and Six Tenths (149.6) acres, more or less; Minerals in the Crown."

The defendant in his statement of defence denies the contract of sale alleged by the plaintiff and therefore the first fact to be determined is whether the alleged contract was in fact made between the plaintiff and the defendant on 27th March 1971. The evidence established the following facts: At all material times the plaintiff was a businessman residing in the City of Saskatoon in this province and for some years he had had a cottage in the country in the Loon Lake district. In March 1971 he also had seven head of cattle in that district which were in the care of one, J. Waugh. At the time of the trial he had increased his cattle to 18.

The defendant was a bachelor residing in the Village of Loon Lake. He worked at odd jobs as a carpenter and painter, did some barbering and at times was employed by the Beaver Lumber Company. The defendant had known the plaintiff for about ten years and had done odd jobs for him on the cottage.

The said parcel of land was homesteaded by the defendant in 1932. This land is situated about 20 miles west of Loon Lake at the edge of settlement. The land is rolling and stony with a small lake on it occupying about 30 acres, in which Waugh had put some trout fingerlings. Several years ago about 25 acres had been cleared. The remainder of the quarter section was bushland and, according to the witness Setrekoff, the cost of clearing this acreage would be more than the land so cleared would be worth. The quarter section was only partially fenced, while to the south and east the area is only open range. The plaintiff had seen this land in 1970.

• • •

The defendant's testimony as to what occurred was as follows: The plaintiff asked him if the land was for sale. In reply he told the plaintiff that he had sold the land to Alex [his brother] in 1963; that since making the cash payment of $100 Alex had not paid him anything; that Alex had also failed to pay taxes, and that he "might" have given the plaintiff "a rough idea" of the amount of tax arrears, which, in fact, were in the vicinity of $300. The defendant produced the agreement with Alex and showed it to the plaintiff. He also told the plaintiff that other people had wanted to buy the property which he was unable to sell because of the Alex agreement and that he had showed the agreement to Conroy J.M.C. He agreed that the plaintiff had told him that, if Alex would sign a quit-claim deed, such would end the agreement and he would then be free to sell the land. The plaintiff told him that he had a quit-claim deed with him and they decided to go to Alex's farm "To see whether my brother wants to pay for the land or give it up". In the event that Alex should neither pay nor sign the quit-claim deed the plaintiff offered to take the Alex agreement to his own lawyer to find out, as the defendant put it, "as to how good it was" (discovery QQ.121-41).

• • •

Alex having signed the quit-claim deed form, the plaintiff and the defendant returned to the defendant's home in Loon Lake. The defendant was pleased that he was now free to sell the land. The plaintiff offered to pay the defendant $300 and also to pay the taxes. This offer the defendant accepted. The plaintiff offered to pay a deposit whereupon the defendant gave him some writing paper. The plaintiff wrote out the following receipt which the defendant signed:

"Loon Lake Sask.

March 27, 1971

"Received from Jack C. Chapman, the sum of Twenty five dollars Deposit on the purchase of N.W. 1/4 Section 31 Township 57 Range 23 West of 3rd Meridian. Balance of total purchase price of Three hundred dollars to be paid subject to clear title.

"[Sgd.] Albert H. Kopitoski"

The plaintiff paid the defendant the $25. At this time the plaintiff wrote into the quit-claim deed the name of "Alexander Christie Kopitoski" as grantor, and "Albert Henry Kopitoski" as grantee. The respective [*sic*] Christian names of "Henry" and "Christie" did not appear in the Alex agreement, and such were given to him by the defendant. On the second page he inserted the description of the land which he got from the Alex agreement. The plaintiff told the defendant that he would have his lawyer prepare and send up a transfer for completion. The plaintiff left and took the Alex agreement and the quit-claim deed to his lawyer.

• • •

From a consideration of all the evidence relevant thereto, inclusive of the evidence hereinbefore referred to, I have no hesitation in finding that on 27th March 1971 the defendant orally agreed to sell and the plaintiff to buy the said land on the terms alleged in para.2 of the statement of claim.

THE STATUTE OF FRAUDS

Paragraph 2 of the statement of defence sets forth the following defence:

In the alternative, the Defendant states that if there was an agreement between the Plaintiff and the Defendant with respect to the sale of land, which fact is not admitted but denied, there was not sufficient memorandum or note in writing of the alleged agreement as required by Section 4 of the Statute of Frauds, 29 C.A.R. II, Ch.3.

The Statute of Frauds, 1677, c.3, s.4, so far as it is pertinent to this case enacts as follows:

4. And be it further enacted that...no action shall be brought...upon any contract for sale of lands, tenements or hereditaments, or any interest in or concerning them...unless the agreement upon which such action shall be bought, or some memorandum or note thereof shall be in writing and signed by the party to be charged therewith or some other person thereunto by him lawfully authorized.

Five years hence the tercentenary of this Statute should be celebrated by the Bar in grateful recognition of the cornucopia of litigation with consequential costs which the Statute has showered upon successive generations of deserving counsel. In such a lengthy period an overabundance of often unreconcilable precedents can be found and the opportunity is now mine to add to the muddying of the waters of this pool of precedents fed by the Statute of Frauds. Numerous precedents were cited to me by learned counsel.

I would first refer to the case of *McDougall et al. v. MacKay*, 64 S.C.R. 1, [1922] 3 W.W.R. 191, 68 D.L.R. 245, where Duff J. (as he then was) defined the nature and effect of the Statute of Frauds at p.4 as follows:

> The agreement, it is true, was an oral one, but it was long ago established that the effect of the Statute of Frauds was only to prescribe the kind of evidence required for proving a contract for the sale of land and not to lay down a statutory condition of the valid constitution of such a contract. The agreement of the 21st of June was a valid contract and enforceable, it is true, speaking generally, only against the party signing a memorandum complying with the requirements of the 4th section of the Statute of Frauds, but a valid contract none the less.

Having proved the oral contract, he alleged in para.2 of his statement of claim that the plaintiff must also prove that there is a "memorandum of note" in writing sufficient to satisfy the requirements of s.4 of the Statute of Frauds. There are many reported cases on the sufficiency of memorandum and, as I read the law, the memorandum a plaintiff relies on must contain all the material parts of the oral contract evidenced by such memorandum.

In *McKenzie v. Walsh*, 61 S.C.R. 312, [1921] W.W.R. 1017, 57 D.L.R. 24, the Court had before it a memorandum in the form of a receipt that was very similar to the receipt the defendant gave in the instant case. Sir Louis Davies C.J.C. said at p. 313.

> …I have reached the conclusion that the memorandum of receipt is sufficient. That it must contain all the essential terms of the contract and must show that the parties have agreed to those terms is conceded by both sides. That it does so, I conclude. The essential terms are the parties, the property and the price.

In *Peterson v.Bitzer*, 62 S.C.R. 384, [1922] 1 W.W.R. 141, 63 D.L.R. 182, Brodeur J. said at p.390:

> The receipt of one hundred dollars signed by Mrs. Bitzer on the 29th of December 1919, and handed over to the plaintiff Peterson, is a document which contains all the essential terms of a contract for the sale of the property therein mentioned. The parties, property and price are all included.

In *McKenzie et al. v. Hiscock et al.* (1965), 54 W.W.R. 163 at 176, 55 D.L.R. (2d) 155 (Sask. C.A.), Brownridge J.A. said:

> Then it was argued that there was not a completed contract because various matters such as taxes, mineral rights, disposition of crop and date of possession were not discussed, nor included in Ex.P.1. The short answer is that the memorandum must include only the essential terms of the contract and these are the parties, the property and the price.

Parties, property and price by their very nature are material parts of every contract but, dependent upon the circumstances, there may be other essential terms of a contract in addition to parties, price and property. Anglin J. (as he then was) in *McDougall et al. v. MacKay, supra* [p. 9], points out that the date of possession may be deemed to be a material term of an agreement or "either an immaterial term or a collateral arrangement only. Fry on Specific Performance (6 ed.), par.368. An arrangement as to date of possession may be of the latter character: *McKenzie v. Walsh* [*supra*]; *Anderson v. Douglas* (1908), 18 Man. R. 254, 9 W.L.R. 378 (C.A.)"

In *Hawkins v. Price*, [1947] Ch. 645, [1947] 1 All E.R. 689, Evershed J. found that an essential part of an oral contract for the sale of property which included a small orchard was that possession should be given to the purchaser on a specified day. The memorandum relied on made no reference to possession. Evershed J. dismissed that action on the ground that the memorandum failed to satisfy the Statute because this "material term" was not evidenced therein, the law requiring "that every material term must be evidenced". See also *Green v. Stevenson* (1905), 9 O.L.R. 671, 25 C.L.T. 354 (C.A.), which was followed and applied by Wetmore C.J. in *Strickland v. Ross* (1912), 5 Sask. L.R. 347, 2 W.W.R. 887, 21 W.L.R. 945, 5 D.L.R. 706.

While all the essential terms of a bargain must appear in the memorandum in order to satisfy the Statute it is not necessary that formal or non-essential terms appear therein, for such will be implied by law. In *McKenzie v. Walsh, supra*, it was objected that the time for completion and the giving of possession were not contained in the memorandum. Sir Louis Davies C.J.C. said that such were "in the nature of appointments merely to carry out the contract and not varying its terms". Again, in *Peterson v. Bitzer, supra*, Brodeur J. said at p.391:

> It is contended by Mrs. Bitzer that the document did not contain any date at which possession was to take place.
>
> The 1st of May, 1920, was stipulated as the date at which the cash payment was to be made and at the same time a mortgage was to be given for the balance of the purchase price. In the absence of a contrary intention appearing possession should take place at that date. The date of payment of the purchase money may be regarded as the date of completion.

In *Rowe et al. v. Fidelity-Phenix Insur. Co. of New York*, [1944] O.W.N. 387, 11 I.L.R. 173, [1944] 3 D.L.R. 441, reversed on other grounds [1944] O.W.N. 600, 11 I.L.R. 266, [1944] 4 D.L.R. 265 (C.A.), the memorandum failed to show a time for completion and Urquhart J. held that the law would infer that the contract was to be performed within a reasonable time. See also *Clark v. Barrick et al*, [1949] 2 W.W.R. 1009 at 1019, [1950] 1 D.L.R. 260, reversed [1951] S.C.R. 177, [1950] 4 D.L.R. 529.

Learned counsel for the defendant submitted that the omission from the memorandum of a fixed date for completion, of a fixed date for payment and of a date for giving possession were omissions of material and essential terms and therefore the receipt of 27th March 1971 was insufficient to satisfy the requirements of said s.4. In the circumstances of this case I find that such were non-essential terms concerned with the carrying-out of the contract itself and did not vary the contract. These three objections to the memorandum therefore fail and are dismissed.

• • •

On 29th March, the defendant secured a postal order for $25 which he enclosed in the letter and mailed to the plaintiff [with a note explaining that his brother Alex now had some money and the land had been sold to him]. The plaintiff received the letter on 30th March and took it to his solicitors, who replied on 31st March, advising the defendant that if he did not carry out his contract a court action would be commenced "for specific performance of your agreement with Mr. Chapman and/or damages". On the 12th April a similar letter was sent to the defendant's solicitor. The defendant refused to proceed with the contract and give the required transfer. On 5th May the plaintiff commenced this action.

The law had long held that the note or memorandum required by the Statute need not be contained in a single document; it may consist of a number of writings sufficiently connected so as to warrant their being read together, and which, when so read, satisfy all the requirements of the Statute as to contents and signature: *see Berry v. Scott* (1906), 6 Terr. L.R. 369, 4 W.L.R. 282 (C.A.); *Peterson v. Bitzer,* 62 S.C.R. 384, [1922] 1 W.W.R. 141, 63 D.L.R. 182; *McLellan Properties Ltd. v. Roberge,* [1947] S.C.R. 561, [1947] 4 D.L.R. 641; *Clark v. Barrick et al., supra,* and *Burgess v. Cox,* [1951] Ch. 383, [1950] 2 All E.R. 1212; and the cases listed in DisCastri, *Canadian Law of Vendor and Purchaser,* p. 85.

The Plaintiff's own evidence was that at the defendant's home prior to meeting Alex, the defendant was concerned about the tax arrears and he at that time stated that he would sell the land for $300 with the purchaser assuming the tax arrears. The plaintiff said that he would buy on this basis if Alex gave a quit-claim deed. In the conversation with Alex the matter of the tax arrears was one of the main matters discussed and the plaintiff pointed out to Alex that if the arrears were not paid eventually the land would be lost. After the quit-claim deed was secured the oral contract was made that the plaintiff would pay both the $300 and the arrears of taxes. The adjustment of taxes between vendor and purchaser at the time of the completion of a sale may well be an immaterial term or a collateral arrangement only. The agreement by the plaintiff to pay all the arrears of taxes in the circumstances of this case was clearly, in my opinion, an essential term of the oral contract. On the authorities above quoted every essential or material term must be evidenced in writing.

I have perused, in searching for a "memorandum" sufficient to satisfy the Statute, the defendant's receipt of 27th March 1971, the defendant's letter of 28th March, and the letters written by the plaintiff's solicitors dated 31st March and 12th April. Not one of these documents refers to payment of tax arrears in any way. The memorandum is therefore insufficient to satisfy the Statute in that it omits a material term which was a part of the bargain, namely, that the plaintiff was to pay the arrears of taxes: see particularly *Green v. Stevenson* (1905), 9 O.L.R. 671, 25 C.L.T. 354 (C.A.). There an oral agreement for the sale of land was made in October 1904, one of the terms of which was that the plaintiff should pay taxes for all of the year 1904. The memorandum made no reference to this term and the action was dismissed without costs. Like Anglin J. in *Green v. Stevenson,* "I find myself compelled to hold for the reasons above indicated that this action cannot succeed", and the action is therefore dismissed.

• • •

NOTES

1. *"Inter alia" means "among other things".*

# Bergen v. Billingham et al.

*(1972) 28 D.L.R. (3d) 99*
*Manitoba Queen's Bench*
*May 23, 1972*

WILSON J.: This is an action for specific performance of an agreement for the sale of land.

The parties farm neighbouring lands, but whereas defendants were the owners of their property, of the 350-odd acres farmed by plaintiff he owned but 51 acres, occupying the remainder under lease from a third party. They knew each other well, and each of them profess a high regard for the neighbourliness and integrity of the other. At times they spoke of the value of farmlands, and were in agreement that a fair value for each of their properties would be $350 per acre.

In the late fall of 1971, plaintiff was arranging to move on to his own land a dwelling-house, available for sale nearby and which he thought could be mounted upon the foundation he proposed to erect for it. According to plaintiff, defendants' son Alfred happened to pass by, learned what was afoot, and invited plaintiff to consider purchase of a strip of land from his father which, according to plaintiff, this young man assured him was for sale and could be bought at a reasonable price.

What follows is to some degree confused because of the production of diaries kept by the two men, these containing entries which, if they are accurate, would make it impossible for the initial meeting claimed by plaintiff to have occurred. In any event, by October 22nd there was an accord between them with respect to 61.24 acres of defendants' property, to be sold at $12 000 cash, payable on or before December 31, 1971. At the values which plaintiff gave himself, this parcel ought to have brought $21 424; plaintiff expressed his amazement that defendants would let him have it for only $12 000. He contends that their arrangement was an outright agreement of sale and purchase; defendants say not so, that all they intended was to provide plaintiff with a paper of some sort which would help him in his negotiations for a loan, to finance the cost of buying and installing the house mentioned above.

Plaintiff says defendants were at his place on Friday evening, October 22nd, when the final terms of sale were agreed, the male defendant undertaking to produce a memorandum of sale to be executed the next day. Early Saturday morning, plaintiff went to defendants' house, only to find them on their way out and with no time to stop so that, according to plaintiff, he was to call back later in the day to sign the agreement. In fact, he spent the day harvesting, did not finish until late in the evening, and was too tired to go, so that he left it until the next day, Sunday, to sign the agreement. He arrived at defendant's house in the early evening, the agreement was ready, he read it over, and it was signed, first by the defendants and then by himself. Dated October 23rd (that is the previous day, Saturday) and written in longhand by the male defendant it reads:

> We, Alfred G. and Bertha Billingham do hereby agree to sell Sixty one, desimal [*sic*] Two Four (61.24) acres known as the north half of lot 48 (Inner two miles) between PTH #8 and PTH #9, described as no. 70500 on the tax roll plan no. 3992, lot 48 W. ST. Paul, at and for the price of Twelve Thousand Dollars ($12 000.00) payable in cash on or before the 31st day of December, 1971.
>
> Including all buildings subject to vendor removing all plywood concrete forms now supporting grain in two buildings and one temporary round plywood bin which are not included in the sale agreement.
>
> We shall require one year from date of adjustment to remove farm effects from property.
>
> We shall reserve the right of free access to remove any or all grain presently stored on the farm during the course of the aforementioned year with no rental or storage charges attached.
>
> We also agree that the date of adjustment will be the 31-Dec-1971 and the date of possession will be the same as the date of cash payment in full to our account through our lawyers, Tupper Adams & Co. 7th floor Bank of Canada Bldg. to facilitate any home construction plans that may require immediate attention by the purchaser Mr. Henry P. Bergen, S. 1/2 Lot 48 R.M. W. St. Paul.
>
> *Alfred G. Billingham*
> *Bertha Billingham*
> *Henry P. Bergen*

Male defendant's version is that he prepared two draft documents before settling on the form accepted for signature, doing all of this on Sunday, October 24th, although he deliberately dated it as of the day before. This, perhaps, matters not at all, both of them knowing that the paper was in fact signed on the Sunday.

Within days another party was after defendants to sell the same land at $350 per acre, submitting his written offer to purchase on October 27th. Male defendant was away, and on his return next day, October 28th, both defendants called on the plaintiff, demanding return of ex.1, which they described as no more than an offer of sale, which offer they now rescinded. If that is all it was, the "offer" could, of course, be withdrawn at any time before acceptance. Viewing their agreement as in fact one of sale, plaintiff insisted upon its performance; the full sum of $12 000 was tendered shortly afterwards, and refused.

Defendants base their refusal upon two grounds; first, that the agreement is illegal as one made on a Sunday, and secondly, that it is a nullity for want of consideration, either by way of deposit paid or other disadvantage suffered by the buyer, or by way of mutual promise between them.

By s.4 of the *Lord's Day Act, R.S.C. 1970, c.L-13:*

> 4.  It is not lawful for any person on the Lord's Day, except as provided herein, or in any provincial Act or law in force on or after the 1st day of March 1907, to sell or offer for sale or purchase any goods, chattels, or other personal property, or any real estate, or to carry on or transact any business of, his ordinary calling, or in connection with such calling, or for gain to do, or employ any other person to do, on that day, any work, business, or labour.

The validity of this legislation is no longer questioned, and it has been the subject of many cases. At one time it was held by our Court of Appeal to be of no effect in transactions between farmers: *Cote v. Friesen et al.,* [1921] 3 W.W.R. 436, 32 Man. R. 334; but that decision was not followed elsewhere, and its invalidity was confirmed with *R. v. Thompson,* [1931] 2 D.L.R. 282, 55 C.C.C. 33, [1931] 1 W.W.R. 26.

The question of course is, what is a "sale" within the meaning of the Act, or putting it another way, what is the effective date of a "sale"? Plaintiffs here contend that their agreement was concluded, verbally, on a juridical day, a Saturday, and that all that happened the day following was signature of a memorandum to evidence their bargain, and they refer to *Beaumont v. Brengeri* (1847), 5 C.B. 301, 136 E.R. 893. There, the defendant ordered a carriage, and on Saturday made arrangements for its delivery the following day in order that he might take a drive in it, so that the carriage was delivered on the Sunday. The Court refused to set aside the contract, holding that the agreement was in fact concluded on the Saturday, a completed bargain and sale prior to Sunday.

Speaking of the comparable English Sunday trading laws, 8 Hals., 3rd ed., p. 142, notes that "A contract is not avoided by the statue unless it is wholly made, or at all events completed, on Sunday..." And see DiCastri, *Canadian Law of Vendor and Purchaser,* p. 236, para. 283.

Of course, the bargain is void where everything happens on a Sunday: *Ciz v. Hauka* (1953), 108 C.C.C. 349, 11 W.W.R. (N.S) 433, 61 Man. R. 370. The statute does not, however, render illegal a contract created by the acceptance later in the week of an offer tendered the Sunday before: *Bailey v. Dawson* (1912), 1 D.L.R. 487, 25 O.L.R. 387, *Gibbons v. Koepke,* (1952) 1 D.L.R. 707, 102 C.C.C. 381, 4 W.W.R. (N.S.) 560; or because part of the negotiations occurred on a Sunday: *Young v. Taylor,* [1921] 3 W.W.R. 882. The contract is caught by the Act when an offer tendered earlier in the week is accepted on Sunday: *Perry v. Anderson* (1970), 12 D.L.R. (3d) 414; or when satisfaction of a condition upon which acceptance is to depend occurs on a Sunday: *Superior Motors Ltd. v. Cade (No. 2)*, [1930] 3 D.L.R. 1003, [1930] 2 W.W.R. 448, 24 S.L.R. 558, where although the sale documents were signed on Saturday, the wife's approval of her husband's choice of their new automobile, a condition of the sale, was not given until she actually saw the car the next day. And, a contract otherwise void because made on a Sunday may be good because affirmed on another day: *Olliviere v. Durand*, [1953] 3 D.L.R. 590, 9 W.W.R. (N.S.) 53, where what occurred on the Sunday was treated as "preliminary" to the actual delivery and acceptance of the goods later in the week.

*Lyle Ltd. v. Rouse* (1956), 19 W.W.R. 373, is analogous to the *Cade* case. In the *Rouse* case, the applicable legislation made delivery of a certain document an integral part of the transaction, and where this was done on Sunday, the contract was void. *Contra*, execution of documents not essential to the basic contract will not save the latter when the statute is violated. *Angevaare v. McKay* (1960), 25 D.L.R. (2d) 521, where sale of a motor-car was void because done on a Sunday, and not validated by execution of finance papers later in the week, these being merely collateral to the existence of the contract of sale.

Seemingly, too, the statute does not apply where the plaintiff was unaware of it breach by the defendant: *Aconley et al. v. Willart Holdings Ltd.* (1964), 47 D.L.R. (2d) 146, 49 W.W.R. 46.

From the foregoing the test is, was the contract in fact completed (in the *Gibbons* case, *supra*, the expression is "substantially completed") on a Sunday? Clearly, this is so where the entire transaction, or acceptance of an offer earlier made, or satisfaction of a condition essential to the contract, occurs on a Sunday. But here, the bargain was completed before Sunday (and I reject defendants' evidence that the conditions in ex.1 were not introduced until Sunday) when all that occurred was the signing in ex.1. And while it may be true that to satisfy the *Statute of Frauds*[1] a contract of sale of land may not be enforceable in the absence of a writing, the cases have repeatedly held that the statute goes no further. It does not provide that, in the absence of writing, the bargain does not exist: Halsbury, *supra*, p. 89: "The effect of the statutory provisions referred to which require a note or memorandum in writing is not to render void contracts which do not comply therewith, still less to make them illegal, but to make a note or memorandum in writing indispensable evidence in proceedings to enforce them." Because writing was not essential to the validity of the contract, it cannot be said that, simply because ex.1 was signed on Sunday, the contract was "wholly made, or at all events completed, on Sunday", and the defence under this heading must fail.

Defendants urge that despite its terms, ex.1 does no more than evidence an offer for sale of the concerned lands. The language of the document does not support this contention, and it must be kept in mind that ex.1 was prepared by defendant Alfred Billingham himself. As presented to plaintiff and signed, it was the end result of two essays in composition, two drafts, so that its language was the considered product of his concentration to that extent.

At no time did defendants protest that ex.1 omitted terms, or incorporated terms not intended. In his answers on discovery, Q.52, the male defendant said in part, "I felt sorry for him and just made a mistake and agreed to sell for twelve thousand dollars." Invited to protest the terms of sale, Q.88, although repreating his insistence that no more was meant than an offer for sale, this witness accepted ex.1 as setting out their bargain. And his protest that the conditions for sale written into ex.1 formed no part of their initial discussions or negotiations is hardly supported by the answer to Q.153, that ex.1 was signed without any discussion, which is not what one would expect, in the ordinary course of things, where one party attempts to vary the terms of a settled bargain by introducing what are, after all, a fairly complicated set of conditions.

The somewhat cryptic statement upon which ex.1 closes, "to facilitate any home construction plans that may require immediate attention by the purchaser Mr. Henry P. Bergen", is not at all inconsistent with the latter's intention to move his new home to the property subject of sale, instead of to the site which he initially had in mind when he first spoke with defendants' son, who, incidentally, was not called to deny plaintiff's account of his meeting with this young man.

If there is any ambiguity, the *contra proferentem*[2] rule requires that it be held to the account of defendants, as being those who prepared the document. The plain language of that exhibit is that they agreed to sell—not offered to sell—the lands in question to plaintiff. And, if it was only an offer, what was the effect of plaintiff's signature, or why was he invited to sign?

I hold that ex.1 correctly recites the terms of an agreement for sale of the land from defendants to plaintiff.

But, say defendants, the contract is void as being *nudum pactum,* for want of consideration.

• • •

So here, because ex.1 does not in express terms oblige plaintiff to buy, defendants claim an absence of mutuality and, because there was no deposit, the contract, they say, is without consideration.

In *Dawson v. Helicopter Exploration Co. Ltd.,* [1955] 5 D.L.R. 404 at p. 411, [1955] S.C.R. 868, Rand J., after quoting with approval from *The "Moorcock"* (1889), 14 P.D. 64 at p. 68, that a business transaction is to be accorded such "business efficacy as both parties must have intended", continued:

> This question is considered in *Williston on Contracts,* vol. 1, pp. 76-77, in which the author observes:
> "Doubtless wherever possible, as matter of interpretation, a court would and

should interpret an offer as contemplating a bilateral rather than a unilateral contract, since in a bilateral contract both parties are protected from a period prior to the beginning of performance on either side—that is from the making of the mutual promises.

"At the opening of the present century the courts were still looking for a clear promise on each side in bilateral contracts. A bargain which lacked such a promise by one of the parties was held to lack mutuality and, therefore, to be unenforceable. Courts are now more ready to recognize fair implications as effective: 'A promise may be lacking, and yet the whole writing may be "instinct with an obligation," imperfectly expressed,' which the courts will regard as supplying the necessary reciprocal promise."

The expression "instinct with an obligation" first used by Scott J., in *McCall Co. v. Wright* (1909), 133 Appl. Div. (N.Y.) 62 is employed by Cardozo J. in *Wood v. Lady Duff-Gordon* (1917), 222 N.Y. 88 at pp. 90-1, in the following passage: "It is true that he does not promise in so many words that he will use reasonable efforts to place the defendant's endorsements and market her designs. We think, however, that such a promise is fairly to be implied. *The law has outgrown its primitive stage of formalism when the precise word was the sovereign talisman, and every slip was fatal...* A promise may be lacking and yet the whole writing may be 'instinct with an obligation,' imperfectly expressed."

The expression appears again, in *Great Eastern Oil & Import Co. Ltd. v. Chafe* (1956), 4 D.L.R. 310, 40 M.P.R. 21. So here, although ex.1 does not recite in express terms an agreement to purchase corresponding to the agreement to sell on defendants' part, yet it is impossible to read the document as devoid of an undertaking to buy, whereby the mutual promises of the parties provide the consideration for their agreement. Bergen is referred to as the "purchaser", and by signing as he did, he must be taken to have accepted this reference to his status under the agreement, with all that follows.

In the result, plaintiff succeeds. Because, however, he was party to the irregular dating of ex.1, out of which sham this litigation in large part arose, there will be no costs,[3] and see *Fallis v. Dalthaster* (1912), 4 D.L.R. 705, 2 W.W.R. 132, 21 W.L.R. 171 *sub nom. Fallis v. Balthaser.*

*Judgment for plaintiff*

NOTES

1. *Please note that the* Statute of Frauds *was repealed in Manitoba on July 1st, 1983.*
2. *"contra proferentem" is a rule which provides that where there is ambiguity in a document, the interpretation will be against the interest of the party who prepared it.*
3. *The plaintiff was deprived of his costs because he had agreed to date the agreement on the Saturday instead of the Sunday, and the judge felt this was partly the reason that the action had to be brought.*

# Starlite Variety Stores Ltd. v. Cloverlawn Investments Ltd.

*(1979) 92 D.L.R. (3d) 270*
*Ontario High Court of Justice*
*December 13, 1978*

• • •

[ed: The plaintiff Starlite is the operator of a chain of small variety stores situated chiefly in Windsor and London, Ontario. It leases the stores and then sublets the property on a franchise basis, in return for a royalty, usually 2%, on the gross sales. It was owned by Don Myers who had his brother Ray as the manager.

The defendant Cloverlawn is a private company which builds and owns shopping plazas. Cloverlawn decided to expand its plaza at the corner of Grand Marais and Longfellow in the city of Windsor, but didn't want to commence construction until a tenant had been obtained.

Frank D'Amico represented Cloverlawn in its leasing affairs. He and James Morrow, a well-known real-estate salesman representing Starlite, orally agreed upon a lease for ten years after which they shook hands and Frank said, "You've got a deal." They then had a "liquid lunch". Later Starlite executed the lease and returned it with a deposit. Cloverlawn retained the agreement but never signed it.

Mr. Justice Stark outlined these facts in some detail and continued.]

Construction on the addition to the plaza was now commenced. A well-known builder, one John Drazic, was asked to tender and in due course his bid was accepted. Construction began early in June of 1977. The store to be occupied by Starlite was designated on the plans as store No. 3. On August 16th, Ray Myers produced a sketch, known as a vellum drawing, which in effect provided for changes in the store front and in the location of certain electric conduits. These changes were made. Other changes were later requested. Drazic contacted Bairstow, an employee of Cloverlawn's who was supervising construction, and he gave verbal approval of the changes, and this approval was later confirmed in writing by Drazic, although Bairstow's letter of acceptance did not arrive until September 27th. The witness Drazic, whose records were very complete, testified that at all times he was given the impression from Bairstow and from other Cloverlawn employees that the tenant of store No. 3 was to be Starlite. The cost of the last-mentioned changes was $851.50. Certain additional changes had been requested but were refused by Cloverlawn.

Throughout the construction period, Starlite was busily engaged in preparing for the occupancy of the new store. They attended at the site and selected their colours. Ray Myers was at the location constantly, observing and pressing for progress. On June 16th, Starlite ordered their new advertising signs for the store, at a price of $1540.80. On August 15th, Starlite ordered shelving for the new store at a cost of $3697.74.

Viewing the evidence as a whole, it seems clear that the various managers of departments at Cloverlawn, acted on the understanding that a deal had been completed, with the single exception of Cloverlawn's president, Kenneth McGowen. Thus, Bairstow, the property manager, authorized structural changes. D'Amico was Cloverlawn's representative who negotiated the deal, just as he had previously negotiated deals on behalf of his company. I accept the evidence of Morrow and Myers that no suggestion was ever made to either of them, that the deal as negotiated with D'Amico was conditional upon formal execution by the company.

The president of Cloverlawn, McGowen, admitted that on August 25th he accepted a better rental offer which he received from Mac's Convenience Stores Limited. He contended that his delay in formal acceptance of the Starlite deal was because of his dissatisfaction with Don Myers' handling of certain rental arrears on another property, leased by another company owned by Myers. McGowen said that he instructed D'Amico to get that settled and then he would consider the proposed lease. He also wanted Myers to take over a certain vacant store in another plaza. Nevertheless, he admitted that he authorized Bairstow to make the specific changes requested by Starlite which I have earlier described. He had also approved of the inclusion of air conditioning for store No. 3, a feature not ordinarily provided for tenants except when specially negotiated. Moreover, it also appeared from the evidence that one of McGowen's senior officers had already approved of a settlement of the rental arrears which had loomed large in persuading McGowen to delay his acceptance of the disputed deal. McGowen admitted his knowledge of the franchise deal with Mrs. Morrow. He said he felt sorry for Morrow but had no regrets for Starlite.

Two defences are raised by Cloverlawn. The first is that no agreement was ever reached between the parties, because the offer to lease was never formally accepted. The second defence is reliance on the *Statute of Frauds*, R.S.O. 1970, c. 444.

In my view, a verbal agreement was in fact reached between the three men, Morrow, D'Amico and Ray Myers, subsequently accepted by Don Myers. The draft memorandum on Cloverlawn's standard forms, embodied certainly the principal points of agreement; and D'Amico's acting as representative of the defendant company never suggested that any formal or different kind of acceptance would be required. The conduct of all parties throughout was consistent with the completion of the deal and inconsistent with an unaccepted unilateral offer. I therefore reject that defence.

I turn now to the alleged failure to comply with the *Statute of Frauds*. Section 4 reads as follows:

> 4.  No action shall be brought whereby to charge any executor or administrator upon any special promise to answer damages out of his own estate, or

whereby to charge any person upon any special promise to answer for the debt, default or miscarriage of any other person, or to charge any person upon any agreement made upon consideration of marriage, or upon any contract or sale of lands, tenements or hereditaments, or any interest in or concerning them, or upon any agreement that is not to be performed within the space of one year from the making thereof, unless the agreement upon which the action is brought, or some memorandum or note thereof is in writing and signed by the party to be charge therewith or some person thereunto by him lawfully authorized.

• • •

[ed: The plaintiff argued that the lease did not have to be signed in order to satisfy the Statute of Frauds. The judge disagreed and continued:]

Finally, there is the doctrine of part performance. The essential elements required to establish the part performance which will exclude the statute are listed in 8 Hals., 3rd ed., p. 110, para. 190, as follows:

(1) the acts of part performance must be such as not only to be referable to a contract such as that alleged, but to be referable to no other title; (2) they must be such as to render it a fraud in the defendant to take advantage of the contract not being in writing; (3) the contract to which they refer must be such as in its own nature is enforceable by the court; (4) there must be proper parol evidence of the contract which is let in by the acts of part performance.

The part performance, in order to take the case out of the operation of the statute, must be by the person seeking to enforce the parol agreement.

The leading Canadian authority is the decision of the Supreme Court of Canada in *Deglman v. Guaranty Trust Co. of Canada et al.*, [1954] S.C.R. 725, [1954] 3 D.L.R. 785, where the above principles are followed. That case made it clear that the mere payment of money, as occurred in the case at bar in the payment of the two deposit cheques, will not qualify as part performance. In view of the recent English decision in *Steadman v. Steadman*, [1974] 2 All E.R. 977, a case which reached the House of Lords, that may no longer be the fixed rule in England; and it seems logical that money clearly referable to the specific contract should no longer be treated as equivocal. However, I am bound by the *Deglman* decision.

As I have indicated there are acts of part performance on the part of Starlite which, in my view, meet the requirements of the common law so as to relieve the burden imposed by the *Statute of Frauds*. The preparation by the plaintiff of the plans to meet its peculiar requirements, the conduct of the plaintiff throughout the whole period of construction, the actions by the plaintiff in the preparation of its advertising signs and the shelving for its products, and the payment of various expenses concerned with these matters, all these are acts of part performance which meet the law's requirements. Accordingly, I hold that the agreement to lease is enforceable, and that the defendant breached the agreement, and that the plaintiff is entitled to damages in lieu of specific performance, which latter remedy is no longer available.

The matter of damages in a case of this kind is one which raises great difficulties. The plaintiff produced figures to show the revenue it receives from various other franchised stores in Windsor. This revenue in each case is based on 2% of the gross sales. The figures filed vary in amount from an annual volume of $576 000 to a low of $240 000. Thus, even if the low figure of $240 000 were accepted an annual income of about $5000 continuing for the lease term of 10 years, would result in a claim for lost income of some $50 000. But there are many important contingencies before such a figure could be accepted. It was admitted that not all franchise stores succeed. Some fail in their attempts. The success of any new store is unpredictable. Much depends on the initiative and capabilities of the franchisee. Much depends on population changes and traffic conditions. Allowance must be made for expenses incurred by Starlite in the collection of its royalties and in the supervision of its franchises. It would be unrealistic not to discount any suggested figures by at least 50%.

One possible measure of the value to Starlite of the loss of the deal, is provided by the higher rental figures which Mac's Convenience Stores Limited undertook in their lease to pay. Exhibit 1 indicates that the total rent to be paid by Starlite for the 10-year period is $110 700. But the rent called for in Mac's Convenience Stores Limited lease, ex. 20, for the 10-year period is fixed at $126 000. Thus, it might be argued that Starlite, by the loss of its contract, has forfeited a property which was worth $16 000 more, over the 10-year period than they were required to pay under their agreement.

Under the above circumstances, and since in my view the plaintiff is clearly entitled to some relief by way of damages, even though those damages are ephemeral and difficult to determine, I would fix the amount to which the plaintiff is entitled for breach of contract at $20 000, as being a not un-reasonable estimate of the damages he has suffered. The deposit payments of $790 should be returned to the plaintiff. I do not allow interest on that amount. Judgment for the plaintiff therefore should issue in the sum of $20 790 plus the costs of this action.

*Judgment for plaintiff.*

[ed: An appeal from this decision was dismissed by the Ontario Court of Appeal, see (1980) 106 DLR (3d) 384.]

# H. Interpretation of Contracts

## Bonnett v. Bonnett

*(1981) 112 D.L.R. (3d) 649*
*Saskatchewan Queens Bench*
*April 30, 1980*

HALVORSON, J.: The plaintiff has sued for the balance owing on a verbal agreement by the defendant to purchase a house and certain equipment. The claim is resisted on the grounds that the property sold was to have been devised to the defendant.

On January 3, 1977, a Mr. Bonnett sold his farm to his nephew, the defendant, but specified in the agreement for sale that the farmhouse should be excluded as the vendor desired to retain it as his home. The wording of that clause was as follows:

> It is agreed by the parties hereto that the house located on the NW 15 is excluded from this sale. The Vendor is to have the right to retain said house on the NW 15 for the remainder of his life, use of the yard, and access thereto. It is further agreed that should the house be sold during the lifetime of the Vendor, the first opportunity to purchase same will be given to the Purchaser.

The wording of this exclusion concerned the defendant because he had no other home in the area of the farm and wished to be assured of being able either to obtain the house on Mr. Bonnett's death or to purchase same if it were offered for sale during Mr. Bonnett's lifetime. The parties were in agreement that this should be the result, but rather than alter the term in the agreement for sale it was decided instead to accomplish this by a codicil[1] to Mr. Bonnett's will. To that end a codicil dated January 8, 1977, was executed wherein Mr. Bonnett devised to the defendant any house which he owned at his death.

On September 24, 1977, Mr. Bonnett married the plaintiff and then died on November 5, 1977.

114

A few days after the death, the defendant, I find, reluctantly agreed with the plaintiff to buy the house together with a tractor and tools for a total consideration of $19 000. The house must be viewed as a chattel because the land to which it is attached belongs to the defendant.

Of the $19 000 the defendant unilaterally apportioned $2500 as the price for the tractor and $2000 as the price for the tools. The plaintiff accepted cheques of $2500 and $2000 in payment for these items. In April, 1978, the defendant took possession of the house and has resided there since.

By the operation of s. 15 of the *Wills Act*, R.S.S. 1978, c. W-14, Mr. Bonnett's marriage invalidated his previous will and the aforementioned codicil. He did not make a new will following his marriage, and, therefore, the plaintiff became the sole beneficiary of his estate under the provisions of the *Intestate Succession Act*, R.S.S. 1978, c. I-13. His estate was worth approximately $275 000.

On behalf of the defendant it was argued that part of the consideration for the purchase of the farm by the defendant from Mr. Bonnett was the latter's verbal covenant to give the farmhouse to the defendant upon the death of Mr. Bonnett, and that I should enforce that covenant.

I accept the defendant's testimony, substantiated as it is by the codicil, that Mr. Bonnett in fact agreed that the defendant should receive the house upon the demise of Mr. Bonnett. The question is whether evidence of the verbal commitment is admissible in light of the written words of the agreement for sale.

Normally, extrinsic evidence cannot be tendered to vary the terms of a written document. In the text, *Chitty on Contracts*, 23rd ed. (1968), p. 302, the rule is stated thusly:

> Where the parties have embodied the terms of their contract in a written document, the general rule is that extrinsic evidence is not admissible to add to, vary, subtract from or contradict the terms of the written instrument. This rule is often known as the "parol evidence" rule. Its operation is not confined to oral evidence, but extends to extrinsic matter in writing, such as drafts, preliminary agreements and letters of negotiation. The instrument itself is the only criterion of the intention of the parties; so extrinsic evidence is excluded even though such evidence might clearly show that the real intention of the parties was at variance with the particular expressions used in the written instrument. "If there be a contract," said Lord Denman C.J., "which has been reduced into writing, verbal evidence is not allowed to be given of what passed between the parties, either before the written instrument was made, or during the time that it was in a state of preparation, so as to add to or subtract from, or in any manner to vary or qualify, the written contract." And this was always the rule of the courts of equity as well as courts of law.

There are certain exceptions to that general principle, one of which is in the area of supplementary terms. The author, Chitty, describes that exception at p. 306 in his text as follows:

> Although extrinsic evidence is not admissible to add to or vary the terms of a written instrument, evidence may be admitted to show that the instrument was not intended to express the whole agreement between the parties. If, for exam-

ple, the parties intend their contract to be partly oral and partly in writing, extrinsic evidence is admissible to prove the oral part of the agreement. But a heavy burden of proof rests upon the party who alleges that a seemingly complete instrument is incomplete and it would seem that the extrinsic evidence must not be inconsistent with the terms of the instrument.

I am of the opinion that the defendant's situation falls within this exception. To assure that the defendant would have the house, the parties agreed in writing that he had the first right of refusal to buy the house, and they agreed orally that if the house was not sold, the defendant would receive it as a gift upon the death of Mr. Bonnett. The verbal agreement is not inconsistent with the written terms of the contract, but, rather, fills a void inasmuch as the agreement for sale did not cover the event of Mr. Bonnett dying while still owning the house.

The plaintiff's claim is dismissed with costs.

*Action dismissed*

NOTES

1. *A codicil is a document which alters a will without re-drawing it. A bequest in a will may be added to, subtracted from, omitted or changed by preparing this formal document. The codicil states the nature of the change or changes and is signed and witnessed in the same manner as was the original.*

# I. Privity of Contract

## Greenwood Shopping Plaza Ltd v. Beattie et al.

*(1980) 111 D.L.R. (3d) 257*
*Supreme Court of Canada (from Nova Scotia)*
*June 17, 1980*

MCINTYRE, J.: This appeal concerns the doctrine of privity of contract and the question of the extent of third party rights under contract.[1] The appellant is the owner of a shopping centre in Greenwood, Nova Scotia. Neil J. Buchanan Limited (the Company) is a corporation whose shares are all beneficially owned by one Neil J. Buchanan who was active in the management of the Company's affairs which concerned the operation of a Canadian Tire Store under franchise. The respondents, Beattie and Pettipas, were at all relevant times employees of the Company. The Company became a tenant of the appellant in 1972, occupying some of the space in the shopping centre. It took over the unexpired term of a lease with the former tenant and, on the expiration of that term, it was renewed. No new lease was executed but an exchange of letters covered the creation of a new term at a new rent subject to the other conditions contained in the lease. It was found at trial, as has not been since contested, that the terms of the tenancy are set out in the earlier lease, save as modified by the exchange of letters. The lease included, in paras. 14 and 15, the provisions which covered insurance of the demised premises. They are set out hereunder:

14. The Lessor shall insure the buildings on the Entire Premises against fire and supplemental risks on the basis of replacement cost to the extent obtainable and shall furnish copies of all policies to the Lessee. The Lessor, if itself unable to procure insurance on this basis, and before insuring on a depreciated cost basis, undertakes to give notice to the Lessee of its inability to procure such insurance and to permit the Lessee to acquire insurance on the basis of replacement cost on behalf of the Lessor and for which the Lessor agrees to pay.

15. Both the Lessor and the Lessee will arrange, provided such arrangement is not contrary to the wishes of any existing or future mortgagee of the Entire

Premises, with their respective insurers not to grant subrogation[2] rights for the recovery of any loss through fire or supplemental perils occasioned by acts of the other, provided such loss is covered by insurance and to the extent only that payment of such loss is made by the insurer.

Neither party to the lease took any steps towards the performance of the agreements mentioned in paras. 14 and 15. The appellant did not insure to replacement cost and neither party took any steps to obtain express waivers of subrogation. The Company did not request and the appellant did not deliver a copy of the policy of insurance mentioned in para. 14. The parties were not, however, wholly without insurance. The Company secured a minimal amount of $10 000 on some of its own property and the appellant insured the buildings on the basis of the cost of construction with a percentage addition but did not procure coverage for replacement cost nor did it make any arrangement regarding the waiver of subrogation rights. On the night of March 3, 1976, a large part of the shopping centre was destroyed or damaged by fire. The fire started in the premises leased by the Company. It was found at trial—and these findings were accepted in the Court of Appeal and have not been contested here—that the fire was caused by the negligence of the respondents, Beattie and Pettipas, acting in the course of their employment, while using welding equipment to erect tire racks in a part of the demised premises used for garage and storage. The action was brought on behalf of Greenwood for the recovery of its uninsured loss and on behalf of its fire insurers by way of subrogation for moneys paid to the appellant by the insurers. The Company, Buchanan personally, and certain other parties were originally involved in this litigation, which involved three separate cases, all of which were consolidated for trial and dealt with in one trial judgment. This appeal, however, concerns only the appellant and the two respondent employees of the Company.

At trial, Cowan, C.J.T.D., found the respondent's negligence caused the fire and held the Company, as the employer, vicariously liable in damages. However,applying the judgments of this Court in *Agnew-Surpass Shoe Stores Ltd. v. Cummer-Yonge Investments Ltd.* (1975), 55 D.L.R. (3d) 676, [1976] 2 S.C.R. 221, 4 N.R. 547; *Ross Southward Tire Ltd. et al. v. Pyrotech Products Ltd. et al.* (1975), 57 D.L.R. (3d) 248, [1976] 2 S.C.R. 35, 5 N.R. 541, and *Smith et al. v. T. Eaton Co.Ltd. et al.* (1977), 92 D.L.R. (3d) 425, [1978] 2 S.C.R. 749, 15 N.R. 315, and upon a consideration of the effect of paras. 14 and 15 of the lease, he limited the recovery of the appellant as against the Company to such damages which exceeded amounts which were or should have been insured against under the insurance provision in paras. 14 and 15. This excluded from the appellant's recovery against the Company both subrogated damages and the appellant's damages consisting of the difference between the amount of insurance and the cost of reconstruction. Rental loss and some incidental expense resulting from the fire were allowed. Damages, however, were not finally fixed at trial or on appeal and remain to be assessed pending the determination of liability.

At the trial [31 N.S.R. (2d) 1], while the respondents were joined as defendants, the question of their separate liability does not seem to have received serious or extensive argument. In supplementary reasons for judgment given on proceedings which were described as "an application for the order" and which followed the trial and the giving of reasons for judgment [34 N.S.R. (2d) 217], Cowan, C.J.T.D., disposed of the matter in these terms [at pp. 218-9]:

A question was also raised as to the position of the defendants, Beattie and Pettipas, and as to whether or not the right of recovery of the Greenwood company against these defendants was similarly limited.

Clause 15 provided that the Greenwood company, as lessor, would arrange with its insurers not to grant subrogation rights for the recovery of any loss through fire or supplemental perils occasioned by acts of the lessee, provided such loss was covered by insurance and to the extent only that payment of such loss was made by the insurer. The defendants, Beattie and Pettipas, were not parties to the lease which was in force between the Greenwood company as lessor and the Buchanan company as lessee. It was suggested that the insurers of the Greenwood company were entitled to subrogation against Beattie and Pettipas, employees of the Buchanan company, acting within the scope of their authority, for whose negligence the Buchanan company is vicariously liable.

Counsel were not able to cite any authority in support of their respective views and the point appears to be one of first impression.

On consideration, it appears to me that the clause in question was intended by the parties to provide that there should be no right of subrogation on the part of the insurers of the Greenwood company in respect of losses, for which the Buchanan company might be liable, either because of its own negligence or because of the negligence of others, for whose actions it would be vicariously liable. That is the effect of the reasons for judgment which I delivered on May 26, 1978.

It seems to me that it follows logically that if there is no right of subrogation against the Buchanan company, in respect of the particular loss, there should be no right of subrogation against the employees of the Buchanan company for whose negligence the Buchanan company is responsible.

In the Court of Appeal, which affirmed the trial decision [99 D.L.R. (3d) 289, 31 N.S.R. (2d) 168, 6 B.L.R. 41], MacKeigan, C.J.N.S., after agreeing that the Company was not liable to Greenwood for losses which Greenwood failed to insure against, or under any subrogated claim on behalf of Greenwood's insurers, dealt with the position of the respondents in these terms [at p. 292]:

Greenwood's final contention, that in any event the respondents Beattie and Pettipas were not protected by the lease, must, in my opinion, fail. Buchanan, in obtaining indirect insurance coverage against liability for its own negligence, must have intended to cover also its employees' liability since its negligence as a corporation only arises vicariously from its employees' negligent acts or omissions.

Greenwood's insurance covers fire caused by any means and by any person, including Buchanan and its employees. Clause 14 gives Buchanan the benefit of that presumed insurance. Greenwood can, it seems to me, no more sue Buchanan's employees than it can sue Buchanan.

After making reference to *Scruttons Ltd. v. Midland Silicones Ltd.*, [1962] A.C. 446, [1962] 1 All E.R. 1 (H.L.), and to the comments on that case by Ritchie, J., in this court in *Canadian General Electric Co. Ltd. v. Pickford & Black Ltd.* (1970), 14 D.L.R. (3d) 372 at pp. 373-4, [1971] S.C.R. 41 at pp. 43-4, 2 N.S.R. (2d) 497, he dealt with those authorities in these terms [at p. 294]:

> I need not try to analyze whether the *Midland Silicones* principle has been diluted by *New Zealand Shipping Co. Ltd. v. A.M. Satterthwaite & Co. Ltd.*, [1975] A.C. 154 (P.C.), and other recent cases, although I have read with profit comments, generally critical of the principle in 55 Can. Bar Rev. 327 (1977) (S.M. Waddams); 40 Mod. L. Rev. 706 (Peter Handford), and 709 (J.L.R. Davis) (1977), and 28 U.T.L.J. 75 (1978) (Graham Battersby). I find the principle does not apply here because the employees of the tenant and of the landlord are not "strangers" to the contract. They are impliedly beneficiaries of the covenant to insure contained in the lease and thus fall within one of Lord Reid's exceptions (p. 474 [in *Scruttons, supra*]) to his "fundamental principle", namely, where the parties to the contract have intended the exemption from liability to extend to the alleged stranger or third party.

He was of the opinion that the landlord's covenant in the lease included a promise to cover the employees and he found an identification of the employees with the employer which saved them from being "strangers to the contract". He continued [at pp. 294-5]:

> Here the landlord's covenant to insure implied, as we have seen, a promise by the landlord to the tenant to assume by insurance the risk of loss by fire caused by any means, including the negligence of the tenant and its employees. That assumption of risk implied a further promise not to sue the tenant for damages which would be covered by that risk. In my opinion, this latter promise must have been intended to extend to the employees through whom and for whom the tenant was responsible.
>
>   This presumed intent to benefit the employees, in my view, arises from the identification, in this type of case, of the employees with their corporate employer, an identification which does not occur, for example, between a shipper and an independent contractor, such as a stevedoring company. Their acts and omissions are the employer's act. All duties imposed on the tenant by the lease are performed by the employees, including the duty not to harm the landlord's property. Any right of the tenant under the lease, such as the right to occupy the demised premises, or to use the parking lot and other common facilities of the shopping centre, is exercised and enjoyed for the tenant by the employees and becomes a right of the employees, e.g., the implied "right" not to be sued for trespass. Why should the implied right not to be sued for negligence be different?

It will be seen that the learned Chief Justice recognized the general common law principle that a person not a party to a contract can neither sue to enforce it nor rely upon it to protect himself from liability. He considered, however, that the doctrine should be applied with some exceptions and that one was to be found in the case at bar, the respondents being identified with the employer and not independent contractors as in the stevedoring cases.

The order giving leave to appeal to this Court provided:

It is ordered that leave to appeal be granted from the judgment of the Supreme Court of Nova Scotia, Appeal Division, insofar as it relates to the claim of the appellant as against the respondents, Robert Walker Beattie and Roy Vincent Pettipas.

This limits the scope of the appeal to the narrow question of whether the respondents, held to have been guilty of negligence which caused the loss, but not parties to the lease and the insuring agreements in paras. 14 and 15, may claim the benefit of those provisions and thereby receive the same protection as that afforded to the Company, their employer, who was otherwise equally liable with them for their negligence.

This question, it was argued by the appellant, had been settled in England since *Tweddle v. Atkinson* (1861), 1 B. & S. 393, 121 E.R. 762. It was restated in *Dunlop Pneumatic Tyre Co., Ltd. v. Selfridge & Co., Ltd.*, [1915] A.C. 847 (H.L.), and put beyond doubt by the more recent *Scruttons Ltd. v. Midland Silicones Ltd., supra*. This authority was approved in this Court in *Canadian General Electric Co. Ltd. v. Pickford & Black Ltd., supra*, and thus the law in Canada has been settled upon this point.

The respondent contended that the case turned on a finding of fact made in the Courts below that the employees of the tenant were within the contemplation of the parties when the agreement regarding insurance revealed in paras. 14 and 15 of the lease was made and they were therefore entitled to this benefit. The effect of the argument was that the employees, if not formal parties to the contract, were nevertheless intended objects of its benefits along with their employer and accordingly the trial judgment was correct. In the alternative, it was contended that the *Midland Silicones* case had not settled the law in Canada and that the point relied upon by the appellant was still open in this Court.

The rule relating to privity of contract has been stated in many authorities in sometimes varying form, but a convenient expression may be found in *Anson's Law of Contract*, 25th ed. (1979), p. 411, in these terms:

We come now to deal with the effects of a valid contract when formed, and to ask, To whom does the obligation extend? What are the limits of a contractual agreement? This question must be considered under two separate headings: (1) the imposition of liabilities upon a third party, and (2) the acquisition of rights by a third party. We shall see that the general rule of the common law is that no one but the parties to a contract can be bound by it, or entitled under it. This principle is known as that of privity of contract.

Paragraphs 14 and 15 of the lease are part of a valid contract between Greenwood and the Company which confers rights and liabilities upon each of them and for which there was the necessary consideration. It is clear as well that in entering into that contract the parties were fully aware of the use to which the employer would put the demised premises and that the Company would engage employees. There was at least some awareness of the risk of fire attendant upon such use because the parties agreed to guard against it by insurance arrangements. Whatever may have been in the minds of the contracting parties, however, the employees who seek the protection of paras. 14 and 15 were not parties to the contract and, according to the common law of contract, may neither sue to enforce nor benefit from it. We have here at most a contract where "A" and "B" entered into certain covenants for their mutual protection, from which it is said benefits were to flow to "C" and "D". There are many authorities for the proposition that save for certain exceptions, of which agency and trust afford examples, "C" and "D" in the illustration above can take no benefit under the contract.

• • •

[ed: The court considered whether the company could be deemed to be either an agent or a trustee for the two defendant employees and decided that it was not. The reasons concluded:]

I would allow the appeal with costs in this Court, set aside the judgment of the Nova Scotia Supreme Court, Appeal Division, as against the respondents Robert Walker Beattie and Roy Vincent Pettipas and vary the judgment of the Trial Division so that para. 4 of the order will read:

4. That Greenwood Shopping Plaza Limited do have Judgment against the Defendants Neil J. Buchanan Limited, Robert Walker Beattie and Roy Vincent Pettipas in the amounts of its damages excepting as against the Defendant Neil J. Buchanan Limited those losses which were insured or which should have been insured by virtue of the provisions of Clauses 14 and 15 of the lease referred to in the Reasons for Judgment, together with its costs of the action to be taxed.

*Appeal allowed.*

NOTES

1. *The authors of some texts think the principle of privity of contract has been eroded by the courts. The Supreme Court of Canada refuted that contention in this case. The landlord, Greenwood and its tenant, Neil J. Buchanan Ltd., agreed that each would arrange with their respective insurers not to sue the other for any loss as a result of fire. Two employees of the tenant, through negligence, caused a fire which severely damaged the landlord's premises. The Supreme Court of Canada unanimously held that as the employees were not a party to the lease they could claim no protection under it. In the result the action against the tenant was dismissed but the two employees were held liable. The damages were not assessed at the trial pending a determination of liability.*

   *This decision must be of concern to trade unions or any employees not covered for negligence by their employer's insurance. The employees here are now personally liable for what might be very substantial damages.*

2. *Subrogation is the principle whereby an insurance company having paid the loss of its insured is entitled "to stand in their shoes" and sue the wrongdoer for the loss it has had to pay to the injured party. In this case the employees sought to take advantage of a provision in their employer's lease whereby such rights would not be granted the insurer. Such an action is maintained by the insurer in the name of their insured and not in their own name.*

# J. Discharge of Contracts

## O'Connell v. Harkema Express Lines Ltd. et al.

*(1983) 141 D.L.R. (3d) 291*
*Ontario County Court*
*December 3, 1982.*

SHAPIRO CO. CT. J.: The transport owner-operators at Harkema Express obtained union certification on January 22, 1981. There were 85 of them. On March 18th their union agents put forward a demand for a wage increase. The demand was for the equivalent of 80% of revenue. Later it was reduced to 70%. At the time Harkema Express, along with many other transport companies in Canada, was in a difficult financial position. This was in part brought about by general economic problems. There were fewer producers and there was less consumer demand. Harkema Express had been in a loss position for three-quarters of a year.

On April 10th, Harkema Express directed an open letter to its employees. It suggested that all employees increase their workload by 10%. This was an alternative to a wage cut of 10%. It did, however, offer the owner-operators an increase of 0.5%. This would have given them the equivalent of 55.5% of revenue. The union held firm on the 70% demand. There was an impasse and a legal strike was called on June 26th.

Terry O'Connell was the regional sales manager for Harkema Express and its sister company Harkema Forwarders. Both companies had union as well as non-union employees. The other union employees refused to cross the owner-operator picket lines. It was hoped that the strike could be settled. Until then O'Connell and other non-union staff were told to take their accumulated vacations and to stand by "on call". They performed no work and they were not paid. O'Connell and his sales staff, no longer having any services to sell to customers, became redundant.

As time went on, the hoped-for strike settlement became more and more unlikely. Finally, in mid-August the two Harkema companies (which hence-forth I shall refer to as Harkema, when speaking of them jointly), faced the reality of the situation. They decided to close down their operations and go out of business. O'Connell and five others brought action for wrongful dismissal. The actions came on the list before me. It was agreed by counsel that I would hear the O'Connell action first. The others would then probably abide by the result.

Upon the evidence I make the following findings:

1. There was an implied term in O'Connell's contract of employment with Harkema that he be given reasonable notice of termination.
2. Harkema terminated O'Connell's employment.
3. Harkema bargained in good faith with the union. Considering the companies' financial status Harkema acted reasonably in not acceding to the union's demand for 70% of revenue.
4. Harkema put O'Connell and other non-union employees "on call" as of June 26th.
5. Harkema could not reasonably foresee, as of June 26th, that the strike would not be settled and that it would be "permanent".
6. Harkema, when it realized in mid-August that the strike could not be settled, acted reasonably in ceasing its operations and closing down the companies.
7. O'Connell pursued other employment in a reasonable manner and within a reasonable time frame.

As may be seen from the above findings, the present litigants were innocent victims of unhappy circumstances. Fortunately for O'Connell he was able to obtain other employment commencing October 12, 1981. Also fortunately for him it was at a higher rate of pay. Counsel for Harkema concedes that the three-and-a-half months O'Connell was out of work would normally be a reasonable compensatable period. Considering his position with Harkema, his length of employment over two separate periods, and his commendable efforts at re-employment, had he not obtained employment when he did it might well be argued that he would be entitled to compensation beyond such three-and-a-half-months' period. At any rate, counsel for Harkema contends that the factual situation in this case relieves Harkema from paying any more than the statutory entitlement under the *Employment Standards Act*, R.S.O. 1980, c. 137, or under the *Canada Labour Code*, R.S.C. 1970, c. L-1. If Harkema were deprived of doing business it had no services to sell. The contract of employment with O'Connell was to sell Harkema's services. Counsel for Harkema argues that as a result of the strike by the union the employment contract between Harkema and O'Connell was frustrated and at an end. Counsel contends that the frustration began as of the commencement of the strike, namely, June 26th.

• • •

The Ontario law on frustration had been expressed in a series of four Court of Appeal cases. These are: *Capital Quality Homes Ltd. v. Colwyn Construction Ltd.* (1975), 9 O.R. (2d) 617, 61 D.L.R. (3d) 385; *Focal Properties Ltd. v. George Wimpey Canada Ltd.* (1975), 14 O.R. (2d) 295, 73 D.L.R. (3d) 387; *Victoria Wood Development Corp. Inc. v. Ondrey et al.* (1977), 14

O.R. (2d) 723, 74 D.L.R. (3d) 528, 1 R.P.R. 141, and *Leitch Transport Ltd. v. Neonex Int'l* (1979), 27 O.R. (2d) 363, 106 D.L.R. (3d) 315, 8 B.L.R. 257 (Business Law Reports). The first three cases involve real estate transactions affected by the *Planning Act* of Ontario. The fourth case arose out of transactions and counter-transactions with respect to share transfers in a corporate reorganization. I quote excerpts from these cases, including references to English authorities.

1. *Capital Quality Homes Ltd. v. Colwyn Construction Ltd.*

Capital Quality Homes contracted with Colwyn Construction for the purchase of 26 building lots from Colwyn. Subsequent to the execution of the agreement but prior to the closing of the transaction amendments were made to the *Planning Act* (Ontario). These amendments curtailed the owner's right to convey his property. They also required the consent of the relevant committee of adjustments prior to any severance. Capital Quality Homes sought to negate the agreement and to recover its deposit. It was successful both at trial and on appeal.

Writing for the Court of Appeal, Evans J.A. (later C.J.H.C.) reviews the law of frustration [at p. 623 O.R., p. 391 D.L.R.]:

> The legal effect of the frustration of a contract does not depend upon the intention of the parties, or their opinions or even knowledge as to the event that has brought about the frustration, but upon its occurrence in such circumstances as to show it to be inconsistent with the further prosecution of the adventure. On the contrary, it seems that when the event occurs, the meaning of the contract must be taken to be, not what the parties did intend (for they had neither thought nor intention regarding it) but that which the parties, as fair and reasonable men, would presumably have agreed upon if, having such possibility in view, they had made express provision as to their several rights and liabilities in the event of its occurrence: *Dahl v. Nelson et al.* (1880), 6 App. Cas. 38.
>
> The supervening event must be something beyond the control of the parties and must result in a significant change in the original obligation assumed by them. The theory of the implied term has been replaced by the more realistic view that the Court imposes upon the parties the just and reasonable solution that the new situation demands.

Evans J.A. then refers to Lord Radcliff's statement in *Davis Contractors Ltd. v. Fareham Urban District Council,* [1956] A.C. 696 at pp. 728-9.

> "So perhaps it would be simpler to say at the outset that frustration occurs whenever the law recognizes that without default of either party a contractual obligation has become incapable of being performed because the circumstances in which performance is called for would render it a thing radically different from that which was undertaken by the contract. *Non haec in foedera veni.* It was not this that I promised to do."

Continuing, Evans J.A. then says [at p. 626 O.R., p. 394 D.L.R.]:

> There can be no frustration if the supervening event results from the voluntary act of one of the parties or if the possibility of such event arising during the term of the agreement was contemplated by the parties and provided for in the

agreement. In the instant case the planning legislation which supervened was not contemplated by the parties, not provided for in the agreement and not brought about through a voluntary act of either party. The factor remaining to be considered is whether the effect of the planning legislation is of such a nature that the law would consider the fundamental character of the agreement to have been so altered as to no longer reflect the original basis of the agreement. In my opinion the legislation destroyed the very foundation of the agreement. The purchaser was purchasing 26 separate building lots upon which it proposed to build houses for resale involving a reconveyance in each instance. This purpose was known to the vendor. The lack of ability to do so creates a situation not within the contemplation of the parties when they entered into the agreement. I believe that all the factors necessary to constitute impossibility of performance have been established and that the doctrine of frustration can be invoked to terminate the agreement.

In the penultimate paragraph of his judgment [p. 630 O.R., p. 398 D.L.R.], Evans J.A. concludes:

If the factual situation is such that there is a clear "frustration of the common venture" then the contract, whether it is a contract for the sale of land or otherwise, is at an end and the parties are discharged from further performance and the adjustment of the rights and liabilities of the parties are left to be determined under the *Frustrated Contracts Act* [now R.S.O. 1980, c. 179][1].

• • •

[ed. The judge reviewed the other three cases in the same way and continued:]

*Smith v. Tamblyn (Alberta) Ltd. et al.* (1979), 9 Alta. L.R. (2d) 274, 23 A.R. 53, is a recent case involving personal services and a defence of frustration. No strike was involved. The plaintiff, a registered pharmacist, had her status changed from a permanent employee to a temporary employee because of an exceptional decline in business. She refused to accept the change in her position and instituted an action for wrongful dismissal. Laycraft J. at p. 279 says:

A common example of discharge of an agreement for personal service by frustration is the case where an employee dies or suffers a long and incapacitating illness. Indeed, the earliest case of frustration in English law involves a contract of service, although the agreement itself was not directly involved in the dispute. In *Taylor v. Caldwell* (1893), 3 B. & S. 826, 122 E.R. 309, a music hall burned down, so that persons who had agreed to sing were unable to do so. In that case, in discharging the agreement for impossibility, Blackburn J. introduced the law of frustration into the English law and therefore eventually into Alberta law. Impossibility of performance cannot be alleged, however, where performance is merely more onerous or less profitable than the parties had hoped would be the case. An agreement of personal service is not impossible to perform because business has fallen 30 per cent, even if the fall is permanent. It seems hardly necessary to expand on that point.

Again the case at bar is easily distinguishable. It is not just a case of business falling off, but of business ceasing.

The most recent Canadian case is one from the Quebec Court of Appeal. It is *Otis Elevator Co. Ltd. v. A. Viglione Bros. Inc.* noted at (1981), 8 A.C.W.S. (2d) 54. The corporate plaintiff was prevented from completing its contractual obligations because its employees were on strike. Here the court finds that there was a bad trade union situation and that the strike was beyond the plaintiff's control. The court indicates that as a general rule strikes do not constitute *force majeure*.[2] It is, however, of the view that the plaintiff was not liable since the cause of the default was beyond its reasonable control....

In applying the above cases, particularly the Ontario Court of Appeal quartet, to the case at bar, it is incumbent upon Harkema to prove that which is italicized below. Its proof follows after each italicization:

1. *A critical rather than a trivial supervening event.* The non-resolvable strike.

2. *An event not of short duration but protracted in time.* Again the strike that could not be settled.

3. *An event not within the contemplation of the parties.* Although O'Connell and Harkema might contemplate a strike there was no evidence that it was within the contemplation of either that there might be an unresolved strike that would completely close down Harkema's business.

4. *An event coming about without fault on either party.* O'Connell, of course, had nothing to do with the strike. The evidence leads to a finding that Harkema acted reasonably in its negotiations with the union and in not acceding to the union's demands.

5. *An event that rendered the parties incapable of performing their contractual obligations.* Harkema no longer had any services to offer. O'Connell no longer had any company services to sell.

6. *The performance of a contract that would radically alter the original agreement into something other than that intended.* O'Connell was employed as a regional sales manager. The sales department was closed down. There were very few people employed after the strike. Those whose employment was continued for a time were specialists at their own positions. No additional ones were needed; nor was there evidence that O'Connell was qualified to have carried out such different type of work.

With these principles in mind I conclude that the employment contract between O'Connell and Harkema has been frustrated by reason of the unresolved strike of the transport owner-operators. The unresolved strike was a supervening event. Strikes might reasonably be within the contemplation of the parties to an employment contract. In the case at bar, however, I find that it was not contemplated that the strike would be never-ending. Nor that it would result in the closing of the Harkema business which was substantial and had existed for 26 years. A few employees were kept for a time after Harkema ceased its trucking operations. These were in accounts receivable or on the senior executive level. There was no evidence that O'Connell could have performed these duties.

A question left to be decided is at what time did the frustration take effect. Is it to be backdated to June 26th when the strike first started and when

O'Connell and other non-union employees were put "on call"? Or is mid-August the effective time?...

• • •

In the case at bar both O'Connell and Harkema had reasonable expectations that the strike would be settled. In the vast majority of labour disputes this is what happens. It was not until mid-August that it was realized that the matter could not be resolved. And it was at that later time that all the elements first converged to constitute at law a frustration of the contract of employment between O'Connell and Harkema. Although a specific calendar date would be preferable the evidence refers to mid-August. This is sufficiently ascertainable to satisfy the requirement of a specific time mentioned in the English case *Davis Contractors* and the Ontario Court of Appeal case of *Focal Properties*.

I therefore allow O'Connell lost of earnings from June 26th to Friday, August 13th (the end of the second week in August). This is a period of seven weeks. At $550 a week that amounts to $3,850. I award 4% of that sum for vacation pay. That is, $154. I consider any accumulated vacation pay O'Connell may have received after June 26th as reflecting his entitlement up to that date. The company car allowance was estimated at $350 per month. Taking into account personal use and fuel and other running expenses I allow $400 as a fair estimate of his loss for car allowance to mid-August. I also allow the claimed amounts for medical expenses, parking, telephone, and tuition. These four items total $202.71. Judgment will therefore go in favour of the plaintiff O'Connell against the named defendants for $4606.71 together with pre-judgment interest from the date of the notice of the claim. Costs to the plaintiff.

*Judgment for plaintiff*

NOTES

1. *Most of the provinces of Canada have now passed acts covering the situation where a contract has been frustrated. This legislation settles which of the parties are to be responsible for the financial losses and expenses arising from the termination of the contract.*

2. *"Force Majeure" means superior or irresistible forces; it is a term frequently used in contracts and insurance policies. It usually has the effect of relieving the parties of any further liability.*

# K. Breach of Contract

## Cornwall Gravel Co. Ltd. v. Purolator Courier Ltd.

*(1978) 83 D.L.R. (3d) 267*
*Ontario High Court of Justice*
*February 10, 1978*

R.E. HOLLAND, J.: This is an action for damages for breach of contract and negligence brought by Cornwall Gravel Company Limited (Cornwall Gravel) against Purolator Courier Ltd. (Purolator) and Bernard Levert and Rheal Boisvenue who, at the material time, were employees of Purolator, arising out of the late delivery of a tender prepared by the plaintiff for submission to the Ontario Ministry of the Environment.

It is admitted that had the tender been delivered in time Cornwall Gravel would have been awarded a contract for $698 246.79 and would have made a profit on the contract of $70 000.

The information for tenderers which governed the submission of the tender provided that tenders were to be delivered on or before 3 p.m. Toronto time on October 2, 1973, at the office of the contracts officer of the Ministry in Toronto and further that under no circumstances would any tender be considered which was received after that time. The tender in question was delivered by Purolator at 3.17 p.m. on October 2, 1973, and was therefore rejected.

The tender was ready for delivery at Cornwall shortly after 6 p.m. on October 1, 1973. Cornwall Gravel had used the services of Purolator to deliver tenders on prior occasions. Ronald Paymemp, who was at the time the controller of Cornwall Gravel, telephoned the office of Purolator around noon on October 1st to advise that there was a pick-up for Toronto that evening. Cornwall Gravel had been supplied by Purolator with bill of lading forms. The bill of lading for the tender was written up by Cornwall Gravel and reads, on its face, in part, as follows:

---

Bill of Lading—
TRANS CANADIAN COURIERS, LTD.          Date.
Oct. 1/73.
RECEIVED AT THE POINT OF ORIGIN ON THE DATE SPECIFIED, FROM THE SHIPPER
MENTIONED HEREIN. THE GOODS HEREIN DESCRIBED, IN APPARENT GOOD ORDER,
EXCEPT AS NOTED (CONTENTS AND CONDITIONS OF CONTENTS OF PACKAGES
UNKNOWN) MARKED, CONSIGNED AND DESTINED AS INDICATED BELOW, WHICH
THE CARRIER AGREES TO CARRY AND DELIVER TO THE CONSIGNEE AT THE SAID
DESTINATION. FOR OTHER TERMS, SEE REVERSE SIDE.

POINT OF ORIGIN.                    DESTINATION.
Cornwall Gravel Co. Ltd.           The Ministry of the
P.O. Box 67—390 Eleventh St. W.    Environment,
Cornwall, Ontario.                 135 St. Clair Ave., W.,
                                   Toronto 195, Ontario.

          CONTENTS.        No. Pes.  Weight.   Charges.
          Tender.              1        .8

(Deliver before 12 noon    )
(      Oct. 2.             )"P"
(September 29, 1973.        )

DECLARED VALUE. MAXIMUM LIABILITY $1.50 per
                POUND UNLESS DECLARED VALUATION
                STATES OTHERWISE.
                IF A VALUE IS DECLARED SEE
                CONDITIONS ON REVERSE HEREOF.
TRANS CANADA COURIERS, LTD.
BY: "Boisvenue".
SHIPPER:
BY: "Paymemp".

---

On the reverse the bill reads, in part, as follows:

---

VALUE
UNLESS OTHERWISE SPECIFICALLY AGREED TO IN WRITING THE CARRIER WILL
NOT TRANSPORT ANY GOODS DECLARED TO HAVE A VALUE IN EXCESS OF $250.
ENQUIRES FOR SUCH SERVICE SHOULD BE DIRECTED TO THE CARRIER'S CLOSEST
REGIONAL OFFICE.

APPLICABLE LAW
IT IS AGREED THAT EVERY SERVICE TO BE PERFORMED HEREUNDER SHALL BE
SUBJECT TO THE LAWS RELATING TO THE TERMS AND CONDITIONS TO BE CONTAINED
IN BILLS OF LADING (WHICH ARE HEREBY INCORPORATED BY REFERENCE) APPLI-
CABLE AT THE PLACE WHERE THE GOODS ORIGINATE WHICH IF NOVA SCOTIA AND
BRITISH COLUMBIA, THE REGULATIONS MADE PURSUANT TO THE MOTOR CAR-
RIER ACTS OF SUCH PROVINCES: QUEBEC, FORM R.T. 200 APPROVED BY THE
QUEBEC TRANSPORTATION BOARD ON AUGUST 5, 1960; AND ONTARIO, THE REG-
ULATIONS MADE PURSUANT TO THE PUBLIC COMMERCIAL VEHICLES ACT.

---

shown as September 29th, which was in error, and was changed to October 2nd by Boisvenue, the driver employed by Purolator.

When the tender was picked up by Boisvenue, there was a conversation between Paymemp, John Fleming, who was an engineer employed by Cornwall Gravel and who had worked on the tender, and Boisvenue. Paymemp and Fleming wished to make sure that the tender would be delivered on time. If there was any question about late delivery one or the other of them would have driven with the tender to Toronto. They were assured by Boisvenue that there would be no problem with delivery. Paymemp had inserted the time as 12 noon rather than 3 p.m. to make the time consistent with other tenders that had previously been delivered to Toronto for other departments where the time for delivery was 12 noon. There was no conversation with Boisvenue or anyone from Purolator as to the amount of the tender.

Boisvenue was not called as a witness at the trial and I was advised by counsel that he was no longer in the employ of Purolator and his whereabouts were unknown. He was examined for discovery and part of his examination was read in by counsel for the plaintiff. He admitted that he was told that the document was very important, that he had read the bill of lading and had noticed the incorrect date which he changed. He was then asked these questions and made these answers:

Q. 76.  I see. At that time you left the office at Cornwall Gravel with this parcel, did you know that it was a tender?
A.      I think so because I had read it, yes.
Q. 77.  Did you at that time know what a tender was?
A.      As a rule I do, yes.
Q. 78.  What did you understand?
A.      Well, I know that it has—it—
Q. 79.  Generally, when someone says, "here is a tender."
A.      Yes?
Q. 80.  Did you believe you understood what a tender was?
A.      Yes.
Q. 81.  What did you understand it to be?
A.      That it is fairly important and it has to be there a certain time to my own personal knowledge.

Bernard Levert testified that he had a conversation with someone from Cornwall Gravel in which he advised that delivery by noon could not be guaranteed. I do not accept his evidence on this point. It is contrary to the evidence that he gave on examination for discovery and I do not accept his explanation for the contradiction between his evidence at trial and on discovery. Mr. Levert also testified that at the material time Purolator used only Econoline vans in Cornwall. This is contrary to the evidence of Marcel Poulant, a defence witness who is presently regional manager who stated that Econoline vans and private cars were used in Cornwall.

The transfer point for delivery of the envelope to Toronto was Kingston. The envelope arrived in Kingston on time but was delayed because the vehicle bringing parcels and envelopes from Montreal had broken down. The envelope finally arrived in Toronto about 10 o'clock in the morning but by that time routine deliveries had already started in Toronto and the envelope was not delivered until 3.17 p.m.

• • •

[ed: The judge considered an argument that the Public Commercial Vehicles Act did not apply to the claim, but concluded that it did. He continued:]

It is my opinion, therefore, that the Act does apply and I must look at the clauses limiting liability in Sch. A. There are a number of sections of the Schedule that are important to a decision and to an interpretation of the words "maximum liability $1.50 per pound unless declared valuation states otherwise".

SCHEDULE A

1. The carrier of the goods herein described is liable for any loss thereof or damage or injury thereto, except as herein provided.

• • •

5. The carrier is not liable for loss, damage or delay to any of the goods described in the bill of lading caused by an act of God, the Queen's or public enemies, riots, strikes, defect or inherent vice in the goods, the act or default of the shipper or owner, the authority of law, quarantine or differences in weights of grain, seed, live stock or other commodities caused by natural shrinkage.

• • •

7. No carrier is bound to transport the goods by any particular public commercial vehicle or in time for any particular market or otherwise than with due despatch, unless by agreement specifically endorsed on the bill of lading and signed by the parties thereto.

• • •

9. Subject to paragraph 10, the amount of any loss, damage or injury for which the carrier is liable, whether or not the loss, damage or injury results from negligence, shall be computed on the basis of,
   (a) the value of the goods at the place and time of shipment including the freight and other charges if paid; or
   (b) where a value lower than that referred to in clause *a* has been represented in writing by the consignor or has been agreed upon, such lower value.

10. Subject to paragraph 11, the amount of any loss or damage computed under clause *a* or *b* of paragraph 9 shall not exceed $1.50 per pound unless a higher value is declared on the face of the bill of lading by the consignor.

• • •

13. The carrier is not liable for loss, damage, injury or delay to any goods carried under the bill of lading unless notice thereof setting out particulars of the origin, destination and date of shipment of the goods and the estimated amount claimed in respect of such loss, damage, injury or delay is given in writing to the carrier at the point of delivery or at the point or origin within ninety days after the delivery of the goods, or, in the case of failure to make delivery, within ninety days after a reasonable time for delivery has elapsed.

• • •

It seems to me looking at the sections as set out above as a whole that there is a distinction between loss, damage or injury on the one hand and delay on the other and that the limitation of liability of $1.50 per pound applies only to loss, damage or injury to the goods themselves. The word "injury" may seem strange but I suppose could well apply to a shipment of livestock. Liability is excluded for delay under para. 5 in certain circumstances set out therein. None of these circumstances existed in the present case. I therefore conclude on the wording of the sections of the Schedule itself that a limitation of liability in this case only applied to the goods being transported and did not cover consequential loss due to delay. In coming to this conclusion I have not construed any of the provisions *contra proferentem* since it was an Act of the Legislature that included the words "in the contract": *Madill v. Chu*, [1977] 2 S.C.R. 400, 71 D.L.R. (3d) 295, 12 N.R. 187.

There remains the question whether or not this loss was in the contemplation of the parties and this takes us back to *Hadley et al. v. Baxendale et al.* (1854), 9 Ex. 341, 156 E.R. 145. At pp. 354-5, Alderson, B., said this:

> Where two parties have made a contract which one of them has broken, the damages which the other party ought to receive in respect of such breach of contract should be such as may fairly and reasonably be considered arising naturally, i.e., according to the usual course of things, from such breach of contract itself, or such as may reasonably be supposed to have been in the contemplation of both parties, at the time they made the contract, as the probable result of the breach of it. Now, if the special circumstances under which the contract was actually made were communicated by the plaintiffs to the defendants, and thus known to both parties, the damages resulting from the breach of such a contract, which they would reasonably contemplate, would be the amount of injury which would ordinarily follow from a breach of contract under those special circumstances; so known and communicated. But, on the other hand, if those special circumstances were wholly unknown to the party breaking the contract, he, at the most, could only be supposed to have had in his contemplation the amount of injury which would arise generally, and in the great multitude of cases not affected by any special circumstances, from such a breach of contract. For, had the special circumstances been known, the parties might have specially provided for the breach of contract by special terms as to the damages in that case; and of this advantage it would be very unjust to deprive them.

In the present case Purolator, through its employee, Boisvenue, knew that the item to be transported was a tender and that it was required to be delivered by 12 noon on October 2, 1973. Boisvenue was told of the importance of the document and must have realized that if delivered late the tender would be worthless and a contract could well be lost. In these particular circumstances it is my opinion that "the special circumstances under which the contract was actually made were communicated by the plaintiff to the defendant" and the damage which in fact flowed from the breach of such contract was damage "which they would reasonably contemplate...which would ordinarily follow from a breach of contract under those special circumstances, so known and communicated".

It is not necessary, in view of my findings, to deal with the allegation that there is liability for the misrepresentation of Boisvenue that the tender would be delivered by 12 noon the next day.

For the above reasons there will be judgment for the plaintiff for $70 000, with interest in accordance with s. 38 of the *Judicature Act*, R.S.O. 1970, c. 228, as amended, from the date of the coming into force of s. 3 of the *Judicature Amendment Act, 1977 (No. 2)*, 1977. c. 51, to the date of judgment, together with costs against the defendant Purolator. The action as against the individual defendants will be dismissed without costs.

*Judgment for plaintiff.*[1]

NOTES

1. *Appeals from this decision to both the Ontario Court of Appeal, and the Supreme Court of Canada were dismissed with very short reasons, see (1981) 115 D.L.R. (3d) 511 and (1981) 120 D.L.R. (3d) 575.*

# Parta Industries Ltd. v. Canadian Pacific Ltd. et al.

*(1975) 48 D.L.R. (3d) 463*
*British Columbia Supreme Court*
*July 4, 1974*

CRAIG. J.:   The plaintiff commenced an action against the defendants (hereinafter referred to as "the defendants") claiming:

a) Special and general damages for breach of contract entered into between the Plaintiff and the Defendants on the 12th day of September 1969, by which contract the Defendants, common carriers, contracted to deliver goods for and to the Plaintiff, and did fail to do so in accordance with the terms, express and implied, of the said contract, which failure caused financial loss to the Plaintiff.

b) In the alternative, damages against the Defendants for negligence in the performance of the aforementioned contract, which negligence caused financial loss to the Plaintiff.

The defendants have denied the plaintiff's claim, generally, and have counterclaimed for the sum of $1548.59 which, they allege, is the net amount owing to them after making financial adjustments between the parties relating to this incident.

In 1968, the plaintiff was incorporated to operate a plant for the production and sale of "wood particle board" products at Grand Forks, British Columbia. Originally, the officials of the company expected that the plant would be in production by April, 1969. This did not happen. Eventually, they set November 14, 1969, as the definite "in production" date.

The plaintiff had to obtain most of the production equipment, namely, about 500 tons, from a Belgian manufacturer and retained Kuehne & Nagel (Canada) Ltd. (hereinafter referred to as "the agent") a national firm of custom brokers, to handle the transportation arrangements and all other matters incidental to the importation of the goods into Canada. Mr. Popoff, president of the plaintiff, said that he gave the agent "sole authority" to handle these matters. Each equipment order was shipped by sea from Antwerp to Vancouver and then transported by truck to Grand Forks.

The final 90 tons of the equipment was to be delivered in 1969 in time to permit the plant to commence production by November, 1969. In the summer of 1969, a dockers' strike in Vancouver caused company officials to find an alternate transportation route in order to ensure delivery of the goods in time to meet the production date. It was decided to ship the goods to Montreal and transport them by rail to Grand Forks.

• • •

On or about September 8th, the equipment arrived in Montreal. On the same day, a representative of the agent telephoned Douglas Mayer, supervisor of the import section of the defendant, located in Montreal, advised him that the equipment had arrived, and instructed him that the equipment was to be loaded by September 9th, and rushed to the plaintiff in Grand Forks.

On the same day, the agent delivered a "straight" bill of lading, in a form authorized by the Board of Transportation Commissioners for Canada, stating that 77 packages of "construction material", totalling 182 834 lbs., was to be delivered to the plaintiff in Grand Forks, British Columbia. Stamped on the front of the bill of lading in large letters was the word "RUSH".

The bill of lading contained eleven authorized conditions, including condition 4, which reads:

Sec. 4. No Carrier is bound to transport said goods by any particular train or vessel, or in time for any particular market or otherwise than as required by law, unless by specific agreement endorsed hereon. Every Carrier in case of physical necessity shall have the right to forward said goods by any railway or route between the point of shipment and the point of destination, but if such diversion be from a rail to a water route liability of the Carrier shall be the same as though the entire carriage were by rail.

The defendant loaded the equipment on three freight cars. While passing through Ontario, some of the freight cars were derailed, including the three cars containing the plaintiff's equipment. As a result of the derailment, some of the equipment was lost, and most of the equipment which was finally delivered was damaged, some of it beyond repair.

The plaintiff was able to repair some of the equipment, but, in many cases, it had to re-order replacement equipment from the Belgian manufacturer, including equipment which might have been repairable but which was not repaired because the manufacturer refused to maintain its original warranty with respect to it.

The plaintiff did not complete the installation of the repaired and replaced equipment until 105 days after November 14, 1969.

Mr. Moran contends that the failure of the defendant to deliver the equipment in usable condition on or before September 19th, or within a reasonable time of this date, was a breach of the contract to "rush" delivery and that the plaintiff suffered damages totalling $129 705. He filed a schedule as ex. "4" which representatives of the plaintiff had prepared, showing how damages were calculated and what items were included. He submitted that these items of damages and the amounts claimed for these items are such damages:

1. "...as may fairly and reasonably be considered as...arising naturally...", or at least,
2. "...as may reasonably be supposed to have been in contemplation of both parties, at the time they made the contract, as the probable result of the breach of it".

citing *Hadley v. Baxendale* (1854), 9 Ex. 341, 156 E.R. 145, and the well-known judgment of Asquith, L.J., in *Victoria Laundry (Windsor) Ltd. v. Newman Industries Ltd.; Coulson & Co. Ltd. (Third Parties)*, [1949] 2 K.B. 528, [1949] 1 All E.R. 997.

Counsel for the plaintiff conceded in argument that the contract which the defendant allegedly had breached was to be found in the bill of lading and the contract had been made with the defendant on September 8, 1969, and by the agent for the plaintiff. He contends that although condition 4 relieves the defendant generally from the responsibility of delivering the equipment at a particular time, the condition, in this case, was qualified by the word "RUSH". He says the effect of this word, read in conjunction with condition 4, means that the defendant would deliver the equipment, if not on September 19th, then within a reasonable time of that date. He submits, also, that I should accept Mr. Popoff's recollection of his dealings with Vanderburgh and that I must impute Vanderburgh's knowledge of the urgency of the situation of the defendants.

Counsel for the defendant, while admitting as a fact that as a result of the derailment a portion of the shipment "...either was lost or damaged and delayed commencement of the plaintiff's manufacturing business", rejects virtually all of the damages claimed by the plaintiff, because in his view, they are not within either branch of the rule in *Hadley v. Baxendale*, or, in other words, the damages are too remote. He contends that the contract was to rush delivery of approximately 90 tons of equipment, simply described as "construction material", and that the defendant did not have knowledge that the plant could not operate without the equipment.

• • •

The contract was made between the plaintiff and defendant in Montreal on September 8th, 1969. Surely, if the plaintiff wanted to emphasize the special circumstances he should have apprised his agents of these special circumstances and insisted that the agent attempt to incorporate these in any contract. The agent did not bring these special circumstances to the attention of the defendant. The agent prepared the bill of lading which stated simply that there were 77 packages of "construction material" weighing "182 834 lbs." to be delivered to the plaintiff in Grand Forks, B.C., on a "RUSH" basis.

In the *Victoria Laundry (Windsor) Ltd. v. Newman Industries Ltd.* case, *supra*, Asquith, L.J., listed six propositions applicable to damages for breach of contract. His judgment has been referred to on numerous occasions. These propositions are as follows [at pp. 539-40]:

1. It is well settled that the governing purpose of damages is to put the party whose rights have been violated in the same position, so far as money can do so, as if his rights had been observed:(*Sally Wertheim v. Chicoutimi Pulp Company*, [1911] A.C. 301). This purpose, if relentlessly pursued, would provide him with a complete indemnity for all loss de facto[1] resulting from a particular breach, however improbable, however unpredictable. This, in contract at least, is recognized as too harsh a rule. Hence,
2. In cases of breach of contract the aggrieved party is only entitled to recover such part of the loss actually resulting as was at the time of the contract reasonably foreseeable as liable to result from the breach.
3. What was at that time reasonably so foreseeable depends on the knowledge then possessed by the parties or, at all events, by the party who later commits the breach.
4. For this purpose, knowledge "possessed" is of two kinds; one imputed, the other actual. Everyone, as a reasonable person, is taken to know the "ordinary course of things" and consequently what loss is liable to result from a breach of contract in that ordinary course. This is the subject matter of the "first rule" in *Hadley v. Baxendale*. But to this knowledge, which a contract-breaker is assumed to possess whether he actually possesses it or not, there may have to be added in a particular case knowledge which he actually possesses, of special circumstances outside the "ordinary course of things," of such a kind that a breach in those special circumstances would be liable to cause more loss. Such a case attracts the operation of the "second rule" so as to make additional loss also recoverable.
5. In order to make the contract-breaker liable under either rule it is not necessary that he should actually have asked himself what loss is liable to result from a breach. As has often been pointed out, parties at the time of contracting contemplate not the breach of the contract, but its performance. It suffices that, if he had considered the question, he would as a reasonable man have concluded that the loss in question was liable to result (see certain observations of Lord du Parcq in the recent case of *A/B Karlshamns Oljefabriker v. Monarch Steamship Company Limited*, [1949] A.C. 196).
6. Nor, finally, to make a particular loss recoverable, need it be proved that upon a given state of knowledge the defendant could, as a reasonable man, foresee that a breach must necessarily result in that loss. It is enough if he could foresee it was likely so to result. It is indeed enough, to borrow from the language of Lord du Parcq in the same case, at page 158, if the loss (or some factor without which it would not have occurred) is a "serious possibility" or a "real danger." For short, we have used the word "liable" to result. Possibly the colloquialism "on the cards" indicates the shade of meaning with some approach to accuracy.

In his judgment, also, Asquith, L.J., said that the case of *British Columbia*

*Saw-Mill Co. v. Nettleship* (1868), L.R. 3, C.P. 499, annexed a rider to the principle laid in *Hadley v. Baxendale* to the effect

>...that where knowledge of special circumstances is relied on as enhancing the damage recoverable that knowledge must have been brought home to the defendant at the time of the contract and in such circumstances that the defendant impliedly undertook to bear any special loss referable to a breach in those special circumstances. The knowledge which was lacking in that case on the part of the defendant was knowledge that the particular box of machinery negligently lost by the defendants was one without which the rest of the machinery could not be put together and would therefore be useless.

Having regard to the evidence in this case and the circumstances generally, I find that the only knowledge possessed by the defendant was that he was to "RUSH" delivery of 77 packages of "construction material". There is nothing in the contract to indicate the nature of the material, nor the use to which it was to be put. Certainly, there is nothing to indicate that it was to be used in a large manufacturing plant and that the plant could not operate without the equipment. In other words, the defendant did not have knowledge of the special circumstances of the situation which would bring into operation the second branch of the rule in *Hadley v. Baxendale*. That being so, what damages, if any, in this case should be considered as "...such as may fairly and reasonably be considered as...arising naturally i.e. according to the natural course of things from the breach of contract..."? In my opinion, the defendant could have reasonably foreseen on the facts which were known to it in this case that a delay in delivery, or a failure to deliver was liable to result in:

a) a delay in actual construction;
b) extra labour costs;
c) interest;
d) depreciation of equipment;
e) additional overhead expenses;
f) cost of repairing and replacing equipment.

While I think that the defendant could have reasonably foreseen a delay in construction, I do not think that the defendant could have reasonably foreseen a delay of 105 days. The assessment of the delay period is to be somewhat arbitrary, but, on reflection, I think that the defendant could have reasonably foreseen a 45-day delay period, particularly as the defendant knew that the goods had been obtained from overseas and the replacements may have had, also, to come from there.

The plaintiff says that it incurred additional labour costs totalling $18 462.18. The evidence indicates that 50% of this time was spent in repairing equipment and the other 50% was on installation. Even if the defendant had had knowledge of the circumstances of this case, then the plaintiff would only have been able to collect 50% of this amount. I allow the plaintiff $4000 for the item of extra labour.

The plaintiff claims a further $7000 representing a total of salaries paid to

Mr. Popoff and Mr. Henniger at the rate of $1000 per month. Mr. Henniger advised that he spent 75% of his time during this period on matters concerning the equipment and that Popoff spent 25% of his time. Accordingly, I think that the allowance of $1500 for this particular item is reasonable.

The plaintiff claims $3363.58 for depreciation which is based on a book value of $467 698. Initially, I considered that this particular claim was too remote. However, on further reflection, I think that it is not. However, an award must be somewhat arbitrary and I award $500 for this item.

The plaintiff has claimed interest totalling $35 076.44. The plaintiff contends that this amount of interest had to be paid by it for the delay in connection with the loans that the company had made since its inception. While an allowance for interest is a proper consideration in assessing damages (see *Sunley (B) & Co. Ltd. v. Cunard Whitestar Ltd.*, [1940] 1 K.B. 740) such a claim appears to be related to "interest on the money invested which was being wasted", *Sunley (B) & Co., Ltd.* case, *supra*. In the absence of special circumstances, I think the interest claim in this case is too remote. However, it seems that the plaintiff is entitled to some interest, although it would appear to be a relatively small amount. If the parties cannot agree, I suggest that the matter be referred to the Registrar for assessment.

The plaintiff has claimed, also, for several items which may be compendiously referred to as overhead, including office expenses in the sum of $5052.04 and building insurance in the sum of $348.87, municipal taxes in the sum of $6687.50, plant heating in the sum of $385 and insurance premiums in the sum of $5144. Overhead is an appropriate item in a damage claim (see *Shore & Horwitz Construction Co. Ltd. v. Franki of Canada Ltd.*, [1964] S.C.R. 589); *C.P.R. Co. et al. v. Fumagalli et al.* (1962) 38 D.L.R. (2d) 110. I award the plaintiff $3500 in respect to this item.

As regards the cost of repairing and replacing equipment, I understand that the parties have agreed on some items relating to this aspect of the case. Obviously the defendants should pay for any equipment which has to be repaired and any equipment which had to be replaced. In its claim, the plaintiff asked for $9023.76 for equipment which had to be replaced because the manufacturer would not stand behind his written warranty in view of the repairs. I think this is a reasonable claim, and I allow it.

As I mentioned at the outset, the plaintiff conceded that the defendant had a valid counterclaim for certain items.

The effect of my judgment is that the plaintiff will receive more than the defendant is entitled to receive. Accordingly, there will be a judgment for the plaintiff for the difference and the plaintiff will be entitled to its costs for success on the main action and the defendant will be entitled to its costs on the counterclaim.

*Judgment for plaintiff.*

NOTES

*1. "De facto" means "in fact" or "actually".*

# PART THREE

# Special Types of Contracts

# A. Sale of Goods

## Sigurdson et al. v. Hillcrest Service Ltd.; Acklands Ltd., Third Party

*(1977) 73 D.L.R. (3d) 132*
*Saskatchewan Queen's Bench*
*December 21, 1976*

ESTEY, J.: This action arises out of a single vehicle accident in which the plaintiffs allege that they did suffer personal injuries. The said vehicle was owned by the plaintiff Mr. K. E. Sigurdson. The plaintiffs allege that the cause of the accident was a faulty brake hose installed on the vehicle in the defendant's garage. The defendant joined Acklands Limited as a third party as Acklands supplied the defendant with the two hydraulic brake hoses which the defendant through its employees installed on the said vehicle.

The plaintiff Karl Edward Sigurdson stated that he was on June 16, 1973, operating a 1963 Ford vehicle owned by him and had as passengers his wife Hannelore and his children Christopher and Michael. At approximately 4:30 p.m. on June 16, 1973, Mr. Sigurdson was approaching the intersection of Avenue H and 20th St. in the City of Saskatoon intending to make a right-hand turn onto 20th St. when he was confronted with a red stop-light at the said intersection. Mr. Sigurdson stated that pedestrians were crossing the intersection in front of his vehicle and when he applied the brakes they failed to operate. He immediately swung his vehicle to the right hitting a power pole. Mr. Sigurdson stated that at the time of the accident his speed was 15 to 20 m.p.h. and that the brakes of the vehicle had up until the time of the accident been operating in a proper manner. The vehicle as a result of the accident was damaged beyond repair. A few days prior to May 1, 1973, Mr. Sigurdson took his vehicle to the defendant's service station for certain repairs as the defendants had previously serviced his vehicle. Exhibit P.10 dated May 1, 1973, is the invoice which Mr. Sigurdson received from the defendant covering the repairs and labour performed on his vehicle immediately prior to the said date. This exhibit shows that two brake hoses were on this occasion installed by the defendant on Mr. Sigurdson's vehicle. Mr. Sigurdson as a result of the accident had three teeth removed and now has a partial denture. His son the plaintiff Michael received minor scratches while the plaintiffs Christopher and Mrs. Hannelore Sigurdson received injuries to which I will later refer. Mr. Sigurdson stated that after receiving his vehicle from the defendant's garage on or about May 1, 1973, the brakes on the said vehicle did until the time of the accident operate in a proper manner and that from May 1, 1973, to the date of the accident he had travelled approximately 1300 miles. Mr. Sigurdson takes the view that the cause of the brake failure was due to a faulty brake hose. Counsel agreed that the brake hose removed from Mr. Sigurdson's vehicle is ex. P.11 and that exs. P.12, 13, 14 and 15 which are portions of a brake hose were cut off P.11 for purpose of examination.

Professor C. M. Sargent, from the faculty of mechanical engineering at the University of Saskatchewan in Saskatoon, examined the said brake hose by means of cutting off portions and found therein at least two particles which were composed of what he described as a "glassy material". His opinion was that due to the operation of the motor vehicle these particles tended to work towards the outside of the brake hose permitting the brake fluid to escape. His evidence was that in order for a garage operator to discover the presence of these "glassy particles" the hose would have to be cut and thereby destroyed.

• • •

Evidence on behalf of the defendant was given by Mr. A. P. Halseth who in May, 1973, was an officer of the defendant company and worked in the company's service station. Mr. Halseth admitted that just prior to May 1, 1973, Mr. Sigurdson's vehicle was in the defendant's service station and that two new brake hoses were installed on the said vehicle. The said brake hoses were obtained by the defendant from the third party Acklands Limited, which company had been a supplier to the defendant since 1958. Mr. Halseth stated that the defendant company relied on the third party to supply proper brake hoses. Exhibit D. 3 is an invoice from the third party referring to two brake hoses. Mr. Halseth stated that after the accident he inspected the plaintiff's vehicle to determine the cause of brake failure. He filled the master brake cylinder with brake fluid but found that there was no build-up of pressure and on examining one of the brake hoses which had been installed by the defendant he found that brake fluid was dripping from the brake hose in the location immediately adjacent to the male end of the hose. The witness stated that he has had considerable experience with brake hoses but does not know of a method of testing a brake hose for leaks prior to installation. Mr. Halseth stated that after installing new brake hoses he puts the fluid under pressure and inspects for leaks. The witness denied that any member of the defendant's staff did anything in the installation of the brake hose which contributed to the rupture of the hose.

The plaintiffs in their statement of claim allege that the cause of their injuries was the failure on the part of the defendant's employee or employees to properly service and repair the vehicle and failure to test and examine the repairs to the vehicle. The plaintiffs also allege the use of defective materials by the defendant in effecting the repairs. The statement of defence pleads the provisions of the *Contributory Negligence Act*, R.S.S. 1965, c. 91, and in the alternative that if liability is found the responsibility for such injuries and damages rests with Acklands Limited as its supplier of automotive parts. The third party's statement of defence admits that the said party is engaged in the wholesale automotive parts business and did on or about May 1, 1973, sell and deliver to the defendant's place of business two brake hoses priced at $6.60. The third party also alleges that the hydraulic brake hoses were supplied to it by a firm know[n] as Echlin Limited and that if there was negligence in the "supply and manufacture of the said brake hose, it was the negligence of Echlin Limited the supplier and manufacturer". It should be pointed out that at the time of the trial of the action the manufacturer of the said brake hoses was not a party to the action.

I will first deal with the actions of Mrs. Sigurdson and her son Christopher. My understanding of the law is that in order for these parties to succeed against the defendant they must establish negligence on the part of the defendant in the repair of the vehicle. I am satisfied from the evidence that one of the brake hoses installed by the defendant was defective in that it contained at least two foreign objects as determined by Professor Sargent and that due to the operation of the vehicle these objects moved causing a rupture in the hose which permitted brake fluid to escape. I am further of the view that the cause of the accident was brake failure caused by the escape of the brake fluid. If there be negligence on the part of the defendant it must be carelessness on the part of its employee or employees in the installation of the brake hose or in the installation of the brake hose which the defendant's employees knew or should have known was defective. From the evidence I am unable to find that there was any negligence in the installation of the brake hose. The evidence further established to my satisfaction that no inspection by an employee of the defendant of the brake hose prior to installation would have determined the defects other than that of cutting the hose as was done by Professor Sargent. Indeed the professor stated that he knew of no test which could be made in the garage which would determine the presence of foreign objects in the hose other than by the destruction of the hose. The question of the necessity for an inspection of the brake hose by the defendant is dealt with in *Charlesworth on Negligence*, 5th ed. (1971), para. 654, pp. 405-6, when the author writes:

> A retailer is under no duty to examine the goods for defects before resale, in the absence of circumstances suggesting that they might be defective, when he obtains them from a manufacturer of repute. If he obtains them from another source, he may be under a duty to examine them, depending on the nature of the goods and the probability or otherwise of danger to be expected from defects to which the goods are subject.

The learned author then goes on to point out that the duty of a retailer applies to all sellers of goods who are not manufacturers whether they sell retail or wholesale. Placing the defendant in a position of a retailer I take the view that there were no circumstances in the present case which would suggest to an employee of the defendant that the brake hose was or might be defective when it was delivered to the defendant's place of business by the third party. Indeed there was, prior to installation of the brake hose, no test or examination which could be conducted by the defendant which would locate the foreign object short of destruction of the brake hose. Moreover, the operation of the vehicle from May 1st to June 16th suggests in itself that the actual installation of the brake hose was proper. There is therefore in my opinion no negligence on the part of the defendant in either the installation of the brake hose or in the failure to inspect such hose prior to installation. As I have held that there is no negligence on the part of the defendant, I dismiss the actions of the plaintiffs Mrs. Sigurdson and her son Christopher.

The liability of the defendant towards the plaintiff Mr. Sigurdson involves other considerations. While I have already held that the defendant's employees were not guilty of negligence the defendant, in so far as the plaintiff Mr. Sigurdson is concerned, is faced with the provisions of the *Sale of Goods Act*, R.S.S. 1965, c. 388, s. 16, which reads:

16. Subject to the provisions of this Act and of any Act in that behalf there is no implied warranty or condition as to the quality of fitness for any particular purpose of goods supplied under a contract of sale except as follows:
   1. Where the buyer expressly or by implication makes known to the seller the particular purpose for which the goods are required so as to show that the buyer relies on the seller's skill or judgment and the goods are of a description that it is in the course of the seller's business to supply, whether he be the manufacturer or not, there is an implied condition that the goods shall be reasonably fit for that purpose.
   2. Where goods are bought by description from a seller who deals in goods of that description, whether he is the manufacturer or not, there is an implied condition that the goods shall be of merchantable quality:
      Provided that if the buyer has examined the goods there shall be no implied condition with regard to defects which such examination ought to have revealed;
   3. An implied warranty or condition as to quality or fitness for a particular purpose may be annexed by usage of trade;

Waddams in his text *Products Liability* (1974) suggests that even in the absence of negligence a repairer may be liable to the plaintiff Mr. Sigurdson for breach of the implied warranty as set out in said s. 16 when the author writes at pp. 18-9:

However, insofar as the defect complained of is caused by defective materials supplied by the installer or repairer, there may be liability even in the absence of negligence for breach of an implied warranty that the materials used are reasonably fit.

The said author points out at p. 76 of his text:

> ...liability for breach of the implied warranties is strict liability in the sense that it is no defence for the seller to show that he exercised reasonable care or that the defect of the goods was undiscoverable.

I am of the view on the facts of the present case that there was by virtue of the *Sale of Goods Act*, an implied warranty or condition that the brake hose would be "reasonably fit" for the purpose for which it was intended. I find that the said brake hose was not "reasonably fit" in that it contained foreign bodies which eventually caused a rupture and brake failure which failure was the cause of the accident.

The defendant's plea of contributory negligence appears to be based on Mr. Sigurdson's failure to keep a proper look-out. The plaintiff was in the situation described by Hodgins, J.A., in *Harding v. Edwards et al.*, [1929] 4 D.L.R. 598 at pp. 599-600, 64 O.L.R. 98 at p. 102 [affd [1931] 2 D.L.R. 521, [1931] S.C.R. 167], when he wrote:

> ...hence I cannot convince myself that he was sufficiently recovered from the shock of the emergency to be judged by standards involving deliberation and opportunity for conscious decision, or by what is called by Lord Sumner "nice Judgment, prompt decision." *SS. "Singleton Abbey" v. SS. "Paludina"*, [1927] A.C. 16, at p. 26.

The plaintiff when confronted with pedestrians in front of him and a failure of his foot-brakes was faced with an emergency and he chose to turn to his right. There was no time for a "conscious decision" to the effect that he should try the hand-brake for by turning right he would hit a power pole. I do not think that contributory negligence attaches to the plaintiff on the facts of this case.

The question now arises as to the damages to which the plaintiff Mr. Sigurdson is entitled. Counsel for the parties agreed to special damages in the amount of $2079.56. I therefore award to the plaintiff Mr. Sigurdson special damages in the amount of $2079.56. I award the said plaintiff general damages in the amount of $2000. The plaintiff Mr. Karl Sigurdson shall be entitled to his tax costs in this matter, such costs to be taxed in accordance with column 4 of the Queen's Bench tariff of costs.

I have not referred to the plaintiff Michael Sigurdson as he is in the same position as the plaintiffs Mrs. Sigurdson and Christopher Sigurdson. Moreover, any injuries he suffered were of a very minor nature. The third party did not take an active part at the hearing. The reason being no doubt that it admitted selling two brake hoses to the defendant. My view is that the defendant may successfully recover from its supplier the third party for a breach of warranty, *i.e.*, that the brake hose was defective or not reasonably fit for the purpose for which it was intended. This point is dealt with by Waddams at p. 189 when the author writes:

> Although it is doubtful that one held liable for breach of warranty has a claim for contribution against the manufacturer of the defective goods as a joint

tortfeasor, he may have a remedy against his own supplier (whether manufacturer or other distributor) for breach of implied warranty.

I therefore award judgment in favour of the defendant against the third party in the amount of the judgment recovered by the plaintiff against the defendant, together with the taxed costs paid by the defendant to the plaintiff.

*Judgment for plaintiff.*

# Burroughs Business Machines Ltd. v. Feed-Rite Mills (1962) Ltd.

*(1974) 42 D.L.R. (3d) 303*
*Manitoba Court of Appeal*
*December 3, 1973*

MATAS, J.A.: This is an appeal from a judgment of Hamilton, J., dismissing a claim by plaintiff ("Burroughs") against defendant ("Feed-Rite"), allowing a counterclaim of Feed-Rite and ordering Burroughs to return certain equipment to Feed-Rite. Costs were assessed against plaintiff.

The cause of action arose out of a sale in April, 1968, by Burroughs to Feed-Rite, of a complete E6494 computer system (the "E6"). It was agreed that, in addition to the components of the E6, Burroughs would provide:

1. The installation of the equipment on Feed-Rite's premises.
2. The preparation and writing of programmes for the following seven applications:
   (a) Accounts receivable statements;
   (b) Aged Analysis;
   (c) Sales Analysis;
   (d) General Ledger;
   (e) Accounts Payable;
   (f) Payroll; and
   (g) Inventory.
3. The training of Feed-Rite personnel to operate the equipment.

The components of the E6 arrived in Winnipeg at different times in late 1968, with the last unit arriving possibly in January, 1969. The computer was assembled at Burroughs' premises and was put in operating condition. In the meantime the first programme was written and was then tested on the new equipment.

Two additional pieces of equipment were purchased by Feed-Rite from Burroughs in March, 1969. A separate contract was entered into covering these items, although Feed-Rite had not been aware that adjuncts to the system would be required.

All the equipment was delivered to Feed-Rite's premises at the end of March, 1969. The first financial information was obtained from the E6 for the month of April, 1969.

There were difficulties of a serious nature from the beginning. Not withstanding concerted efforts by plaintiff's personnel, a series of different problems continued to bedevil satisfactory use of the equipment. Matters came to a head in November, 1969, when Feed-Rite wrote the following letter to Burroughs (ex. 18): (see following page)

Following receipt of this letter, Burroughs made further attempts to have the system function as it was supposed to but its efforts were not successful. Feed-Rite began plans for transferring part of its accounting function to an outside data service company.

At the end of December, 1969, Burroughs' local office, in an effort to retain Feed-Rite as a user of Burroughs' equipment, made a proposal for use of a different unit. The proposal was accepted by Feed-Rite, but rejected by plaintiff's head office. On February 24, 1970, Feed-Rite shut down the E6 and requested Burroughs to disconnect the system. Plaintiff, while disagreeing with this decision, compiled with defendant's request (exs. 24 and 29).

In July, 1969, Feed-Rite had made a payment of $30 000 to Burroughs. The cheque (ex. 42) had the following notation written on its face: "subject to machine performance".

The learned trial Judge found no fault with Feed-Rite personnel in discharge of its responsibilities and found that "all of the defects in the machine or in the installation of the program were caused solely by the failure of Burroughs to perform the contract in accordance with its terms, that is to provide equipment, to program it, to train the Feed-Rite operators and to have it function as intended".

As well, Hamilton, J., found that Burroughs was in the business of supplying accounting machines, including computers; that defendant relied on the skill and judgment of plaintiff and that the equipment was not reasonably fit for the purpose of performing defendant's accounting function: the *Sale of Goods Act*, R.S.M. 1970, c. S10 (the "Act"), s. 16.

We are all of the opinion that there was ample evidence to support those findings. We agree with them.

Counsel for plaintiff argued that defendant had accepted the E6. Section 37 of the Acts reads:

> The buyer is deemed to have accepted the goods when he intimates to the seller that he has accepted them, or when the goods have been delivered to him, and he does any act in relation to them which is inconsistent with the ownership of the seller, or when after the lapse of a reasonable time, he retains the goods without intimating to the seller that he has rejected them.

In support of this submission Mr. Smethurst outlined a number of facts which, according to his argument, would support defendant's allegation that, at best, Feed-Rite was entitled only to damages for breach of warranty (the

Burroughs Business Machines Ltd.
1381 Portage Avenue
Winnipeg, Manitoba
Gentlemen:

We have come through another stattering (*sic*) month-end, with more than the usual month-end breakdown of equipment which delayed what could have been a very successful closing.

The new program did not run off as well as we had expected and leaves a lot to be desired. The statement run did not materialize in one hours running time and is more than likely in excess of two hours if everything goes well. We had considerable trouble in running the Aged Analysis which had to be corrected by adding machine by your people. The Sales Analysis was another chore which, through lack of comprehensive program instructions our people had to wait at times until Mr. Martindale led them, step by step, through the operation which was trying enough for him.

We are still waiting for the ledger card up-dating program to update our ledgers with interest, in the meantime we must use our Aged Analysis to secure account balances.

We gave you a deadline to get this system operating. It was November 1, 1969, or the time required to take off the October statements which should be (by your own admission) one but no more than two working days. This, as you know, did not happen.

We are, therefore, giving you written notice by registered mail that you have until the end of November to successfully take off, without breakdown, or program bugs, in a reasonable period (two days) our statements for that period. We will, through better scheduling on your direction, be even better prepared than we were for October. We are prepared to do anything we can to make this system work. So far you have handled it like you were on a "survival course", always scrambling in at the last possible moment with programs and running into trouble.

We have had no programs from you regarding the Payroll, Accounts Payable, General Ledger, and Inventory Control. How long do we have to wait for this?

Failing the expected performance we will, on January 1, 1970, have you remove the entire E6000 system, return our typing sensimatic with punch type and verifier along with the $30 000.00 paid subject to equipment performance.

Trusting you understand our intent, I remain,

Yours truly,
FEED-RITE Mills (1962) LTD.
"C. L. Anderson"
C. L. Anderson

CLA:jeo
P.S. SALES ANALYSIS
All Territories $4611.00 our from Control
Adding all Territories together $6807.00 from Control
RECEIVABLES
Tabbed and balanced day by day throughout month, unable to reconcile after your using for program check.
C.L.A.

Act, s. 13(3)), and not to rescission. But in our view the learned trial Judge was right in his conclusion that Feed-Rite had never "accepted" the computer: *Lightburn v. Belmont Sales Ltd. et al.* (1969), 6 D.L.R. (3d) 692 at p. 699, 69 W.W.R. 734; *Barber v. Inland Truck Sales Ltd.* (1970), 11 D.L.R. (3d) 469 at p. 474; *Polar Refrigeration Service Ltd. v. Moldenhauer* (1967), 61 D.L.R. (2d) 462 at p. 468, 60 W.W.R. 284.

Payment of $30 000 in July, 1969, was clearly made subject to performance. The E6 never did reach the stage of performing satisfactorily. Defendant's efforts in co-operating with plaintiff in an effort to make the equipment work cannot be used to negate the absence of legal acceptance. All that happened was, that defendant accepted the computer conditionally and continued for a reasonable time to permit plaintiff the opportunity of producing a computer which would perform the functions for which it had been purchased.

In our view, cases cited by appellant on this point, namely, *Massey-Harris Co. Ltd. v. Skelding*, [1934] 3 D.L.R. 193, [1934] S.C.R. 431; *Yeoman Credit, Ltd. v. Apps*, [1961] 2 All E.R. 281, and *R.W. Heron Paving Ltd. v. Dilworth Equipment Ltd.* (1962), 36 D.L.R. (2d) 462, [1963] 1 O.R. 201, are all distinguishable on their respective facts.

Was there a fundamental breach of the contract? On this point the learned trial Judge held:

> Feed-Rite purchased a computer to do its complete accounting. Due to defects in the equipment and the failure of the plaintiff to fully programme the unit there was a breach of the contract of such severity that it went to the root of the matter. The defendant was deprived of the whole benefit it was intended to obtain from the contract. In the result, Feed-Rite is entitled to treat the contract as at an end and to compensation for the damages it sustained.

In *Western Tractor Ltd. v. Dyck* (1969), 7 D.L.R. (3d) 535, 70 W.W.R. 215, Woods, J.A., said at p. 536:

> A fundamental breach is one going to the root of the contract so as to entitle the other party to treat it as a repudiation. In order to decide whether or not there is a fundamental breach, it is necessary to look to all the facts and circumstances of the contract.

The following appears in *Anson's Law of Contract*, 22nd ed. (1964), p. 155:

> Whether there has been a breach of a fundamental term is a question of degree depending on the facts of the case and the inference of law to be drawn from those facts....

And see *Lightburn v. Belmont Sales Ltd. et al., supra; Barber v. Inland Truck Sales Ltd., supra; Johnson v. Lambert* (1956), 17 W.W.R. 545; *Public Utilities Com'n for City of Waterloo v. Burroughs Business Machines Ltd. et al.*, (1973), 34 D.L.R. (3d) 320, [1973] 2 O.R. 472; *Beldessi et al. v. Island Equipment Ltd.* (1972), 29 D.L.R. (3d) 213 [reversed in part 41 D.L.R. (3d) 147].

We are all of the opinion that the learned trial Judge was correct in his conclusion that there was a fundamental breach. Defendant was entitled to return the E6 to plaintiff, was entitled to the return of its equipment, or damages in lieu thereof, and to be repaid $30 000 which it had paid to plaintiff; defendant was properly allowed $11 296.14 by way of damages, without deduction for value of any benefits alleged to have been obtained by it in respect of the use of the E6.

Appeal is dismissed with costs.[1]

NOTES

1.   *An appeal to the Supreme Court of Canada was dismissed, see (1976) 64 DLR 767.*

# B. Insurance

## Ramsay v. Home Insurance Company

*8 Insurance Law Reporter, (1941) 155*
*New Brunswick King's Bench*
*March 1, 1941*

RICHARDS, J.: The plaintiff claims for damages to an automobile under a policy of insurance issued by the defendant company. The automobile was badly damaged on November 11th, 1939.

The policy sued on was issued on May 17th, 1939. At that time the plaintiff lived in and conducted a rooming-house at No. 24 Weldon Street, in the City of Moncton. Among her roomers was one E. C. Bowers. On May 17th, 1939, Bowers bought a new automobile, a 1939 Plymouth Sedan, from A. O. Fownes Ltd., the Plymouth dealers in Moncton. The price, with equipment, was $1195.00. In payment he turned in an old car, gave some cash and a lien note for $360.00. The plaintiff says that Bowers gave her the car—according to her statement it was an outright gift and came as a surprise. There was no writing of any kind. At any rate the car was registered in her name. The certificate of registration is evidence. Exhibit "B". He gave her the keys and she considered the car was hers absolutely. At the hearing in Moncton on February 4th, instant, she produced the keys of the car (one set). She said the car was still hers. There had been no change in the ownership since it was given to her.

Apparently on the same day that Bowers bought the car, May 17th, he also applied to the defendant company for insurance. The application for the insurance was made in the name of the plaintiff, it was signed in the plaintiff's name, by Bowers, and in accordance with the application the policy was issued in her name.

On November 11th, 1939, this car, while being driven by Bowers, got out of control and crashed into a building near the corner of Mountain Road and Botsford Street, in the City of Moncton. The insurance company was notified, an insurance adjuster from the company, Donald Elderkin, made an inspection, and appraised the damages to the car at $589.91. As a result of further investigation and information the insurance company refused to pay the plaintiff's claim. Hence this action, in which the plaintiff claims the sum of $589.91.

The main defences are put forward: (1) That the said E. C. Bowers, and not the plaintiff, was the actual owner of the car—there was in fact, and in law, no gift to the plaintiff—and the plaintiff had no insurable interest in the car; and (2) In the alternative that the insurance was obtained by false representations on the part of the insured, to the prejudice of the defendant company. At the conclusion of the hearing the evidence completely satisfied me as to two points: First, that there was, in fact, no gift of the car to the plaintiff, the so-called gift was a pure sham; and, second, that false representations were made in the application for the insurance. There were two features in respect of which, as I remarked at the time, I felt that I should give some further consideration, namely, the question of "insurable interest" and "the materiality of the representations".

• • •

The question still remains: Why does E. C. Bowers put the car in the plaintiff's name if it is not a gift? The answer is plain and simple. He gave it to Donald Elderkin, the appraiser from the defendant company, when the latter was appraising the damage. Elderkin testified that Bowers said to him that he had licensed the car in Mrs. Ramsay's name to avoid payment of taxes on it in Moncton. This is not denied. Bowers, who is the one person who could have denied it—if it were not true—does not appear at the hearing. He leaves his partner in fraud to bear the whole burden. And this scheme to escape taxes in Moncton was not the whole fraud. The car was registered as follows:

"Name—Mrs. D. C. Ramsay.

Address—R.R. No. 2, Moncton, N.B."

and in addition to that we find the same address upon the application for insurance, with the further notation:

"Occupation or Business—Farmer.

Business Address—Upper Coverdale."

What is the explanation? It is clear again—so that the plaintiff may escape taxes on the car in Moncton; and that, in fact, is what resulted. "R.R. No. 2, Moncton", is in Albert County in the Parish of Coverdale, opposite the City of Moncton. This is her father's address. He lives on a farm, which was formerly in his name, but is now in the plaintiff's name, subject to a mortgage. But to represent the plaintiff as a farmer is another sham. And this subterfuge suggests the further question: Would Bowers be likely to indicate the plaintiff's address as "R.R. No. 2, Moncton", without the knowledge and privity of the plaintiff? It is possible, but hardly credible. Other circumstances might be cited to support the finding I have made, but enough has been said, I think, to show conclusively that there never was, in fact, any gift from Bowers to the plaintiff. The real ownership was, and remained, in Bowers.

In 15 *Halsbury*, 715, sec. 1246, it is said:

Where a person buys property and pays the purchase-money, or part of it, but takes the purchase in the name of another, who is neither his child, adopted child, nor wife, there is *prima facie* no gift, but a resulting trust for the person paying such money or part. The presumption may be rebutted by sufficient evidence, even though it may be that of the person in whose name the purchase has been made.

In the present case the whole chain of circumstances strongly support the presumption.

If I am right in the finding that the plaintiff was not the owner of the car, it follows, I think, that she had no "insurable interest". I do not suggest that a person holding even a small interest in some property or article may not insure the whole property or article, and for the full insurable value. In *Keefer v. Phoenix Insurance Co.* (1900) 31 S.C.R., 144, an unpaid vendor of a house insured for the full value. Upon a loss he recovered the full amount. He, of course, could retain only his own share, holding the balance in trust for the purchaser. But the interest to be insurable must be a monetary interest. In *Welford's Accident Insurance*, 2nd Ed., p. 13, it is said: "An interest, to be insurable, must have a pecuniary value." citing *Halford v. Kymer* (1830), 10 B. & C., 724. *Laverty's Insurance Law of Canada*, 2nd ed., p. 77, gives the following as a statement of what is covered by the term "insurable interest":

If you are liable to suffer a *direct, and immediate, loss or liability, appreciable in money*, from the happening of a certain event, then that event is one upon which you can obtain insurance, provided there is nothing *contra bonos mores*[1] or public policy.

The defendant cited *Rockmaker v. Motor Union Ins. Co.* (1922) 70 D.L.R., 360; 52 O.L.R. (C.A.). In this case it was held that the insured was the owner though he had purchased under a lien agreement that the property in the car was not to pass until fully paid for and he had assigned his interest as security for a debt. But in that case the insured had a real monetary interest in the car.

*Veterans' Sightseeing and Transportation Co. Ltd. v. Phoenix Ins. Co., et al.*, (1924) 2 D.L.R., 674, also cited by the defendant, was similar to and followed the Rockmaker case.

All the "interest" which the plaintiff had in the car was the privilege of using it. This is hardly an insurable interest. In my judgment this finding is sufficient to dispose of the whole case.

I think, however, that it is advisable to deal with the alternative defence; that of false representation in respect of the application for insurance. This is based on the assumption that the plaintiff was the owner, or at least, has an insurable interest in the car.

The two particulars to which I shall first refer are those which are set out in the defence as filed. By amendment at the trial, subject to objection, other particular false representations were relied upon. The two alleged false representations cited are:

1. In answer to the question, in the application, Item 2, "Is the automobile fully paid for?" the answer given was "Yes", whereas at the time of the accident the car was not paid for and was subject to a lien in favour of A. C. Fownes, Ltd.
2. In answer to the question, in the application, Item 4(a), "Will the automobile be operated by any person suffering from the loss of an eye, hand, foot or limb, or who is otherwise bodily deformed or maimed?" the answer given was "No", whereas, as it is said by the defendant, the car was intended to be operated, to the knowledge of the plaintiff, by E. C. Bowers, who at the time of the application suffered from the loss of a leg. He had a wooden leg.

These representations are said to be contrary to the provisions of sec. 173(1) of *The Insurance Act*, 1937. This section is as follows:

> Where an applicant for a contract falsely describes the automobile to be insured, to the prejudice of the insurer, or knowingly misrepresents or fails to disclose in the application any fact required to be stated therein or where the insured violates any term or condition of the policy or commits any fraud, or makes any wilfully false statement with respect to a claim under the policy, any claim of the insured shall be rendered invalid and the right of the insured to recover indemnity shall be forfeited.

In respect of the application for the insurance the applicant is the plaintiff, but Bowers is her agent, he actually makes the application and she must be held responsible for all that he said in connection with the application. She is the plaintiff and is claiming on a policy, based on this application. Now the answer as to the payment of the car is clearly false—it was not paid for and the lien was not disclosed—and this false representation was made knowingly, by Bowers, and must be so accepted by the plaintiff. The same is true in respect of the second item, the loss of a leg by Bowers. On this item the plaintiff contended that if the plaintiff be regarded as the applicant she could not be held to make the false representation knowingly: She would not know that Bowers would use the car, or that there was any intention that he would use the car. Even assuming that the plaintiff was the owner it is impossible to accept such a view. The circumstances speak too strongly against any thought that Bowers was to be excluded from all use of the car. As a matter of fact, I have not the slightest doubt, from the evidence, that each of them, Bowers and the plaintiff, knew and believed that the car would be used by each of them—as in fact it was. Neither, I think, can there be any doubt that the plaintiff knew of Bowers' physical disability. The plaintiff also contended in connection with this item that Miss Smith, the local agent for the defendant company, knew that Bowers had lost a leg. This was a fact, but to her the applicant was the plaintiff; she had no reason to know or believe that Bowers would use the car. In my opinion each of these representations was made knowingly.

The question now arises as to the materiality—are these facts material to the risk, and in any case must the misrepresentation or non-disclosure be of material facts. I would have thought that the principle was well-established that misrepresentation or non-disclosure to avoid a policy of insurance or to afford a basis to reject a claim thereunder must be of facts material to the risk. But in this case the defendant raised the point that under section 173(1), quoted above, materiality is not necessarily essential; the clause contained in the section "knowingly misrepresents or fails to disclose in the application any fact required to be stated therein" does not specify a *material* fact. And does not carry any relation to "prejudice of the insured". Therefore the mere fact of the misrepresentation or non-disclosure, without more, is sufficient to avoid the policy or afford a defence.

But I do not think it is necessary to determine this question, for in my view each of the two features now being considered constitutes a fact material to the risk. No comment seems necessary in respect of the use of a car by one who has a wooden leg. Mr. White, Special Agent and in charge of part of New Brunswick for Douglas, Rogers & Co., Ltd., testified that knowledge of this fact would have meant refusal of the policy. And this view seems obvious. The question as to payment for the car and the lien also seems very material. Mr. White said it was material in relation to the value and ability of the owner to complete payment and his measure of interest in the article. It is true he said on cross-examination that this feature alone might not prevent issuing of the policy, but he had previously stated that it was a matter that would suggest an investigation. Inquiry in this case would have disclosed the lien and, no doubt, the true ownership. In any event the Act itself seems to determine the matter. Statutory Condition No. 1(a)(ii), section 170, provides that any mortgage, lien or encumbrance affecting the automobile after the application for the policy shall be a "change in the risk material to the contract". Such a circumstance then must be a fact material to the risk when the policy is made, that is, in the application.

In *Johnson v. The British Canadian Ins. Co.* (1932) 4 M.P.R., 280 (N.S.), the plaintiff in the application for insurance stated that the automobile would be chiefly used for private purposes only. In the contract it was stipulated that the defendant would not be liable for any loss or damage while the car was rented or leased. It was found as a fact that the plaintiff rented or leased the car for considerable periods. Notice of this circumstance was not given to the defendant. It was held that the letting of the car was a change material to the risk.

In *Holdaway v. British Crown Assurance Corp. Ltd.* (1925) 51 O.L.R. 70 (C.A.), it was held, per Latchford, C.J., p. 82, that misrepresentation as to cost was material in fact. He cited as the test of materiality the statement of the Privy Council in *Mutual Life Ins. Co. of N.Y. v. Ontario Metal Products Co.* (1925) A.C. 344, where at page 351 it is said:

In Their (Lordships') view, it is a question of fact in each case whether, if the matters concealed or misrepresented had been truly disclosed, they would, on a fair consideration of the evidence, have influenced a reasonable insurer to decline the risk or to have stipulated for a higher premium.

On this alternative basis, restricted to those features cited in the original defence, the plaintiff must fail.

Subject to strenuous objection by plaintiff's counsel, I allowed the defendant to add, by way of defence, at the trial, certain other items of false representation. I do not believe that the plaintiff was in any way prejudiced. I think counsel had sufficient time and opportunity to meet these new features. These other false representations were:

1. False residential address.
2. False description of business or occupation.
3. False business address.

These three items may be shortly considered, and together. There is no doubt that each answer to the relevant question is false. And I have stated above that the obvious reason was to assure that the plaintiff would not have to pay taxes on the car in Moncton. The materiality of these facts is also obvious. The risk is much greater in respect of a car owned and operated by one living in a city than by a farmer living in the country. Mr. White gave the ratio of risk as 80% for the city and 20% for the country.

The plaintiff's action will be dismissed, with costs.

NOTES

1. *"Contra bonos mores" literally means "against good morals" or as the quotation indicates "against public policy". Such a contract would be unenforceable and quite possibly void.*

# C. Bailment

## Manitoba Public Insurance Corp. v. Midway Chrysler Plymouth Ltd.

*[1978] 1 W.W.R. 722*
*Manitoba Court of Appeal*
*December 12, 1977*

O'SULLIVAN J.A.: This action for damages to an automobile turns on whether the care exercised over the automobile by the defendant meets the standard required of a bailee for reward. It was agreed by both parties to the appeal that the plaintiff is subrogated[1] to the rights of a bailor, who brought his automobile to the defendant's place of business for repair under a warranty agreement. The status of the defendant as a bailee for reward is not in dispute. Furthermore, it is agreed that if the defendant is liable for negligence then the plaintiff's judgment should be in the sum of $2003.97 and costs.

The trial was held before Hewak Co. Ct. J. on agreed facts. When the automobile was brought to the defendant, it was found that the repairs could not be done the same day and it was necessary to leave it overnight. The defendant has a storage compound in the open air surrounded by a chain-link metal fence, six feet in height, on top of which is an additional two feet of barbed wire, sloped outward. There is one gate, which was locked with a chain and padlock. Fence and gate were in good repair. The storage compound is illuminated at night by three incandescent lamps. A police cruiser car drives by during the night on a random spot check basis.

The defendant's standard practice has been to store automobiles in the storage compound, to remove the keys from the ignition and place them on a board in a locked office and to lock the gate. The automobile in question had an anti-theft mechanism such that the steering wheel locks and cannot be turned without the key being in the ignition.

Contrary to the standard practice of the defendant, its employee, a car jockey who placed the automobile in the storage compound, left the keys in the ignition rather than removing them at the end of the day. During the night, someone scaled the fence and drove the automobile away through the locked metal gate. When the automobile was recovered, it was in a damaged state. Hence this lawsuit.

It is accepted by both parties that a bailee such as the defendant is not an insurer of the goods in his custody and it is not liable for the acts of independent third parties, such as thieves; but a bailee cannot rely on the defence of theft if the bailee has failed to take reasonable care of the goods. The learned trial judge said he could not find that the acts or omissions of the defendant amounted to the "causa causans"[2] of the damage inflicted on the automobile. I agree that the "causa causans" was the theft and not the failure of the defendant to take care, but liability on bailees does not, with respect, depend on a finding that the bailee's negligence is the "causa causans" of the loss of or damage to the thing bailed. Counsel for both parties to the appeal argued it on the basis that the sole issue before us was to determine whether or not in all the circumstances the bailee had taken the care required of it by law.

Counsel for the respondent cited and the learned trial judge accepted as good law a statement by Laidlaw J.A. of the Ontario Court of Appeal in *Brown v. Toronto Auto Parks*, [1955] O.W.N. 456 at 457, [1955] 2 D.L.R. 525:

> In law, the position of a custodian who undertakes to keep goods in his possession for reward is that he is under a duty to exercise due care and diligence in keeping the article in trust to him on behalf of the bailor. It has been said that the duty is to exercise that care and diligence which a careful and diligent man would exercise in the custody of his own articles and goods in the same circumstances. When a chattel, such as this motor car, is lost, the onus is on the custodian to show that the injury or the loss did not happen in consequence of his neglect to use such care and diligence as a prudent and careful man would exercise in relation to his own property.

Before us, both counsel referred to *Sask. Govt. Ins. Office v. Mid-West Motors Ltd.*, 36 W.W.R. 254 at 258, [1961] I.L.R. 1-041 (Sask.), where Friesen D.C.J. quoted with approval from 2 Hals. (3rd) 114, as follows:

> The standard of care...must be that care and diligence which a careful and vigilant man would exercise in the custody of his own chattels of a similar description and character in similar circumstances.

Accepting such statements of law, the learned trial judge said:

> The fact that the key was left in the ignition could not in my view be described as such negligence that would attach liability to the defendant company any more than leaving the key in one's own car in a locked garage could be considered negligence.

In this court, counsel for the respondent submitted that a prudent man could not be said to be guilty of being careless about his own goods if he left keys in a car otherwise carefully secured.

In my opinion, a more accurate statement of the law is contained in 2 Hals. (4th) 711, para. 1539:

> A custodian for reward must exercise due and reasonable care for the safety of the article entrusted to him. The standard of care and diligence imposed on him is that demanded by the circumstances of the particular case, and is higher than that required of a gratuitous depositary; it should be the rather greater care that a reasonable man would take of other people's articles lent to him at his request for his convenience.

This is one of those cases in which a trial judge had no special advantage of weighing evidence, since the trial proceeded on agreed facts. While giving due consideration to the opinion formed by the learned trial judge, we have the duty on an appeal of this kind to subject the facts as found to a fresh evaluation. At the conclusion of the hearing, we were all of the view that the defendant should be held responsible for its employee's negligence.

It is true that we must be cautious about regarding every breach of a safety procedure adopted by a bailee as being in itself indicative of negligence, since a bailee may adopt a system of more than ordinary care and such bailee should not be penalized by having its extraordinary system treated as imposing on it a higher standard of negligence than is imposed on those who do not adopt such extraordinary systems. Nevertheless, a breach of a system established by a commercial defendant for the protection of goods entrusted to its care is some evidence of negligence. In our opinion, even on the basis of an ordinary system of care to which a bailee for reward should reasonably be expected to conform, the failure of the defendant's employee to take the keys out of the ignition and to place them in the defendant's office amounted to actionable negligence for which the defendant is vicariously responsible.

Accordingly, we allowed the appeal and directed that judgment be entered for the plaintiff against the defendant for the sum of $2003.97 and costs here and below.

NOTES

1. Subrogation—*see note 1 at the end of the* Greenwood Shopping Plaza Ltd. *v.* Beattie. *case (Privity of Contract)*
2. Causa causans *means the immediate effective cause or the last link in the chain of causation.*

# D. Principal and Agent

## Palinko (Palinka) v. Bower

*[1976] 4 W.W.R. 118*
*Alberta Supreme Court (Appelate Division)*
*April 23, 1976.*

MOIR J.A.: The appellant is a married woman. She encountered difficulties in her marriage. She and her husband separated. As a result, the appellant and her husband reached a settlement. By the terms of that agreement the husband transferred his interest in the matrimonial home to the appellant.

The appellant had few assets. She decided to sell the house. She listed it on 17th February 1972 with Buxton Real Estate at a price of $34 900. She soon became impatient with them. She was allowed to cancel that listing on 18th April 1972. She immediately listed the property with City Savings & Trust Company at a price of $37 900. No sale was made. The appellant was anxious. On 2nd August 1972 she signed what purported to be a guaranteed sales agreement. This agreement provided that the property would be offered for sale until 3rd September at $34 900. For the next month it was to be offered at a price of $33 900. Finally, the property was to be sold at $32 500 to City Savings & Trust. This is the purport of the agreement as explained to us by counsel although one would have difficulty in interpreting the agreement as explained.

One D. G. Thomas was the agent of City Savings & Trust who took the listing on the property from the appellant. He also dealt with the appellant on a number of occasions. All of the City Savings & Trust agents inspected the house to familiarize themselves with the property. One of the agents who inspected the property was the respondent. Throughout the whole of the time the respondent was a real estate agent in the employ of City Savings & Trust. He was actively engaged in trying to sell the property.

On 15th August 1972 the respondent made an offer of $32 500 for the property. Thomas took the offer to the appellant. He told the appellant the respondent was a real estate agent and should be employed by City Savings

& Trust. The appellant accepted the offer although it is clear that she was not too happy about it. She saw no one but Thomas, the listing agent. She did not receive independent advice as to whether or not she should accept the offer. She did not know the true value of her property except as advised by City Savings & Trust. The valuation which was obtained for mortgage purposes through the Toronto-Dominion Bank of $34 000 was not disclosed to the appellant.

The appellant was distressed about the offer. She was in tears when the mortgage appraiser arrived a few days later. She then visited her then solicitor along with a branch manager of City Savings & Trust. Next she changed solicitors. Although time was of the essence of the agreement which called for a payment of $15 300 on 28th September 1972, the respondent's solicitor sent to the appellant's previous solicitor a cheque in the sum of $2449 together with an assignment of mortgage proceeds. The respondent's solicitor wrote directly to the appellant on the same date requesting a transfer in favour of the respondent. This letter was delivered on 30th September 1972. Prior to this, at the time of making the offer, the respondent had deposited $1000 with City Savings & Trust as a deposit for his due performance of the agreement.

The appellant refused to complete the transaction. She was sued for specific performance or, in the alternative, for damages. A statement of claim was issued on 23rd October 1972 and a defence was filed on 14th November 1972. The chief defence was the fact that the appellant husband had never consented to the disposition of the "homestead" property as required by *The Dower Act*[1] of Alberta, being R.S.A. 1970, c. 114. In addition, the appellant alleged coercion, breach of condition, failure to complete by the time specified and, finally, that the respondent was in breach of his duty to the appellant because his duty and interest conflicted when the respondent sold to himself.

The trial of the action took place on 30th October and 1st November 1973. The learned trial Judge found that *The Dower Act* was not a valid defence in that the appellant was estopped from relying upon that defence. He granted an order for specific performance, and in the alternative the respondent was to have judgment for damages against the appellant in the sum of $1429. The formal judgment so providing was not entered until 9th May 1975. Notice of appeal was filed on 2nd June and the notice of cross-appeal was filed on 20th June 1975. The appeal came on to be heard in November 1975.

On the appeal the main argument was that the respondent, being an agent for sale, had sold to himself without full disclosure and that in the circumstances it would be inequitable to grant specific performance of the alleged agreement. The dower argument was pressed as well.

It seems to me that we should examine the respondent's conduct in the light of the position he occupied. There are several rules which must be adhered to when one occupies the position of agent for a principal. The best known of these rules is that an agent must not put himself in the position where his duty to his principal conflicts with the agent's own interests. As stated by Brodeur J. in *Stahl v. Miller*, [1918] 2 W.W.R. 197, 56 S.C.R. 312 at 322-23, 40 D.L.R. 388:

> The fairness of the transaction is immaterial; and the agent might be acting with the best of good faith; but it does not make any difference, because an agent will never be allowed to place himself in a situation in which, under ordinary circumstances, he would be tempted to do that which is not the best for his principal. *Bank of Upper Can. v. Bradshaw* (1867), L.R. 1 P.C. 479.

The next rule is that an agent shall not make any profit from his position except that remuneration agreed upon between the principal and the agent. This too is clearly and emphatically stated by Brodeur J. in *Hichcock v. Sykes* (1914), 49 S.C.R. 403 at 422, 23 D.L.R. 518:

> The principle of law and equity is that an agent or a partner shall make no profit to himself out of his employment other than the amount payable to him by his employer or by the partnership.
>
> That principle is an exceedingly just one calculated to secure the observance of good faith between principal and agent or between partners and to prevent the agent sacrificing the interest of the employer and obtaining gain and advantage for himself.

The next rule is that an agent should not use his position as agent, or information gained by virtue of that position, unjustly and to his own ends. This is clear from the judgment of Lindley L.J. in *Lamb v. Evans*, [1893] 1 Ch. 218 at 226:

> What right has any agent to use materials obtained by him in the course of his employment and for his employer against the interest of that employer? I am not aware that he has any such right. Such a use is contrary to the relation which exists between principal and agent. It is contrary to the good faith of the employment, and good faith underlies the whole of an agent's obligations to his principal. No case, unless it be the one which I will notice presently, can I believe be found which is contrary to the general principle upon which this injunction is framed, viz., that an agent has no right to employ as against his principal materials which that agent has obtained only for his principal and in the course of his agency.

See, too, Bowen L.J. at p. 230 of the same case and *Regal (Hastings) Ltd. v. Gulliver*, [1967] 2 A.C. 134, [1942] 1 All E.R. 378.

The principles are clear. These principles must be applied to the facts. The learned trial Judge found that the appellant knew that the purchaser was a real estate agent with City Savings & Trust. The appellant knew this as she admitted on examination for discovery. On the other hand, the respondent admits to having purchased the property. He was asked if Thomas signed up the buyer and he replied "I signed up the buyer, which was myself." There is no suggestion in the evidence that any other disclosure was ever made.

In my opinion there are numerous legal obstacles in the way of an order for specific performance at the suit of the respondent. Firstly, there was the listing agreement itself. The price at the time was $34 900 reducing to $33 900 and finally to $32 500. The respondent knew of this arrangement as he was attempting to sell the house. It is clear that six weeks prior to the price being reduced to $32 500 the respondent knew that was to be the final sale price. He offered precisely that amount. He must be taken to have used this information to his advantage. As I understand the principle of *Phipps v. Boardman*, [1965] Ch. 992, [1965] 1 All E.R. 849 at 857, affirmed [1967] 2 A.C. 46, [1966] 3 All E.R. 721, Lord Denning stated: "He gained an unjust benefit by the use of his principal's property or his position and must account for it."

Although the principle so stated does not cover precisely this point (because a profit has not been made), it is a ground to resist the present action. This application of the principle was given by Galligan J. in *D'Atri v. Chilcott* (1975), 7 O.R. (2d) 249, 55 D.L.R. (3d) 30 (Ont.).

Secondly, for a period of some two weeks it was the duty of the agent to sell the property for $34 900 or more. After that period the agent was to sell at $33 900. The respondent by offering to purchase the property at a lesser price put himself in a position where his interest and duty might conflict. As agent for the appellant he was duty bound to find a purchaser at the best possible price. As purchaser his interest was to secure the property as cheaply as possible. In placing himself in this position the respondent cannot expect us to inquire as to the goodness of the bargain. The appellant wants to be free of it and that is sufficient.

Thirdly, the listing agreement called for a payment to the agent (City Savings & Trust) of 7 per cent or $2275. This commission was to be divided 40 per cent to the listing salesman and 60 per cent to the selling salesman. The respondent told the learned trial Judge that he did not have to pay the 60 per cent commission due to the selling agent and City Savings & Trust on an equal division because of an internal arrangement. This meant the respondent really obtained the property for $31 135. This was not disclosed to the appellant. In my opinion a full, frank and complete disclosure was necessary. The respondent as agent should not be permitted to have this secret advantage.

The respondent obtained a decree of specific performance at trial. In the light of his conduct, was the respondent entitled to such a decree? To my mind, the use by the respondent of the listing agreement to obtain the guaranteed sale price, the possibility of the conflict of interest and the failure to disclose the fact that the respondent was obtaining the property at a reduced price are fatal to the claim for specific performance. That action should be dismissed.

None of these reasons would make the contract void or voidable. However, specific performance is an equitable remedy. Here we are entitled to take into account the conduct of the respondent. It is the conduct of the purchaser that must be assessed in this type of action. To my mind the use by the respondent of the listing agreement to obtain a guaranteed sale price, the possibility of a conflict of interest, the failure to disclose the fact that the respondent was obtaining the property for $31 135 and the failure to advise as to the real value of the property are fatal to the claim for specific performance.

The respondent argues that all of these things may be perfectly true insofar as City Savings & Trust are concerned but this has nothing to do with the respondent. They argue that City Savings & Trust was the agent. It is claimed that the respondent owed no duty to the appellant—even though he was actively engaged in attempting to sell the property. However, it appears to me that limited companies can only act through agents or salesmen and that duty falls on the agent or salesman. He cannot escape by hiding behind the employer who was the agent in law. In this respect, I agree with the reasoning of Meredith J. in *Kramer v. Cooper*, [1975] 2 W.W.R. 1 (B.C.), where he says at p. 4:

> In this case the plaintiff, it might be said, was not strictly speaking the agent of the defendant. Canada Permanent was the agent and the plaintiff but an employee, not directly assigned by the company to sell the property. Nevertheless the obligation of the agent, namely, that he will not put his interest in conflict with that of his principal without the fullest of disclosure, must, I think, extend to the employees of the agent, whether actively engaged in promoting the sale of the property or not. Obviously an employee not directly involved in the sale is not responsible to advance the interests of the client, but I think he is responsible not to derogate from the client's interest or to put his interest in conflict with that of the client. Mr. Kramer wanted to buy as cheaply as possible. Mrs. Cooper wished to obtain the maximum price for her property. The conflict was apparent. The plaintiff in the employ of the agent was duty-bound as I see it to fully disclose his interest. That he did not do so was obvious on the evidence. I think Mrs. Cooper did not know, certainly it was not brought home to her, firstly, that the plaintiff was himself in fact the purchaser, and, secondly, that he was in the employ of the trust company.
>
> The failure to disclose his interest as purchaser is fatal to the plaintiff's claim whether it be for damages or for specific performance. But I think as well that the plaintiff was obliged in the circumstances to disclose to Mrs. Cooper at least the possibility, which I find existed, that he would share in the commission which Mrs. Cooper agreed to pay to her agent. The plaintiff does not escape by simply saying that his entitlement to share was not settled until after the agreement to buy was concluded. Clearly the matter was one which 'would be likely to operate upon the principal's judgment' and should accordingly have been disclosed.

In my opinion the claim for damages in lieu of specific performance must also be dismissed. It is only where specific performance would be decreed but where damages are a more suitable remedy that damages are awarded. That is not the situation here and accordingly the alternative claim for damages is dismissed.

• • •

In the result, the appeal is allowed and the respondent's action for specific performance and in the alternative for damages is dismissed with costs in both Courts. Costs are to be taxed on col. 5 of the Consolidated Rules of the Supreme Court, no limiting rule to apply.

[The concurring reasons of Mr. Justice McDermid are omitted.]

NOTES

1. *For reference to Homestead and Dower rights see note 1 to* Bomek v. Bomek *under the heading "Mistake".*

# Cypress Disposal Ltd. v. Inland Kenworth Sales Ltd.

*(1975) 54 D.L.R. (3d) 598*
*British Columbia Court of Appeal*
*January 21, 1975*

FARRIS, C.J.B.C.: This is an appeal by the defendant from a judgment holding it liable for damages for the fraud of its salesman, Mr. Nontell, in effecting the sale to the plaintiff of two garbage disposal trucks for the sum of Fifty Thousand, One Hundred and Fifty ($50 150) Dollars. The trial Judge held that when the fraud was perpetrated Nontell was not acting within the scope of his actual authority. He held, however, that there was such a holding out by the defendant of the salesman's authority as to fix it with liability for his conduct. I do not agree. It was clear from the order form that Nontell had no authority to bind the company. There was no conduct of the defendant that could reasonably be interpreted as enlarging his powers. When the fraud was committed the agent was not acting within the scope of his authority, actual or ostensible. Therefore there is no basis for holding the defendant liable and the appeal must be allowed.

There is no dispute as to the facts. On August 17, 1972, the plaintiff (represented by its manager Mr. Gazsity), following negotiations with the defendant's salesman Nontell, signed an order form for the purchase of two Kenworth garbage disposal trucks which were to be custom-made. Delivery of the trucks was to be at Victoria, B.C., by October 18, 1972. A provision was inserted in the form to the effect that the defendant would be charged $300 per day for every day of late delivery.

The order form provided: "This order...is not binding on the Vendor until accepted by one of its officers." Below this is a box space headed "Vendor's signing area" containing the words:

Inland Kenworth Sales (Nanaimo)
submitted by
            A. P. Nontell (and his signature)
            Salesman
Accepted by...

At the time the order was given (or a day or so later) the plaintiff gave Mr. Nontell a deposit of $2000 by way of a cheque payable to the defendant and post-dated August 21, 1972.

When the order was submitted to the defendant's head office at Nanaimo, a day or so later, its manager, Dunn, advised Nontell that it would not agree to the penalty clause for late delivery. He initialled on the form "not accepta-ble". Nontell then told Gazsity that the defendant would not agree to the penalty clause as written, but if Gazsity would agree not to invoke the clause if there was a delay of only six or seven days there would be no problem. Gazsity agreed that there would be no claim in such an event.

Nontell then, without the knowledge of Gazsity, filled out another form without the penalty clause and providing for "delivery as soon as possible". He forged Gazsity's name to it and forwarded the document to the head office. This was accepted and signed by Dunn. Normally the sending of a copy of the completed form to the customer would be done by the salesman. Nontell, of course, did not send it to Gazsity and Gazsity never asked for a copy of the completed order form that he had signed containing the penalty clause showing acceptance by the defendant.

The defendant deposited the plaintiff's cheque for $2000 as it understood from the second order and assurances by Nontell that there was no problem.

The order for the trucks was proceeded with but the delivery date of October 18, 1972, was not met. Delivery was 28 days late.

On November 16, 1972, Gazsity took delivery of the trucks and signed a conditional sales agreement. When the claim for the penalty was made the fraud of Nontell was discovered.

In order for the plaintiff to recover $300 per day for late delivery, it must establish a contract containing the penalty clause. This it cannot do. The order form clearly told the plaintiff that the order was not binding on the defendant until accepted by it. There never was any such acceptance. A contract containing the penalty clause never came into existence because the parties were never *ad idem*.

Gazsity could not rely on the assurance of Nontell that if the plaintiff would make no claim for a short delay there would be no problem because he knew that Nontell had no authority to contract. The order form told him it had to be accepted by an officer of the defendant.

This case falls within the principle set out in *Russo-Chinese Bank v. Li Yau Sam*, [1910] A.C. 174 at p. 184:

> It is undoubted that a person who deals with an agent, whose authority he knows to be limited, as the plaintiff knew in this case, does so at his peril, in this sense, that should the agent be found to have exceeded his authority his principal cannot be made responsible. While the several authorities cited by Mr. Scrutton, from *Grant v. Norway*, 10 C.B. 665 down to *Ruben v. Great Fingall Consolidated*, [1906] A.C. 439, establish, in their Lordships' opinion, the proposition that, in order that the principle of "holding out" should in any given case of agency apply, the act done by the agent, and relied upon to bind the principal, must be an act of that particular class of acts which the agent is held out as having a general authority on behalf of his principal to do; and, of course, the party prejudiced must have believed in the existence of that general authority and been thereby misled. In other words, if the agent be held out as having only a limited authority to do on behalf of his principal acts of a particular class, then the principal is not bound by an act done outside that authority, even though it be an act of that particular class, because, the authority being thus represented to be limited, the party prejudiced has notice, and should ascertain whether or not the act is authorized.

There is no room here for the application of the doctrine of ostensible authority. As was said in *A.-G. Ceylon v. Silva*, [1953] A.C. 461 at p. 479:

All "ostensible" authority involves a representation by the principal as to the extent of the agent's authority. No representation by the agent as to the extent of his authority can amount to a "holding out" by the principal.

The only representation by the principal was that the salesman had no authority to contract. Any statements made by Nontell to the contrary cannot change that.

It was argued that Nontell had authority to communicate with third parties. Therefore it was submitted, if in the course of the authorized act of communication the agent represented that his principal accepted the modified penalty clause, the principal is bound. In support of this, the decision of the majority of the Manitoba Court of Appeal in *Berryere v. Fireman's Fund Ins. Co.; Murray, Third Party* (1965), 51 D.L.R. (2d) 603, [1961-65] I.L.R. 663, was cited.

This submission is without merit. Nontell's authority to communicate with third parties was not an authority to orally communicate an asserted acceptance of the contract by the defendant. The order form prescribed the method of acceptance, *viz.*, a signature by an officer of the defendant in the space headed "Vendor's signing area".

The *Berryere* case turns on its particular facts. There the agent had wide powers to bind the company, which had given him "definite indicia of authority". The agent was much more than a mere soliciting agent or salesman. Accordingly, when the agent communicated falsely to an applicant that his application for insurance had been approved, and issued a pink card to that effect (the cards having been supplied to him by the company), it was held the company was liable.

In the present case Nontell was not "much more than a mere soliciting agent". He had "no indicia of authority". The defendant did nothing which could lead Gazsity to reasonably believe that the requirement of acceptance as prescribed by the order form had been abandoned.

A more pertinent case is *Jensen et al. v. South Trail Mobile Ltd. et al.* (1972), 28 D.L.R. (3d) 233, [1972] 5 W.W.R. 7, where on facts very similar to the present case, the Alberta Court of Appeal held that a false representation by the agent that he had received approval from head office did not bind the principal. The Court relied on the *Silva* case, *supra*, that no representation by the agent as to the extent of his authority can amount to a "holding out" by the principal.

It follows that the plaintiff failed to establish any contractual right to penalty for late delivery and the appeal must be allowed.

[The dissenting judgment of Mr. Justice Seaton is omitted.]

# E. Employment

## Betz Laboratories Limited v. Klyn and Clycon Chemicals Ltd.

*(1969) 70 WWR 304*[1]
*B.C. Supreme Court (Chambers)*
*August 26, 1969*

RUTTAN, J. The plaintiff moves for an interim injunction[2] restraining, until trial of the action, the defendants and each of them from accepting employment or acting as agents, manufacturer's representative, partner, officer or self-employed person in any business or field of endeavour competitive with the plaintiff company in the province of British Columbia.

The injunction here sought is to enforce a restrictive covenant entered into by the individual defendant, Peter Klyn, with the plaintiff company at the time when he was an employee of the plaintiff and acting as its sales representative for the province of British Columbia. The covenant he entered into at that time is clause 9 of an agreement entitled "Employees Non-Disclosure and Non-Competitive Agreement."

The particular clause 9 reads as follows:

> When and if my employment with Betz is terminated for any reason whatsoever (including but not restricted to resignation, discharge or mutual agreement of the parties), for a period of eighteen (18) months after such termination, I will not, in any area or territory or in part of any area or territory in which I represented Betz or any of its subsidiaries or affiliates in a sales capacity, at any time during the twelve (12) months immediately preceding such termination, accept employment or act as an agent, manufacturer's representative, partner, officer or self-employed person in any business or field of endeavour competitive with Betz Laboratories Limited, or any of its subsidiaries or affiliates.
>
> Such competitive fields of endeavour shall include, but shall not be limited to the fields of industrial water treatment for boilers, cooling towers and paper mills; anti-scaling agents, corrosion inhibitors, flocculating agents, anti-foams, industrial biocides for industrial water; and corrosion inhibitors and emulsion breakers for oil field and oil well equipment."

While still an employee of the plaintiff company in June, 1968, the defendant Klyn and one, Konrad Tittler, at that time also an employee of the plaintiff company, incorporated a company by name Clycon Chemicals Ltd. in the province of British Columbia, which company is the second defendant herein. The objects for which the company was formed were to engage in the production and sale of chemicals and chemical products of the same type and description as those produced by the plaintiff company. The first defendant left his job with the plaintiff on January 3, 1969, and immediately went to work with the second defendant and sold and offered for sale boiler water and cooling water treatment agents of the same type he formerly sold for the plaintiff company. The plaintiff alleges that Klyn also has been selling chemicals known as "slimicides," and though this is denied on affidavit by the defendant, it is sufficient for my purpose that if proved this allegation also amounts to a breach of his covenant. It is admitted that if any injunction shall go against Klyn it may also lie against the company through which he is carrying out his activities.

The defendant's objection to the granting of this injunction is that the restriction is void as unduly restrictive and there is therefore no subject matter upon which even an interim injunction can be based. His submission is that every restraint, partial as well as general, is contrary to public policy and is *prima facie* void[3] and the presumption of invalidity can only be rebutted by showing the restraint is reasonable. In this case the restraint seeks to impose upon a former employee the prohibition of carrying out his employment, and such restraint is never reasonable unless there is some proprietary interest owned by the master or owner or employer, which requires protection.

But it does fall within the definition of proprietary interest where an employer seeks to protect his customer connections, that is to say, to prevent his customers from being enticed away from him by an employee who formerly was on his staff. The covenant contained in clause 9 of the agreement is similar to the one defined in *Gilford Motor Co. v. Horne* [1933] 1 Ch 935, 102 LJ Ch 212, by Lord Romer at p. 966 as "a covenant against solicitation." His lordship went on to describe the covenant in these terms:

> • • • that is to say, it is a covenant by an employee that he will not, after his employment shall have ceased, solicit orders from customers of his employers' business who were such at the time of the cessation of his employment or had been such during the existence of that employment. • • • The question whether it be necessary or not depends upon the nature of the business carried on by the employer and the nature of the employment that is being given to the employee."

Cheshire and Fifoot in their textbook on *The Law of Contract*, 6th ed., p. 330, question this test of Lord Romer as being too wide, and prefer the definition of Lord Parker in *Herbert Morris Ltd. v. Saxelby* [1916] 1 AC 688, at 709, 85 LJ Ch 210, where his lordship stressed that, before any restraint is justifiable, the servant must be one who will acquire not merely knowledge of customers but, in addition, influence over them. But even this more restricted definition of reasonable restraint is applicable to the present case. The defendant as a sales representative was the only officer of the plaintiff company who came in contact with certain important customers in the province of British Columbia, that is to say, large paper mills operated by such companies as MacMillan Bloedel Ltd. and Crown Zellerbach Ltd. As such he was in a position to exert influence on these customers and persuade them to change their custom from one type of chemical to another.

One may wonder why a period of only 18 months would be of value to the plaintiff company to prevent loss of business through the competitive salesmanship of its former employee. However, as explained by Mr. Merritt for the plaintiff, to break the continuity of service by a sales representative such as the defendant, who one day appears on behalf of the plaintiff company and the next day acting for a competitor, a period of 18 months would be helpful and sufficient to protect the plaintiff in maintaining and developing its own customer outlets.

In any event, for the purpose of this motion, I am prepared to agree that the plaintiff has established a proprietary interest which is imperilled by the actions of the defendant in contacting all his former customers.

The area of restraint, i.e., the province of British Columbia, and the duration of restraint being 18 months from the time of the termination of employment are not unreasonable.

However, I am not prepared to grant the injunction in exactly the terms requested in the notice of motion or in the terms of clause 9 in the employment agreement. Restrictive covenants will not be maintained to prevent competition where the plaintiff has no prior interest. The defendant is not to be stopped from carrying on his activities as a salesman but only not to interfere with the plaintiff's legitimate prior interests which he himself may have developed on behalf of the plaintiff. In one affidavit filed by the plaintiff, a Mr. Durkin, after listing several paper mills as customers of the plaintiff who purchased a slimicide known as RX-17, said there were no other paper mills in the province which were customers for the said RX-17. He may be wrong and there may be other paper mills that were customers for this and other of the plaintiff's products. The defendant will know who those customers are and must govern himself accordingly. But as was held in *Gilford Motor Co. v. Horne, supra*, restrictions cover only customers and areas where the plaintiff has already established customer relationships and does not extend to areas which have never been visited.

It was submitted that in granting the injunction I could not do so by varying the terms of the restrictive covenant. It was agreed that in certain circumstances an agreement in restraint of trade which is in part reasonable and in part unreasonable, may be severed and the part which is reasonable enforced. However, the severed parts must be independent of one another and to seek to create a restrictive covenant that meets the requirements of the law by redrawing the agreement is challenged as an attempt to "emasculate the covenant as to leave nothing recognizable. The court will not rewrite the covenant:" See *T. S. Taylor Machinery Co. v. Biggar* (1969) 67 WWR 246, at 257 (Man. C.A.).

However, in the present circumstances, to restrict the covenant as I have indicated is not to emasculate it. The trial judge may still widen or narrow the scope of the covenant depending on the evidence adduced.

I therefore direct that the individual and corporate defendants be restrained from carrying on operations within the terms of clause 9 of the agreement within the territory of British Columbia and until the trial of this action, or 18 months from the time of the termination of the employment with the plaintiff company, whichever is the earlier time, but that added to the end of clause 9 be a proviso that the employment of the personal defendant to which the restriction applies is solely that of a salesman. Moreover the competitive fields of endeavour shall be those as spelled out at the bottom of clause 9 and shall be limited to those fields save for the addition of slimicides.

NOTES
1. *Affirmed on Appeal—(1969) 70 WWR 742 (B.C. Court of Appeal).*
2. *Interim injunction refers to an order of the court awarded during the period pending trial prohibiting the parties from violating the apparent terms of the contract. This type of order is granted by the court where damages would ultimately not be able to restore the parties to their original position.*
3. *See "General Explanatory Notes," Part 4b.*

# Burton v. MacMillan Bloedel Limited

*[1976] 4 W.W.R. 267*
*British Columbia Supreme Court*
*March 18, 1976*

MUNROE J.: In this action the plaintiff claims damages for alleged wrongful dismissal by the defendant, one of the largest corporations doing business in British Columbia.

By letter dated 9th December 1974 the plaintiff, then aged 47, was discharged, effective 31st December 1974, from his position with the defendant as manager of the Engineering Service Department (Pulp and Paper Division), a position which he had occupied for three years under an oral contract of employment of indefinite term. The plaintiff had worked for the defendant for ten years and had been promoted from time to time. His services were entirely satisfactory and his competency is admitted. The parties considered that the employment was to be of a permanent character.

At the time of his dismissal the plaintiff was being paid an annual salary of $34 500 and was in receipt of fringe benefits having a value equivalent to 22 per cent of his salary. The defendant paid to the plaintiff his salary to 31st December 1974.

Counsel for the defendant submits that the plaintiff was discharged for cause and thus was not entitled to any notice or salary in lieu thereof.

In *Port Arthur Shipbuilding Co. v. Arthurs*, [1967] 2 O.R. 49 at 55, 62 D.L.R. (2d) 342 (sub nom. *Regina v. Arthurs; Ex parte Port Arthur Shipbuilding Co.*), reversed [1969] S.C.R. 85, 70 D.L.R. (3d) 693, the right of an employer to terminate the employment of an employee for cause was expressed by Schroeder J.A. as follows:

> If an employee has been guilty of serious misconduct, habitual neglect of duty, incompetence, or conduct incompatible with his duties, or prejudicial to the employer's orders in a matter of substance, the law recognizes the employer's right summarily to dismiss the delinquent employee.

Here, the defendant asserts that the plaintiff refused to continue to perform his duties as manager of the Engineering Service Department and thus was guilty of "wilful disobedience to the employer's orders in a matter of substance". The plaintiff asserts that his refusal on and after 12th September 1974 to remain as such manager was justified because the effect of the re-organization of the defendant's hierarchy as of that date amounted to an unjustified demotion for him—a breach of contract and dismissal by conduct—a unilateral essential alteration in the terms and conditions of his employment. On that date the defendant advised the plaintiff of a corporate re-organization whereunder he would thereafter be reporting and responsible to a group vice-president to whom he had previously reported and with whom he had had serious differences of opinion and clashes of personality, but during that earlier period the plaintiff was one of six heads of departments so reporting whereas under the new organization he alone reported to such vice-president. The plaintiff felt that the new organization meant in effect that the said vice-president was to become the real manager of the Engineering Service Department and that the plaintiff would become his second in command of that department, a feeling supported by the evidence that is confirmed to some extent by subsequent events since the position occupied by the plaintiff has not since been filled and the duties of that position have since been performed by the vice-president in question. While the plaintiff would not have suffered any loss of income or benefits had he remained as manager of the Engineering Service Department, or accepted other positions offered to him, upon the evidence I find that his role in such event would have been substantially different and limited. The words of Anderson J. in *O'Grady v. Insur. Corpn. of B.C.*, [ [1975] 63 D.L.R. (3d) 370] are relevant and apply to the facts of this case. Anderson J. said:

He would have suffered a substantial loss of prestige with consequent embarrassment and humiliation and would have been required to work under a general manager with whom he had had a serious confrontation. The abolition of his former role and the completely different and subordinate role he was offered amounted to a fundamental breach of contract. On the issue of mitigation, it was not unreasonable for him to reject the new position offered.

As McCardie J. said in *Rubel Bronze and Metal Co. v. Vos*, [1918] 1 K.B. 315 at 323:

Dismissal may be effected by conduct as well as words. A man may dismiss his servant if he refuses by word or conduct to allow the servant to fulfill his contract of employment...If the conduct of the employer amounts to a basic refusal to continue the servant on the agreed terms of employment, then there is at once a wrongful dismissal and a repudiation of the contract.

In *Hill v. Peter Gorman Ltd.* (1957), 9 D.L.R. (2d) 124 at 132 (Ont. C.A.), Mackay J.A. said:

Where an employer attempts to vary the contractual terms...the employee... may refuse to accept it and if the employer persists in the attempted variation the employee may treat this persistence as a breach of contract and sue the employer for damages...
   I cannot agree that an employer has any unilateral right to change a contract or that by attempting to make such a change he can force an employee to either accept it or quit.

See also *Allison v. Amoco Production Co.*, [1975] 5 W.W.R. 501, 58 D.L.R. (3d) 233 (Alta.).

Upon the evidence I find that the defendant committed a breach of its contract of employment with the plaintiff in September 1974 and that the plaintiff was dismissed in December 1975 without proper cause or lawful excuse. In view thereof, it is unnecessary for me to adjudicate upon the submission of counsel for the plaintiff that by agreement made between the parties on 3rd December 1974 the issue of liability of the defendant was no longer in issue and that only the quantum of the plaintiff's damages remained in dispute, though I accept as truthful and accurate the evidence of Mr. Butler.

I hold that the plaintiff is entitled to payment of 15 months' salary in lieu of reasonable notice of termination of his employment: *Bardal v. Globe and Mail Ltd.*, [1960] O.W.N. 253, 24 D.L.R. (2d) 140. The plaintiff, for his part, was under a legal duty to take all reasonable steps to mitigate the loss suffered by him: *Paziuk v. Ethelbert* (1963), 45 W.W.R. 216 (Man.), and he did so. On 3rd November 1975 he obtained permanent employment with B.C. Hydro & Power Authority at an annual starting salary of $27 270 plus fringe benefits having a value equivalent to 22 per cent of his salary.

The defendant attempted in September 1974 to vary the terms and conditions of the plaintiff's employment. The said variation was never accepted by the plaintiff. Until the contract of employment was terminated by proper notice, the plaintiff was entitled to insist on performance of the original contract where, as here, he did not relinquish his rights thereunder: *Hill v. Peter Gorman Ltd.* at p. 132. Prior to his dismissal in December he was offered a choice of dismissal, resignation or a subordinate job. Thus the only offer which was before the plaintiff was the offer of employment on terms that he abandoned such legal rights as he had for damages for breach of contract against the defendant. This he was not required to do: *Washer v. B.C. Toll Highways & Bridges Authority* (1965), 53 W.W.R. 225, 53 D.L.R. (2d) 620 (B.C.C.A.). Accordingly, I hold that the time for the giving of reasonable notice is to be computed from 9th December 1974 and not from 12th September 1974.

I assess the damages sustained by the plaintiff at the sum of $35 014.50, calculated as follows:

| | | |
|---|---|---|
| 15 months' salary | $43 125.00 | |
| Plus 22% thereof—fringe benefits | 9 487.50 | |
| | | 52 612.50 |
| *Less* | | |
| Received by the plaintiff from the defendant for the period 9th December to 31st December 1974— salary and fringe benefits | 2 602.00 | |
| Received by the plaintiff from new employer for salary and fringe benefits for the period 3rd November 1975 to 9th March 1976 | 11 645.00 | |
| Unemployment insurance received by the plaintiff | 3 351.00 | |
| | 17 598.00 | |
| | $35 014.50 | |

The claim of the plaintiff for aggravated or exemplary damages is not supported by the evidence and is disallowed.

The claim of the plaintiff for loss of pension benefits is disallowed since no damage in respect thereof has been proved. The fringe benefits of 22 per cent of salary include pension benefits and the plaintiff's new employer has a pension plan conferring benefits similar to those of the defendant's plan.

Judgment accordingly. Costs will follow the event.

# F. Negotiable Instruments

## Royal Bank of Canada v. Pentagon Construction Maritime Ltd.

*(1983) 143 D.L.R. (3d) 764*
*New Brunswick Court of Queen's Bench*
*January 6, 1983*

MILLER J.: This action has been brought by the plaintiff seeking to recover the proceeds of a cheque issued by the defendant upon which cheque a "stop payment" order was issued.

The plaintiff claims to be a holder in due course and this is the real issue for determination. The facts are not complex and the parties have agreed to them in large measure.

Miramichi Glass Works Ltd. ("Miramichi Glass") was a customer of and indebted to the plaintiff at its branch in Newcastle, New Brunswick. On September 13, 1979, it entered into a subcontract with the defendant.

On February 7, 1980, Miramichi Glass assigned all money due it under the contract to the plaintiff, which in turn gave notice of the assignment to the defendant. On the direction of the plaintiff all payments on the contract were made payable to Miramichi Glass and the plaintiff.

It is uncontradicted that problems arose for Miramichi Glass—cash flow problems and contract progress problems. Miramichi Glass was in an overdraft position with its bank, the plaintiff.

On June 6, 1980, David Griffiths, then Maritime manager of the defendant, met with a representative of Miramichi Glass concerning the lack of progress on the contract. At that time Griffiths agreed to make two more advances of approximately $10 000 each on the understanding that Miramichi Glass would have all materials on site and proceed with installations.

He advised his head office to issue two cheques each in an amount of $9996 payable June 6, 1980 and June 13, 1980. Griffiths advised Feges of Miramichi Glass that if he did not perform his part of the bargain the cheque would not be paid. The two cheques were picked up by Miramichi Glass and delivered to the plaintiff.

The real factual issue between the parties is the question of what knowledge the plaintiff had of this arrangement. There is a conflict in the evidence but it is my opinion that Griffiths was much more precise in his testimony than either of the bank employees. On cross-examination he stated that he told Mr. Dorey, then the assistant manager of the bank, that the June 13th cheque would be honoured only if Miramichi Glass carried out the agreement made on June 6th. I accept this to be true.

Miramichi Glass did not carry out its agreement and the defendant stopped payment on its cheque dated June 13, 1980. It is on this particular cheque that this action is taken.

On June 13, 1980, the cheque was deposited by the bank to the account of Miramichi Glass but it was eventually returned by the defendant's bank unpaid because of the stop payment ordered issued by the defendant on June 13th.

The assistant manager of the bank at the relevant times, Dorey, admitted during testimony that the bank's rights under the assignment flowed from the contractual relationship between Miramichi Glass and the defendant—if nothing was owing to Miramichi Glass under the contract nothing would be payable to the bank under the assignment.

The plaintiff's argument was directed to the contention that the bank was a holder in due course and therefore entitled to recover from the defendant.

The plaintiff relies on s. 56 of the *Bills of Exchange Act*,[1] R.S.C.1970, c. B-5, which reads as follows:

56 1. A holder in due course is a holder who has taken a bill, complete and regular on the face of it, under the following conditions, namely:

   (b) that he took the bill in good faith and for value, and that at the time the bill was negotiated to him he had no notice of any defect in the title of the person who negotiated it.

In *Lewis v. Clay* (1897), 67 L.J.Q.B. 224, Lord Russell of Killowen C.J. held that a "holder in due course" does not include the original payee of a cheque. This opinion was considered to be dictum only in *Herdman v. Wheeler*, [1902] 1 K.B. 361. But in *R. E. Jones Ltd. v. Waring & Gillow, Ltd.*, [1926] A.C. 670, the opinion of Lord Russell was accepted and followed in the House of Lords.

The question was considered in *Dominion Bank v. Fassell & Baglier Construction Co. Ltd.*, [1955] 4 D.L.R. 161, [1955] O.W.N. 709, where Hogg J.A. for the Ontario Court of Appeal referred to *Lewis v. Clay, supra*, but accepted the contrary opinion in *Herdman v. Wheeler, supra*. He did not refer to the later opinion of the House of Lords in *R. E. Jones Ltd. v. Waring & Gillow Ltd.*

In *Dominion Bank v. Fassell & Baglier Construction Co. Ltd., supra* the court was considering a claim that the bank was a holder in due course of a cheque issued by Fassell payable to the bank under the terms of an assignment to the bank from its customer.

Hogg J.A. said [at p. 165]:

I think that this particular question should be approached from the standpoint that the appellant Bank could, *if the circumstances permitted*, be a holder in due course and that when the cheque was deposited on February 5th to Carter's account the appellant became *prima facie* a holder in due course. The presumption that the Bank was a holder in due course may be rebutted by the surrounding circumstances.

(Emphasis mine.)

The court did not expound on what was meant by the words "if the circumstances permitted".

On the particular facts the court held that the bank was not entitled to recover on the cheque but the plaintiff here relies on that judgment as authority for its position that the plaintiff is the holder in due course of the cheque issued by the defendant.

But even if the bank as a payee of the cheque could be considered a holder in due course it is my opinion that the facts in the present matter indicate that, in the words of s. 56(1)(*b*), it cannot be said that the plaintiff took the cheque "in good faith" and that it "had no notice of any defect in the title of the person who negotiated it".

As was said by Hogg J.A. in *Dominion Bank v. Fassell & Baglier Construction Co. Ltd., supra* [at p. 167]: "When the term 'good faith' is used it must not be thought that any element of fraud is involved. There is nothing in the case which raises a suspicion of fraud."

The plaintiff bank was aware that it was entitled to receive money from the defendant only if money was owing and payable by the defendant to Miramichi Glass. I have found that the plaintiff bank was also aware that the cheque in question was only payable and would be honoured by the defendant only if Miramichi Glass honoured its obligation—which it did not do.

It seems to me to be an untenable position to contend that it could recover as a holder in due course what it could not recover as a payee. It was aware of the condition under which the post-dated cheque was issued and it took delivery of the cheque subject to that condition.

I am satisfied that on the authority of *R. E. Jones Ltd. v. Waring & Gillow Ltd.* the plaintiff was not a holder in due course and I am also satisfied that on the particular facts the plaintiff cannot meet the requirements of s. 56(1)(*b*) of the *Bills of Exchange Act* to so qualify it as a holder in due course.

The plaintiff also relies on s.165(3) of the *Bills of Exchange Act*, which reads:

3.  Where a cheque is delivered to a bank for deposit to the credit of a person and the bank credits him with the amount of the cheque, the bank acquires all the rights and powers of a holder in due course of the cheque.

The fallacy in this argument is that the cheque was not delivered to the bank for "deposit to the credit of a person…". It was delivered to the bank as a payee by the defendant as required by the assignment of moneys due. The plaintiff bank demanded that any money payable by the defendant to Miramichi Glass be paid to the bank. The defendant submitted to this direction when it delivered the cheque—but when the condition under which the cheque was issued failed, the defendant was entitled to stop payment on it.

The plaintiff's claim therefore fails and the action is dismissed with costs which I allow in an amount of $1750.

NOTES

*1. The* Bills of Exchange Act *is legislation passed by the Federal government and applies to all of the provinces and territories in Canada. The Act governs the use of "negotiable instruments" of which the three most usual types are bank drafts (bills of exchange), promissory notes and cheques.*

# William Ciurluini Ltd. v. Royal Bank of Canada

*(1972) 26 D.L.R. (3d) 552*
*Ontario High Court*
*March 16, 1972*

PARKER, J.: This is an action on a cheque drawn by the plaintiff, a used car dealer, against the defendant, a chartered bank. On September 4, 1969, the plaintiff was a customer of the defendant and had an account at the Bloor and Jane Streets Branch in the City of Toronto. On that day the plaintiff issued a cheque payable to J. Jung for $3900, in payment for a motor vehicle. Mr. Jung took the cheque to another branch of the defendant at Chestnut and Dundas Sts. in the City of Toronto where he received $2900, in cash and deposited the balance of $1000 in his account. Later the same day a telephone call was made by Mr. Ciurluini, president of the plaintiff company, to the branch at Bloor and Jane Sts. asking that payment be stopped on the cheque. The following day, September 5th, Mr. Ciurluini signed a stop payment order. On September 11th the plaintiff's account was debited for $3900. This action was commenced to recover that amount.

Mr. Ciurluini testified that he issued the cheque in question to Mr. Jung [who] he understood was the owner of a 1968 Cadillac convertible and gave the cheque to John Hodder, the used car manager of Elgin Motors, a car dealer in Toronto. On the back of the cheque he wrote "Payment in full re 1968 Cadillac C8367F8150836. Car is free and clear of all liens and encumbrances". He stated that this was about 10:30 or 11 o'clock in the morning and that he advised Mr. Hodder not to turn over the cheque until he had searched for liens. Mr. Ciurluini was advised about 2 or 2:30 p.m. that a lien was registered against the car. He immediately telephoned Mr. Hodder and instructed him not to release the cheque. Mr. Hodder then told him that he had already released it. Mr. Ciurluini testified that he then called his bank, spoke to Mrs. Zioba, who looks after business accounts and asked her to put a stop payment on the cheque. He said that she told him that someone had already phoned in to see if the money was there. The next morning he attended at the bank and signed the stop payment order.

Mrs. Zioba, an employee of the Royal Bank at Bloor and Jane Sts., was called by the plaintiff. She testified that when Mr. Ciurluini telephoned her on September 4th to stop payment, she filled in particulars on a form and looked at the clock on the wall to get the exact time. It was 2:55 p.m. This was normal procedure. She also wrote in the date of the cheque, the name of the payee and the name of the account. Mrs. Zioba testified that she told Mr. Ciurluini when he phoned that the cheque had already been presented.

Mr. James Aftlin, an accountant at the Chestnut and Dundas Streets Branch of the defendant testified that on September 4, 1969, at about 12:30 p.m. he was asked to initial a cheque presented by Mr. Jung for payment. At that time he examined the ledger card of Mr. Jung, checked his address, phone number, and place of employment. He also compared the endorsement on the cheque with the specimen signature card. He then telephoned the Bloor and Jane Streets Branch, described the cheque and enquired whether it was good. He was told it was "okay". He then initialed the cheque for payment. The next day he learned that a stop order had been placed against this cheque and at that time pointed out that the cheque had been cashed at 12:30 p.m. He recalled that the incident took place before he went out for lunch. He subsequently wrote a letter outlining what had taken place.

Considering the evidence of Mr. Aftlin and Mrs. Zioba and the admission by Mr. Ciurluini as to his conversation with Mrs. Zioba when he telephoned her, I am satisfied that the cheque was cashed by the Chestnut and Dundas Streets Branch before Mr. Ciurluini telephoned to stop payment.

The plaintiff claims that after the countermand was given the defendant lacked authority to honour the cheque. As a bill of exchange, the cheque could only be presented for payment at the place set out in the bill. That place was the Bloor and Jane Streets Branch. Because of the countermand that branch had no authority to pay. The defendant does not dispute this so far as the Bloor and Jane Branch is concerned, but takes the position that the Dundas and Chestnut Branch, having given value before the countermand, was a holder in due course and entitled to recover from all prior parties including the drawer. Counsel for the defendant submitted that the branch at Bloor and Jane did not pay the cheque after it was countermanded, but the defendant entered a debt owing to it as a holder in due course against the plaintiff's account.

The plaintiff took the position that a holder in due course was governed by s. 56(1) of the *Bills of Exchange Act*, R.S.C. 1907, c. B-5, which reads:

56 1. A holder in due course is a holder who has taken a bill, complete and regular on the face of it, under the following conditions, namely:

    a. that he became the holder of it before it was overdue and without notice that it had been previously dishonoured, if such was the fact;

    b. that he took the bill in good faith and for value, and that at the time the bill was negotiated to him he had no notice of any defect in the title of the person who negotiated it.

Counsel for the plaintiff submitted that the bill was not complete and regular on its face because of the endorsement on the back that the car was free and clear of all liens and encumbrances and that therefore the defendant could not be a holder in due course. He relied on the case of *Bank of Nova Scotia v. Kelly Motors Danforth Ltd.*, [1961] O.W.N. 34, as authority. After deciding that an endorsee of a postdated cheque takes it subject to the right of the drawer to stop payment before its ostensible date, Macdonell, Co.CT.J., said [at p. 36]:

> In the case at bar there is another reason why, in my opinion, the plaintiff's action fails. By s. 17(1) it is provided that "a bill of exchange is an unconditional order in writing..." It seems to me that the endorsement written upon the cheque sued upon clearly shows that payment of the cheque is conditional upon the motor car being free of all encumbrances and liens. If the document is not a bill of exchange it follows that the plaintiff cannot be a holder of it in due course.

I cannot agree with the submission of counsel that the words endorsed on the back of this cheque made the order to pay conditional. The endorsement may describe the understanding between the drawer and payee, but is not a condition so far as a holder in due course is concerned: *Merchants Bank of Canada v. Bury* (1915), 33 O.L.R. 204, 21 D.L.R. 495.

Counsel for the plaintiff submitted that the Dundas and Chestnut Branch did not act in good faith, since the manager paid out the money to a customer that had been with the bank for only 17 months, whose account was small, and whose ledger card showed three addresses during that time. Although the accountant might have been more cautious I do not think the evidence indicates bad faith. In this case there was no pleading of fraud, duress, fear or illegality, but in any event I find there was none.

In further support of his submission that the plaintiff was not a holder in due course, counsel for the defendant relied upon the case of *Royal Bank of Canada v. Boyce*, [1966] 2 O.R. 607, 75 D.L.R. (2d) 683. That case also involved a cheque given in payment for a motor vehicle. Payment was stopped by the drawer, but not before the cheque had been cashed at another branch of the same bank. The bank sued the payee to recover the money paid. The learned Judge found that because of the way the cheque was drawn it was presented at the proper place within the meaning of s. 88 of the *Bills of Exchange Act* and that the bank had paid the cheque as drawee, and could therefore not be a holder in due course. I cannot agree with counsel for the plaintiff that the case holds that where a customer has his account in one branch, another branch of the same bank cannot be a holder in due course. Many other cases have held to the contrary: see *White v. Royal Bank of Canada* (1923), 53 O.L.R. 543, [1923] 4 D.L.R. 1206; *Bank of Nova Scotia v. Archo Industries Ltd.* (1970), 11 D.L.R. (3d) 593.

Section 74(a) and (b) of the *Bills of Exchange Act* provides:

> 74. The rights and powers of the holder of a bill are as follows:
> a) he may sue on the bill in his own name;
> b) where he is a holder in due course, he holds the bill free from any defect of title of prior parties, as well as from mere personal defences available to prior parties among themselves, and may enforce payment against all parties liable on the bill;

In the present case the defendant having paid $2900 cash to the payee and having given credit for $1000 for the balance of the cheque, is a holder for value in due course. The fact that payment was countermanded for failure of consideration, if not fraud, does not affect the position of a holder in due course if it is not shown to have had notice of the defences when it acquired the cheque: *Huron & Erie Mortgage Corp. v. Rumig*, [1907] 2 O.R. 204, 10 D.L.R. (3d) 309.

The defendant in its capacity as a holder in due course would therefore be entitled to enforce payment against the plaintiff, free from any personal defences the plaintiff might have against the payee in respect of the cheque.

The action is therefore dismissed with costs.

# Royal Bank of Canada v. Siemens

*[1978] 2 W.W.R. 298*
*B.C. County Court*

27th January 1978. FULTON J.: The plaintiff sues for the balance of principal and interest owing under a promissory note made by the defendant on 17th October 1975 on which no payments have been made since September 1976. The defendant says the promissory note is void because, although it is a "consumer note" as defined in Pt. V [en. R.S.C. 1970, c. 4 (1st Supp.), s. 1] of the *Bills of Exchange Act*, R.S.C. 1970, c. B-5, and amendments, it is not stamped or marked on its face with the words "Consumer Purchase" as required by s. 190 of that Act. There are a number of alternative defences raised which can be more appropriately stated after a review of the facts.

The defendant and one Harold Dupuis were living together in Vancouver and Burnaby in 1974 and 1975. The defendant intended marriage, although

Dupuis apparently did not. The defendant was working as a nurse's aide in the Vancouver General Hospital; Dupuis was not working steadily, although he was for much of the time in question in receipt of unemployment insurance. In April 1974 the defendant opened a personal chequing account at the Kingsway and Rhodes branch of the Royal Bank of Canada. She had previously had an account with the plaintiff's Chilliwack branch, where she had borrowed $1750 to purchase a 1972 Ford Pinto car. Payments on this loan were maintained satisfactorily, and at the end of January 1975 the balance outstanding was only $75.

The defendant seems to have been easily influenced by Dupuis at this period, and he certainly took advantage of her. He persuaded her that if he had a car he could more easily find employment. On 29th January 1975 she borrowed $1400 at the plaintiff's branch, where she then had her account, and gave the proceeds to Dupuis to buy a Ford Comet. She told the bank that the purpose of the loan was to purchase furniture. This loan was in her name only. In February 1975 Dupuis told her that he needed a better car, and persuaded her to borrow more money so that he could purchase a 1968 Dodge Charger.On 21st February 1975 the two attended at the bank and made a joint application for a loan of $3000. The total cost of the loan with interest was $3330.78 and both signed a promissory note in this amount, payable at $185 per month. Security for the loan was given by chattel mortgage, also executed by both the defendant and Dupuis, covering her Pinto car and the Charger purchased with the proceeds. The Pinto was valued at $1500. The evidence is that the Charger was purchased from The Car Corner for a total price of $2400, satisfied as to $800 by trade-in of the Comet purchased with the earlier loan and as to the balance by cheque from the proceeds of the new loan.

With respect to the loan transaction itself, the proceeds of $3000 were paid into a savings account of the defendant opened for the purpose, the sum of $1402.75 was debited to this account to retire the January loan of $1400 and interest, and the balance of $1597.25 was transferred to a joint personal chequing account opened at the suggestion of the bank's loan manager in the joint names of the defendant and Dupuis, and a certified cheque for $1597 was issued to The Car Corner to complete the purchase of the Charger.

Dupuis, then being in receipt of unemployment insurance, made the first few payments on this loan. In April 1975 he left the defendant temporarily and in August he left permanently, driving off in the Charger, ostensibly for Toronto. The defendant has not seen him or the Charger since and does not know his present whereabouts. She was not able to maintain regular payment of the $185 a month due under the February loan, and after several telephone calls from the loan manager, Mrs. Mills, pressing for payment and indicating that the bank would have to have recourse to its security if payments were not kept up, the defendant called at the bank to discuss the situation with Mrs. Mills. She says her purpose in this discussion was to persuade the bank that the loan was the responsibility of Dupuis and that the bank should look to him and realize on the security of the Charger under its chattel mortgage. She says her concern was that otherwise her own credit rating would be damaged and that the bank might seize her Ford Pinto.

It is common ground between the parties and the evidence confirms that as a result of the discussions on 17th October 1975 it became apparent that the defendant could not maintain the payments on the February loan at the rate of $185 per month. Alternatives were discussed, and in the outcome arrangements were made for a new loan, to the defendant alone, to cover the balance outstanding on the February loan plus an overdraft in the Siemens-Dupuis joint account together amounting to $2725. Interest on the new loan over the term thereof was calculated at $604.05 (Ex. 6). The total of $3329.05 was to be paid by instalments of $109.05 on 17th November 1975 and $92 per month on the 17th day of each month thereafter (as compared with the earlier requirement of $185 per month under the February loan). Although the figures are not precisely established, it appears that the amount of the overdraft in the personal chequing account was in the order of $280: it is thus clear that the purpose of the new loan of $2725 was to return and replace the obligation for the balance owing under the joint February loan of $3000 for which both the defendant and Dupuis were liable and which was secured by the chattel mortgage covering both the Charger and the Pinto automobiles, and to cover an overdraft in the joint account then being operated by the defendant alone.

In pursuance of the arrangements for the loan of 17th October 1975 ("the October loan") the defendant signed a promissory note to the bank on that date for $3329.05 and gave a chattel mortgage of the same date to secure the amount thereof, covering her 1972 Ford Pinto. It is common ground and the evidence so establishes that the bank through Mrs. Mills advised the defendant that as a result of this arrangement the bank would and could no longer look to Dupuis as a co-debtor on the February promissory note and that the security of the chattel mortgage with respect to the Charger car would be released. It is also established that the defendant did not then take independent legal advice as to the consequences of this transaction. It is further established that neither the February 1975 promissory note nor the October 1975 promissory note was marked or stamped with the words "Consumer Purchase". And, finally, it is established that payments under the October note were maintained by the defendant with reasonable regularity until September 1976, when she took legal advice as to her position and, as a result thereof, discontinued payment. This action, seeking judgment for the balance owing pursuant to the terms of that note, is the result.

• • •

[ed: The Judge's references to certain alternate defences have been omitted.]

In connection with the first defence, that the October note is void because it does not bear on its face the words "Consumer Purchase", it is necessary to consider the relevant provisions of the *Bills of Exchange Act* ("the Act") as they bear on all three of the transactions described above. In the context of this case, those provisions are as follows:

188. In this Part
"consumer purchase" means a purchase, other than a cash purchase, of goods or services or an agreement to purchase goods or services
(a) by an individual other than for resale or for use in the course of his business, profession or calling, and
(b) from a person who is engaged in the business of selling or providing those goods or services;

"goods" means any article that is or may be the subject of trade or commerce, but does not include land or any interest therein;
"purchaser" means the individual by whom a consumer purchase is made;
"seller" means the person from whom a consumer purchase is made;...

189.
1. A consumer bill is a bill of exchange
   (a) issued in respect of a consumer purchase, and
   (b) on which the purchaser or any one signing to accommodate him is liable as a party,...
2. A consumer note is a promissory note
   (a) issued in respect of a consumer purchase, and
   (b) on which the purchaser or any one signing to accommodate him is liable as a party.
3. Without limiting or restricting the circumstances in which, for the purposes of this Part, a bill of exchange or a promissory note shall be considered to be issued in respect of a consumer purchase, a bill of exchange or a promissory note shall be conclusively presumed to be so issued if
   (a) the consideration for its issue was the lending or advancing of money or other valuable security by a person other than the seller, in order to enable the purchaser to make the consumer purchase; and
   (b) the seller and the person who lent or advanced the money or other valuable security were, at the time the bill or note was issued, not dealing with each other at arm's length within the meaning of the *Income Tax Act*...

190.
1. Every consumer bill or consumer note shall be prominently and legibly marked on its face with the words 'Consumer Purchase' before or at the time when the instrument is signed by the purchaser or by any one signing to accommodate the purchaser.
2. A consumer bill or consumer note that is not marked as required by this section is void, except in the hands of a holder in due course without notice that the bill or note is a consumer bill or consumer note or except as against a drawee without such notice.

191. Notwithstanding any agreement to the contrary, the right of a holder of a consumer bill or consumer note that is marked as required by section 190, to have the whole or any part thereof paid by the purchaser or any party signing to accommodate the purchaser is subject to any defence or right of set-off, other than counter-claim, that the purchaser would have had in an action by the seller on the consumer bill or consumer note.

I have no evidence that any note was given in respect of the January transaction or as to whether, if one was given, it was or was not marked

"Consumer Purchase". The evidence establishes that neither of the notes given with respect to the February or October loan was marked "Consumer Purchase". It is therefore necessary to consider whether any of the notes issued when the loan in question were made were issued "in respect of" a consumer purchase so as to be consumer notes as defined.

With respect to the October note, the defendant says it is a consumer note because it was issued in respect of a new loan arrangement made for the purchase of replacing the February loan and note which, it is claimed, were in turn respectively made for the purchase of and issued in respect of a consumer purchase, so that the February note was also a consumer note. In my view this argument fails because, for reasons which will appear, I hold that there were reasons and considerations for the giving of the new note other than the mere cancelling of the February note.

However there is an argument which requires to be dealt with in the contention that a loan made for the purpose of repaying a previous loan which was taken out for the purpose of enabling the borrower to purchase goods is a loan "in respect of" a consumer purchase, and that a note issued in respect of that subsequent loan is therefore also issued "in respect of" a consumer purchase. It is thus necessary still to consider whether the February note was issued in respect of a consumer purchase. The defendant does not rely on the conclusive presumption raised by s. 189(3), so that none of the notes can be consumer notes unless they can be shown to fall within the terms of s. 189(2)(a) as having been issued in respect of a consumer purchase.

In my opinion none of those notes were consumer notes within the definition of or as contemplated by the Act. There are two lines of reasoning which lead me to this conclusion, both based on a consideration of the intent and effect of the legislation and the actual wording of its provisions. It is clear from s. 191 (set out above) that the intent is that where a consumer purchase is involved notice shall be given to all subsequent holders of a note issued in respect thereof, by the stamping of a note, that they take subject to the equities that may exist as between the issuer and the seller. The first requirement, in order for the note to be within the class where this result follows, is that the note be issued "in respect of" a consumer purchase.

Normally, a note issued to a bank which lends or advances cash to or at the request of a borrower would be held to be issued in respect of that loan or advance and not "in respect of" some transaction into which the borrower enters with a third party. The bank or other lender has parted with its cash, the borrower has had the full use of it, and there is no equity as between the borrower and the lender. There is no reason of policy or principle of interpretation which would lead one to hold that that note was issued other than "in respect of" the loan or advance from the lender. Hence the inclusion of subs. (3) of s. 189, to provide that, where the purpose of the loan or advance is to enable the borrower to make a consumer purchase and the lender and the seller of the goods are not at arm's length, then the note issued in respect of the loan or advance shall be conclusively presumed in fact to have been issued in respect of that purchase. This is obviously necessary to prevent the defeat of the purpose of the legislation by the type of dealer who, operating with the "friendly finance company", gets the cash which has been advanced by that finance company but, because the note is in favour of the lender, who is acting in concert with the seller, between them they have defeated the equities.

But as I have said, there is no reason why the legislation should apply to the case of a *bona fide* loan or advance to a borrower-purchaser by a lending institution which is acting quite independently of the seller. In my view it would be straining the meaning of the words to hold that a promissory note issued for a loan or advance from a lender in such circumstances was issued in respect of the purchase transaction: clearly it was issued in respect of the loan.

It would be otherwise, of course, if the note were issued by the purchaser to the seller, who then discounts it and any other security he has taken with a lending institution, whether or not they are at arm's length: for in such case there is no loan or advance by the seller and the only transaction in respect of which that note could have been issued is the purchase in question.

The other ground upon which I hold that none of the notes in question were consumer notes is that, in my view, none of the purchases involved were "consumer purchases" as defined. This ground applies whether or not I be right in concluding, as I have, that the notes were not issued in respect of those transactions but rather in respect of the loans actually made: the notes could be consumer notes only if the transactions of sale and purchase were consumer purchases.

A consumer purchase is defined as a "purchase, other than a cash purchase, of goods". The evidence here establishes conclusively that the goods purchased were: in January, a Ford Comet car and, in February, a Dodge Charger. The evidence, which I have reviewed above, also establishes that on each occasion the transaction was one where payment for the goods was made and accepted as payment in full by the seller and the goods were delivered at that time and title thereto passed to the purchaser. No equities arose between the seller and the purchaser. In the light of these facts I can conclude only that the transaction as between the seller and the purchaser on each occasion was in fact a cash purchase and therefore did not fall within the definition of "consumer purchase".

• • •

I hold in the light of all these considerations that the purchase of the Comet in January and of the Charger in February, being purchases of goods the price of which was payable and was paid at the time of delivery, were both cash purchases as being in each case in opposition to a purchase on credit, and that therefore neither was a consumer purchase. It follows that the February note was not a consumer note and the October note, even if the sole consideration for its issue had been to replace the February note, is not rendered void by reason of the fact that it was not marked "Consumer Purchase".

[ed: Although the Court ruled against the defendant with respect to the *Bills of Exchange Act* defence, the defendant was successful with an alternate defence. The final judgment resulted in a dismissal of the plaintiff's action with costs to the defendant.]

# PART FOUR

# Business
# Organizations

# A. Partnership

## Reitmeier v. Kraft and Exner et al.

*(1970) 75 W.W.R. 97*
*Saskatchewan Court of Appeal*
*May 28, 1970*

[ed: The judgment of BROWNRIDGE, J.A. (dissenting) in the Court of Appeal was adopted by the Supreme Court of Canada. Accordingly the dissenting judgment is given below. Mrs. Reitmeier's appeal was allowed and the judgment at trial restored. The plaintiff received court costs for all levels. See [1971] 5 W.W.R. 384, 12 D.L.R. (3d) 627 S.C.C.]

BROWNRIDGE, J.A. (dissenting) This is an appeal from the judgment of Davis, J. (1969) 68 W.W.R. 16, in which he held that the plaintiff should recover from the defendants, jointly and severally, the sum of $31 451.39, with interest at seven per cent per annum from and after April 11, 1967.

The defendants George Exner and Frederick Exner filed a notice of appeal but at the opening of the appeal their counsel filed minutes of settlement in which it was agreed that the appeal of George Exner be allowed without costs and the appeal of Frederick Exner be dismissed without costs. The defendant Andrew Exner did not appeal. This appeal is, therefore, confined to the defendant Kraft.

In the action for money had and received, the plaintiff claimed that in the year 1962 she retained the services of the firm of real estate agents known E. K. Agencies in the City of Regina, in the Province of Saskatchewan, to assist her in the sale of her interest in a motel located at Aberdeen, in the State of South Dakota, one of the United States of America. She alleged that on or about June 15, 1964 the proceeds of the sale of the said motel in the amount of $33 045.09 were received by E. K. Agencies for the account of the plaintiff and that she instructed the defendant Andrew Exner that the funds should be retained by E. K. Agencies in trust pending her approval of specific first mortgage security loans to be negotiated by E. K. Agencies on her behalf. Andrew Exner admitted that, instead of doing so, he invested the moneys in E. K. Construction Ltd., a private company in which the defendants Andrew Exner and Felix Kraft owned all the shares. This company became insolvent in the summer of 1965. In the years following the misappropriation of the funds by Andrew Exner, the plaintiff was falsely led to believe that her moneys were in the hands of E. K. Agencies and bearing interest at the rate of seven per cent per annum. This was achieved by falsifying and sending to the plaintiff on the stationery of E. K. Agencies elaborate statements to this effect. The most recent of such statements received by the plaintiff was dated April 7, 1967 and showed a balance owing to the plaintiff of $31 451.39, and indicated that the plaintiff was entitled to interest on the said sum at the rate of seven per cent per annum.

E. K. Agencies was a partnership of Andrew Exner and Felix Kraft, formed in 1958, to sell real estate and insurance. E. K. Construction Ltd. was incorporated in April, 1964. The business of the company was laying pipe lines for gas transmission. The only shareholders were Andrew Exner and Felix Kraft, and each owned one common share of a par value of one ($1) dollar. They were both officers and directors of the company.

On October 1, 1965, the partnership of Exner and Kraft in E. K. Agencies was dissolved and under the terms of the dissolution agreement Andrew Exner took over all assets and liabilities of the partnership and agreed to save Kraft harmless from all liabilities connected with the partnership. Notice of dissolution was published in the *Saskatchewan Gazette*[1] dated November 12 and November 19, 1965.

Immediately upon the dissolution of the old partnership, Andrew Exner formed a new partnership between himself and his two sons, Frederick Exner and George Exner, under the same name of E. K. Agencies, but publication of the new partnership did not appear in the *Saskatchewan Gazette* until February 10, 1967.

In his judgment the learned trial Judge made it clear that the defendant Kraft played no part whatsoever in the misappropriation of the plaintiff's funds, his only fault being that he trusted Andrew Exner and was not more alert. He held that Kraft's responsibility, if any, must arise through his partnership in the firm of E. K. Agencies when the misappropriation took place.

At the trial the defendant Kraft raised two principal defences: Firstly, that the misappropriation was that of Andrew Exner acting in his personal capacity and not as a partner and, alternatively, that the plaintiff, by her conduct, had accepted the obligation of Andrew Exner and had released Kraft from responsibility. These same defences were argued by counsel for the appellant on the appeal. In disposing of the first defence, the learned trial Judge (at p. 21) referred back to what he had said earlier on this defence, which was raised by all of the defendants:

••• They contend that the plaintiff engaged Andrew Exner in his personal capacity as a friend of her late husband and not in his capacity as a partner in the Agencies. Andrew Exner has pledged his oath to this—with the hope and expectation of relieving his sons from any responsibility. He has come forward and attempted to assume full responsibility. He can well afford to do this as he is judgment proof. There is no substance whatever in this contention; the evidence to the contrary is so overwhelming I need say no more about it other than to add that I do not accept the testimony of Andrew Exner to that effect.

Counsel for the appellant referred to a number of "errors" in the recital of facts made by the learned trial Judge which, he suggested, made it appear that Kraft had participated in the sale of the plaintiff's interest in the motel in Aberdeen, South Dakota, to a greater extent than he did in fact. For instance, counsel said the plaintiff did not authorize "them", that is, Exner and Kraft, to go to Aberdeen, but only Exner; that while both of them went to Aberdeen, Kraft was merely the pilot in the plane owned by the partners; that the negotiations with one Gorder were carried on by Exner, but not by Kraft, etc. However, in view of the finding by the learned trial Judge that Kraft's responsibility, if any, arose out of the fact of the partnership, nothing turns on the various items referred to by counsel. They do show, however, that Kraft was aware that his partner was acting for Mrs. Reitmeier as early as 1963, and the evidence is he was also aware of the fact that Exner had put her money into the E. K. Construction Company as a shareholder's loan in his name. Exner swore that he told Kraft "within a few days" of his doing so but Kraft said he did not learn this until six or seven months after June, 1964. In any event, he learned of it while he was still a partner in the firm of E. K. Agencies and while the partners were still operating E. K. Construction Ltd.

Moreover, Kraft testified that he had only one dollar invested in E. K. Construction Ltd., and that the capital for the operation of the company came from shareholder's loans. He received no dividends or director's fees and earned only $1000 for 18 months of work on behalf of the company. It was he who suggested the dissolution of E. K. Agencies: "In my view of what happened to E. K. Construction Ltd., and the strains it had put on E. K. Agencies, at that particular time I could not see how I could continue making my living in the partnership."

All of the plaintiff's money went into E. K. Construction Ltd., in the first instance, but later at least $11 094.13 went from the construction company into E. K. Agencies while Kraft was still a partner.

Andrew Exner testified that E. K. Agencies "advanced" Mrs. Reitmeier the sum of $4344.92 with which to purchase a new car. This was the cheque dated September 11, 1964, issued by E. K. Agencies under the signature of Andrew Exner and with the notation "in settlement of Francis Reitmeier". Then on September 14, 1964, a cheque was drawn by Andrew Exner on E. K. Construction Ltd. in favour of E. K. Agencies in the amount of $11 094.13. Exner said that of this amount, $4344.92 represented repayment of the said advance, and the balance was for him.

On March 10, 1965, a cheque was drawn on E. K. Agencies in favour of Mrs. Francis Reitmeier for $200 and this was signed by Felix Kraft. Then on June 25, 1965 a further cheque in favour of Francis Reitmeier was drawn on E. K. Construction Ltd. for $846.89 and was signed by A. Exner.

In addition, Ex. P.1, dated May 18, 1965, and Ex. P.9, dated June 26, 1965, are statements of accounts, copies of which are attached as part of the judgment of the learned trial Judge, which show what was represented by E. K. Agencies to the plaintiff during the time that Felix Kraft was a member of the partnership. These documents established beyond doubt that part of the plaintiff's money was dealt with as partnership money and all of it was represented as money held in trust by the partnership.

Counsel for the appellant submitted that, on the evidence, Andrew Exner was acting in a personal capacity and not as a partner of E. K. Agencies, but after a most careful examination of all of the evidence I respectfully agree with the finding of the learned trial Judge.

It was then argued that even if Andrew Exner were acting as a partner he was not doing so in the ordinary course of the business of the firm, because that business was real estate and insurance, not investment. However, there is no doubt that Andrew Exner advised the plaintiff that her money should be invested in first mortgages and he even attempted to justify his action of putting her money into E. K. Construction Ltd. on the ground that she had authorized him to do so.

So far as Kraft was concerned, there was the uncontradicted evidence of Mrs. Marion Reitmeier, daughter-in-law of the plaintiff, of a conversation which took place at the office of E. K. Agencies before the plaintiff's moneys had arrived from the United States. She said that the plaintiff, her husband and she were talking to Andrew Exner about investment of the money, and he advised that first mortgages would be the best. Felix Kraft was standing in the doorway of Exner's office and, "he agreed with Andy that first mortgages were actually one way of making good money on an investment." Nowhere in the evidence did either Exner or Kraft suggest that investment of money on behalf of clients was no part of their business. The evidence is all the other way.

In my view the evidence established that Andrew Exner was acting in the ordinary course of the business of E. K. Agencies and within the scope of his apparent authority and received the plaintiff's money as a partner and misapplied it, thus making the firm liable under secs. 12 and 13 of *The Partnership Act*, RSS, 1965, ch. 387. As Lord Macnaghten observed in *Lloyd v. Grace, Smith & Co.* [1912] AC 716, at 738, 81 LJKB 1140: "It is a hardship to be liable for the fraud of your partner. But that is the law under the *Partnership Act*."

I turn now to the alternative defence argued, namely, that if the plaintiff is found to be a creditor of the first partnership, then, by her course of dealing with the new partnership and with Andrew Exner, she must be taken to have agreed that Kraft, the retiring partner, was discharged from any liability of the first partnership to her.

Sec. 19 (3) of *The Partnership Act* provides:

19.—(3) A retiring partner may be discharged from existing liabilities by an agreement to that effect between himself and the members of the firm as newly constituted and the creditors, and this agreement may be either expressed or inferred as a fact from the course of dealing between the creditors and the firm as newly constituted.

Counsel argued that the inference should be drawn from all of the evidence that Kraft was discharged, but after carefully examining the evidence I have come to the same conclusion as the learned trial Judge that there is nothing in it to indicate that the plaintiff ever intended to release Kraft from any obligation he may have incurred and that the evidence goes no further than to show that the plaintiff at all times dealt with Andrew Exner and had no dealings of consequence with Kraft.

Nor are the letters written in the handwriting of Andrew Exner on plain white paper, between December 16, 1966 and August, 1967, to the plaintiff inconsistent with this view of the evidence. In these letters Andrew Exner acknowledged that he owed the money and would repay it but, in my opinion, that does not mean that the firm did not owe the money or that the plaintiff was accepting the personal obligation of Andrew Exner in place of the partnership obligation or that she was in any way agreeing to discharge Kraft.

Counsel relied upon *Br. Homes Assur. Corpn. v. Paterson* [1902] 2 Ch 404, 71 LJ Ch 872, as approved by the Supreme Court of Canada in *Vieweger Const. Co. v. Rush & Tompkins Const. Ltd.* [1965] SCR 195, at 203, 48 DLR (2d) 509, reversing 45 DLR (2d) 122. In the former case Farwell, J. said the provisions of the *Partnership Act, 1890* (Imp.), 53 & 54 Vict., ch. 39, did not apply because the plaintiff intentionally contracted with Atkinson as an individual, knowing that he was not acting or appearing to act for the firm at all. In the latter case, the trial Judge concluded that Layden Construction Ltd. was dealing with Vieweger Construction Ltd. as principal. The Court of Appeal held that it was dealing as agent. The Supreme Court held that whether the two were partners or not was irrelevant, because, having elected to enter into contractual arrangements with Layden Construction Ltd. alone, the respondent could not now attempt to hold the appellant company liable and require it to perform the contract of Layden Construction Ltd., even if it were a partner of Layden Construction Ltd.

These cases do not assist the appellant because here the learned trial Judge found, and in my view correctly, that Andrew Exner was not dealing with the plaintiff on his own behalf but on behalf of the firm of E. K. Agencies.

The appeal is dismissed with costs.

NOTES

1. *The Gazette refers to the Saskatchewan edition of an official publication produced by the federal government and each provincial government in Canada. The purpose of each gazette is to provide legal notice of important events such as the effective dates of legislation or, as in this case, the dates of the creation or dissolution of a legal entity such as partnership.*

# B. Company

## Bank of Nova Scotia v. Radocsay

*(1982) 125 D.L.R. (3d) 651*
*Ontario Court of Appeal*
*October 6, 1981*

WEATHERSTON J.A.: The issue in this appeal is whether the defendant
Radocsay is liable to the plaintiff bank on a promissory note for $12 500
dated July 20, 1976, which he signed to cover an overdraft in the account of
Classic TV and Sound. The trial Judge has found that he is not liable; that
the bank account was understood by him to be that of a corporation, Radocsay Television Limited, and that "he believed he was signing only on behalf of
the corporate account and having regard to this total misunderstanding
which was not his fault" he was not therefore personally liable.

Early in 1974 Radocsay agreed to buy a business known as "Classic Lite &
Sound" from William Jakubcsik, and he took over the operation of the store
on June 16th. On June 19th a new account was opened with the bank, by
Radocsay and Jakubcsik as partners in the firm of Classic TV and Sound.
On June 25, 1974, Radocsay Television Limited was incorporated. Then on
September 26, 1974, a number of banking documents were signed. There was
a copy of a resolution of the directors of the new corporation to open an
account at the Bank of Nova Scotia, and which authorized the president and
the secretary-treasurer (or any two of them) to carry out the usual banking
transactions. The date of that document was typed as September 26, 1974,
but that date was altered on a copy found in the bank's files to 1977. There
was also a certified copy of a by-law respecting the borrowing of money by
the company. One copy of that by-law was dated September 26, 1974, but
bears no seal of the corporation. Another copy, sealed, and dated September
26, 1977, was produced from the bank's files. The by-law is on the bank's
form, and both copies refer, in a box, to account No. 248-13 which was the
account number of Classic TV and Sound. There are other banking documents, some of which are undated. There was no personal guarantee, and no
copy of a declaration under the *Partnerships Registration Act*, R.S.O. 1970,

c. 340 [now R.S.O. 1980, c. 371], that the corporation would carry on business as Classic TV and Sound. It would be obvious to an accountant or lawyer that the bank did not have all the papers usually required to open a new account. Radocsay was neither a lawyer nor an accountant: he had emigrated from Germany in 1957, but he had carried on his own business in Canada since 1962.

The account continued to be carried on as before. Statements were sent out monthly to Classic TV and Sound, without any indication as to the name of the real customer of the bank. The bank dealt solely with Radocsay; it had no dealings with Jakubcsik, either as a partner or a signing officer of the corporation.

The learned trial Judge [6 A.C.W.S. (2d) 226] said:

> I am satisfied that the defendant notified the bank that this limited company was taking over the business of Classic TV and Sound. I am satisfied that the defendant filed with the bank documents indicating the corporate ownership of the business and, therefore, the account. I am satisfied that in spite of that notification most of the bank documents did not appear to reflect that change of ownership.
>
> I find that the failure of the bank documents to reflect such a change is the fault of the bank and not of the defendant. From that time on, which was September or perhaps October, 1974, at the latest, the defendant dealt with the bank on the understanding and belief that they, the bank, knew of and accepted the new corporate ownership of the business and, therefore, of the account. This understanding and belief arose as a result of the defendant filing what he believed to be the requisite documents with the bank. He believed this because he filed with the bank, corporate documents that were requested of him by the then assistant manager. There was no reason, therefore, when the defendant was called by Mr. Smith, the manager, in 1976 to sign a promissory note to cover the overdraft in the business account, that Mr. Radocsay would even suspect that he was being called there other than as an officer of the limited company. I am satisfied that he attended as an officer of the limited company and in that capacity and in that capacity alone he signed ex. 4, the note. I am satisfied that it was not explained to him that he was signing a personal note.

• • •

> I am satisfied that Mr. Radocsay signed this note, as an officer of Radocsay Television Limited, that it was intended to cover the account which was or at least should have been known by the bank to be the corporate account. Even Mr. Smith did not know that it was a corporate account.

As Aron Salomon discovered in 1897 [*Salomon v. A. Salomon & Co. Ltd.*, [1897] A.C. 22], the incorporation of a business enables a merchant to carry on his business much as before, but with the singular advantage that he is no longer liable for the debts of the business if things go wrong. But the merchant must be careful that the debts are those of the corporation, not his. He is the one to reap the advantage of this wonderful new creation, and he is the one who must demonstrate that old contractual relationships have been severed, and new ones created.

The difficulties in this case arose from the failure to recognize that this corporation was a completely different legal person from Radocsay. The purchase of the business by the corporation may have included the money in the bank account, but it did not carry with it a novation of the contractual relationship between the bank and its customer; for that there had to be an actual assent by the bank to the substitution of this corporation for Radocsay. There was simply no evidence that both parties dealt with the account on the footing that the new customer was the corporation, not Radocsay. The furthest the trial Judge goes is to say that the bank should have known that this was a corporate account. That is not a sufficient basis for a novation, or (and this was not argued) an estoppel.

But even if we accept that the overdraft in the account was the debt of the corporation and not of Radocsay, that does not mean that Radocsay's belief that he was signing a corporate note is any defence to this action. The note is unqualified—there is not the slightest hint that Radocsay signed in a representative capacity. Section 52 of the *Bills of Exchange Act*, R.S.C. 1970, c. B-5, says:

> 52 1. Where a person signs a bill as drawer, endorser or acceptor, and adds words to his signature indicating that he signs for or on behalf of a principal, or in a representative character, he is not personally liable thereon; but the mere addition to his signature of words describing him as an agent, or as filling a representative character, does not exempt him from personal liability.
>
> 2. In determining whether a signature on a bill is that of the principal or that of the agent by whose hand it is written, the construction most favourable to the validity of the instrument shall be adopted.

The converse is true. If the maker of a note does not add words to his signature indicating that he signs for on on behalf of a principal, or in a representative character, it is his note. I agree with everything Blair J.A. said on this aspect of the appeal.

Radocsay's misunderstanding as to the capacity in which he signed the note was not induced by a misrepresentation by the bank. Radocsay's own evidence is clear, that there was no discussion between him and the bank official as to who was to be responsible for the note. The mere fact that the bank accepted some uncompleted documents from the corporation does not constitute a representation by the bank to Radocsay that thereafter the bank would deal with the corporation as its customer. Even if the bank official knew or ought to have known that Radocsay was not personally liable for the overdraft, there was no duty on him to explain to Radocsay that a new liability was being created. Radocsay does not fall within those classes of persons for whom the law provides a special protection.

In the result, I would allow the appeal with costs. The judgment will be set aside, and in place thereof there will be judgment for the plaintiff for $12 349.45 together with interest on $12 000 from May 24, 1978, until January 21, 1980, at 12%, and thereafter interest in accordance with s. 38 [rep. & sub. 1977, c. 51, s. 3(1)—now s. 36] of the *Judicature Act*, R.S.O. 1970, c. 228 [now R.S.O. 1980, c. 223], and its costs of the action.

[The dissenting judgment of Blair J.A. is omitted.]

# Re D & D Holdings Ltd.

*[1981] 4 W.W.R. 13*
*Alberta Queen's Bench*
*February 3, 1981*

PROWSE J.: In these proceedings Thomas Keith Leslie (hereinafter referred to as "the petitioner") petitions for the winding-up of D & D Holdings Ltd. (hereinafter referred to as "the company") pursuant to s. 197(*e*) of the *Companies Act*, R.S.A. 1970, c. 60, and therefore he must establish that it is just and equitable that the company should be wound up.

The decisions cited by counsel appear to support the court issuing a winding-up order under s. 197(*e*) whenever the evidence adduced establishes that one or more of the following circumstances exist, namely:

1. The company was primarily incorporated for a specific object or purpose which no longer exists: see *Re Dom. Steel Corp. Ltd.*, 59 N.S.R. 398, [1927] 4 D.L.R. 337 at 349 (C.A.); or

2. There is a voting deadlock in the company and future operation of the company is jeopardized by the deadlock and the inability of management to make necessary decisions: *Re Yenidje Tobacco Co. Ltd.*, [1916] 2 Ch. 426; or

3. The minority petitioning shareholder is being "squeezed out" or excluded in exercising his right and the majority shareholders are guilty of misconduct and/or lack probity in managing and using the company assets and as a result the minority have a justifiable lack of confidence in the management by the majority shareholders: see *Loch v. John Blackwood Ltd.*, [1924] A.C. 783 at 788, 796 (P.C.); or

4. The company is a private company carrying on the business formerly operated by shareholders as a partnership or, alternately, the share-holders are carrying on the business of the company as a partnership under the guise of a company, and the original mutual trust and confidence of the shareholders in each other has ceased to exist and thus it is equitable to wind up the company: see *Re Yenidje Tobacco Co. Ltd.*, *supra* and *Ebrahimi v. Westbourne Galleries*, [1973] A.C. 360, [1972] 2 All E.R. 492 (H.L.).

The circumstances referred to in paras. (1) and (2) clearly do not apply here.

Counsel for the petitioner, in the evidence adduced and submissions, sought to establish circumstances which would justify a winding-up order by reason of the existence of the circumstances referred to in paras. (3) and (4) and I will therefore review the facts which are, in my opinion, pertinent.

The company was incorporated in 1968 and all of its issued shares were purchased by William S. Baker and his brother Bryan Baker in October 1970. The company did not carry on any business during the period 1970 until in or about July 1974.

In June 1974 William S. Baker and Bryan Baker, who were still the only shareholders of the company, caused a special resolution to be enacted amending the objects of the company authorizing it to carry on as a hotel, motel and restaurant business.

By agreement in writing dated 4th July 1974 William S. Baker and Bryan Baker acquired a lease-option of real property upon which a motel and restaurant property existed and a hotel was being erected.

By a further agreement in writing dated 5th July 1974 the said William S. Baker and Bryan Baker assigned their interest in the said lease-option agreement to the company.

By further agreements in writing dated 2nd October 1974 the said William S. Baker and Bryan Baker sold shares in the company to the petitioner and others so that upon the registration of the transfers all of the issued shares of the company were owned (and still are) as follows:

| | |
|---|---|
| William S. Baker | 50 common |
| Bryan Baker | 50 common |
| Auke Elzinga Investments Ltd. | 49 common |
| Auke Elzinga | 1 common |
| Wayne Baker | 25 common |
| T. Keith Leslie | 25 common |

Under the said agreement between William S. Baker and Bryan Baker (as vendors) and the petitioner (as purchaser), dated 21st October 1974, whereby the petitioner became the owner of 25 common shares of the company, the said William S. Baker and Bryan Baker have the right to purchase all or a portion of the shares of the company owned by the petitioner in the event: (a) he ceases to be an employee of the company; (b) he decides to sell his shares; or (c) he dies.

The said William S. Baker and Bryan Baker in their said agreements of 2nd October 1974 have the right to purchase the shares of the company sold to Wayne Baker and Auke Elzinga Investments Ltd. in the event either of them decides to sell the shares.

On 2nd October 1974 the petitioner, William S. Baker, Bryan Baker, Wayne Baker and Auke Elzinga were elected directors of the company and they are the only directors of the company at the present time.

Since 2nd October 1974 the officers of the company have been (and still are): president—Bryan Baker; vice-president—William S. Baker; and secretary-treasurer—Auke Elzinga.

In or about April 1973 the petitioner was employed by Baker Investments Ltd. as manager of a restaurant which it operated on the property which was subsequently, in July 1974, leased to the company.

In October 1974 the petitioner was hired by the company as manager of the hotel which was erected on the property subject to the said lease-option agreement. The petitioner continued to be employed as the manager of the said hotel until March 1980 when he quit or his employment was terminated. He was the only shareholder employed by the company.

On the same date this petition was issued, the petitioner issued a statement of claim against the company claiming damages for wrongful dismissal. The company filed a defence to that action on 19th August 1980 denying liability to the petitioner and no further steps in that action have been taken to date.

On 10th July 1979, the company exercised its option to purchase the property it was leasing (under the assignment dated 5th July 1974 from William S. Baker and Bryan Baker) at a cost of approximately $1 437 000. In order to obtain working capital and to exercise the option, companies owned and/or controlled by William S. Baker and/or Bryan Baker and/or Auke Elzinga loaned the company $246 000 and a term loan of approximately $1 260 000 was advanced by a chartered bank. There is no suggestion that the interest payable on any of the loans is other than reasonable. Unfortunately long-term mortgage financing of the loans is not advisable under the present terms available.

Until 1979 the hotel operations made a reasonable profit but in and since 1979 the revenue from it has substantially decreased, resulting in an operation loss for the company. Changes had to be made and additional funds had to be borrowed and will have to be borrowed. These problems in this period of high interest rates have caused friction between the petitioner and the other shareholders who are business associates in other ventures and have been able to loan funds to the company. This downturn in the financial success of the operations of any company is a forseeable possibility and when it is primarily due to events beyond the control of management and requires the investment or borrowing of substantial moneys to safeguard the assets acquired it is bound to create some dissatisfaction among the shareholders. This dissatisfaction becomes more vocal where the shareholders have not an equal ability to raise money and loan funds to the company.

It is against this background that one must judge the complaints of the petitioner which result primarily from the fact he is no longer employed by the company, he contributes or feels he contributes nothing to the decisions of management and his opinion is not sought. While he owns one-eighth of the issued shares of the company he cannot realize on that investment. In June 1979 the hotel owned by the company was appraised for mortgage purposes at approximately $3 000 000.

While the position of the petitioner is not enviable, it is nevertheless the position in which many persons with minority interests in companies find themselves. Is it just and equitable that the company should be wound up because of the dissatisfaction of the petitioner?

I am of the opinion it would not be just and equitable to wind up this company.

In 1974 when the petitioner was employed by the company and executed his share purchase agreement with the majority shareholders, William S. Baker and Bryan Baker, he knew or ought to have known of the fixed rental lease of the restaurant property to Baker Investments Ltd. He ought to have foreseen the possibility he might not be retained as an employee and the effect of the option given to William S. Baker and Bryan Baker to re-purchase all or any of his shares. I am satisfied the shares sold to the petitioner were to give him, as an employee, additional incentive to serve the company well and not as evidence of any partnership relationship with the other shareholders. There is nothing disclosed in the evidence that can reasonably support an inference that the relationship among the shareholders was similar to partners and there is no evidence that the majority shareholders are guilty of misconduct or lack probity in the management of the company.

This application is therefore dismissed with costs to the company.

# W.J. Christie & Co. Ltd. v. Greer and Sussex Realty & Insurance Agency Ltd.

*[1981] 4 W. W. R. 34*
*Manitoba Court of Appeal*
*March 3rd, 1981*

HUBAND J.A.: The defendant Donald W. Greer was a long-time employee of the plaintiff W. J. Christie & Co. Ltd. ("W. J. Christie"). He was, and is, a minority shareholder in the company. For about ten years he was also a director and an executive officer of the company. In the fall of 1978, along with two other employees, the defendant Greer left the plaintiff company to establish a new corporation, the co-defendant Sussex Realty & Insurance Agency Ltd. ("Sussex"). The defendant Greer solicited several customers of the plaintiff and persuaded them to transfer their business to the new firm. Hamilton J. [3 Man. R. (2d) 431] held the defendant Greer and the co-defendant Sussex both liable to the plaintiff and he assessed damages at $23 862. The defendants now appeal on both the liability and the damages. The plaintiff cross-appeals as to damages.

## LIABILITY

The plaintiff company has been in business in Winnipeg since 1946. It is involved in both real estate and insurance. W. J. Christie manages a number of revenue properties for clients. Most of these properties are residential but some are commercial. W. J. Christie is also licensed to sell real estate, and endeavours to earn commissions when the opportunity presents itself. W. J. Christie is also an insurance agency, providing insurance coverage on the properties which it manages for customers. Beyond that, however, W. J.

Christie is in the business of arranging insurance for customers, including motor vehicle insurance, as agent for the Manitoba Public Insurance Corporation.

The defendant Greer began his employment with W. J. Christie in 1955. When his employment terminated in October 1978 he was property manager and manager of its insurance department. He had been the general manager of the company until the majority of the shares of W. J. Christie were purchased by John C. McKinnon on March 1977. As general manager, Greer had been responsible for the overall operation of the company. Even after McKinnon purchased a majority interest and assumed the role of general manager, Greer continued to be a key management person at W. J. Christie.

The defendant Greer became a director and was appointed secretary of the company around 1st September 1966 and maintained those positions until his resignation on 10th October 1978.

As director, officer, and senior management employee, the defendant stood in a fiduciary relationship towards W. J. Christie. The fiduciary nature of the relationship between director and company was confirmed by the House of Lords in *Regal (Hastings) Ltd. v. Gulliver*, [1942] 1 All E.R. 378. Section 117(1)(*a*) of the Corporations Act, 1976 (Man.), c. 40 (also C.C.S.M., c. C225)), reaffirms that director/officers of a corporation stand in a position of trust towards the company:[1]

> 117 1. Every director and officer of a corporation in exercising his powers and
> discharging his duties shall
> (*a*) act honestly and in good faith with a view to the best interests of the
> corporation.

The issue in this case is whether the defendant Greer abused his trust relationship with W. J. Christie to his advantage.

In the month of August 1978 the defendant Greer was giving active consideration to the possibility of leaving W. J. Christie. One of the major clients of the company was having some renovation work done to his properties and in a conversation during the month of August Greer advised the client that he might not be an employee of W. J. Christie by the time the renovations were completed. In early September 1978 another long-time employee of W. J. Christie, Henry Gauthier, travelled to Vermont in the United States to speak to the major clients of W. J. Christie to ascertain whether those clients would transfer business to follow Gauthier, should he leave W. J. Christie and establish a new firm. Those assurances were obtained. The defendant Greer, along with Henry Gauthier, then decided that they would leave W. J. Christie and establish a new firm. Henry Gauthier, like the defendant Greer, was also a shareholder, director, and officer of W. J. Christie. They also discussed their plans with yet another employee, Mr. Ron Campbell, and he too decided to leave the employ of W. J. Christie in order to become a shareholder, director, officer and employee of the new firm.

The defendant Greer announced his plans to Mr. John C. McKinnon, president and general manager of W. J. Christie, on 22nd September 1978. During that discussion, the defendant Greer indicated his intention to leave, along with Henry Gauthier and Ron Campbell, in order to set up a competitive company. He indicated that the major clients approached by Gauthier would be transferring business to the new firm. He expressed the opinion that many of the remaining clients would do so as well, since their connection with W. J. Christie in the management of their properties was through the defendant Greer. The defendant Greer did not resign his employment immediately, though he offered to do so. He inquired of McKinnon, however, whether McKinnon and the other shareholders of W. J. Christie, apart from himself and Gauthier, might be interested in selling W. J. Christie to the defendant Greer, Henry Gauthier, and Ron Campbell. McKinnon's response was negative.

On 10th October 1978 the defendant Greer, Henry Gauthier and Ron Campbell resigned as employees, and Greer and Gauthier as officers and directors. The new company, Sussex Realty and Insurance Agency Ltd., was incorporated on 5th October 1978. Before the new corporation could really get started, Henry Gauthier died suddenly in early November. The defendant Greer, along with Ron Campbell, proceeded with their plans, but the death of Gauthier resulted in the major clients of W. J. Christie, who had been solicited by Gauthier in Vermont, remaining in its fold rather than transferring business to Sussex. Sussex established offices and the defendant Greer made direct approaches to a number of clients of W. J. Christie to solicit their business for the new firm. Seven clients accepted the invitation of the defendant Greer to transfer their business to Sussex. The transfers took place as of 1st December 1978. In the main, that business was property management but five of the clients also generated business by way of insurance commissions, in addition to property management fees.

There is no dispute that the clients in question were directly solicited by the defendant Greer and transferred their business as a consequence of that direct solicitation. The entire issue is whether the solicitation was contrary to a continuing fiduciary responsibility owed by the defendant Greer to W. J. Christie.

As long ago as 1726 the judgment of Lord King in the leading case of *Keech v. Sandford* (1726), 2 Eq. Cas. Abr. 741, 25 E.R. 223, established that a person occupying a fiduciary position—in that case a trustee—was not entitled to obtain a profit from the position contrary to the interest of the *cestui que trust*. In *Regal (Hastings) Ltd. v. Gulliver, supra*, that principle was applied to directors of a company. In his judgment Lord Russell wrote, at p. 389.,

> ...I am of opinion that the directors standing in a fiduciary relationship to Regal in regard to the exercise of their powers as directors, and having obtained these shares by reason and only by reason of the fact that they were directors of Regal and in the course of the execution of that office, are accountable for the profits which they have made out of them. The equitable rule laid down in

*Keech v. Sandford* [*supra*] and *Ex parte James* (1803), 8 Ves. 337, 32 E.R. 385, and similar authorities applies to them in full force.

But, it is argued, the trustee in *Keech v. Sandford*, and the directors in *Regal (Hastings) Ltd. v. Gulliver* were still acting as such when the profits were made. In this instance, the defendant Greer, along with Henry Gauthier, resigned as officer and directors as well as employees, on 10th October 1978, before direct solicitation of those clients who subsequently transferred their business to Sussex some seven weeks later.

It must be observed that Gauthier, with the apparent concurrence of the defendant Greer, had indeed made a direct solicitation of business from the major clients of W. J. Christie before they resigned, and indeed before the defendant Greer, made known their intentions in the meeting with Mr. McKinnon on 22nd September. It is true that because of the death of Henry Gauthier those particular clients changed their minds and did not transfer allegiance to Sussex. But that contact should be seen as part of a total effort on the part of the defendant Greer, Gauthier and Ron Campbell, to shift business from W. J. Christie to the company which they were about to form. That process, in obvious violation of fiduciary responsibility, commenced before resignation as directors, and continued thereafter.

But even if one were able to ignore the solicitation made by Henry Gauthier, it is my view that the direct solicitation of clients by the defendant Greer after his resignation on 10th October constitutes a breach of fiduciary duty redressable in damages. In *Can. Aero Service Ltd. v. O'Malley*, [1974] S.C.R. 592, 11 C.P.R. (2d) 206, 40 D.L.R. (3d) 371, the Supreme Court of Canada, in a unanimous judgment by Laskin J., made it clear that the fiduciary relationship persists after a formal employment relationship has ceased. In that case, two of the defendants had been officers, directors, and top employees with the plaintiff company. They left the plaintiff company, established a new firm, and then negotiated to obtain a lucrative contract for their new company—a contract towards which they had been negotiating when they were with the plaintiff company. Laskin J. wrote in these terms, at p. 382:

...the fiduciary relationship goes at least this far: a director or a senior officer like O'Malley or Zarzycki is precluded from obtaining for himself, either secretly or without the approval of the company (which would have to be properly manifested upon full disclosure of the facts), any property or business advantage either belonging to the company or for which it has been negotiating; and especially is this so where the director or officer is a participant in the negotiations on behalf of the company.

An examination of the case law in this Court and in the Courts of other like jurisdictions on the fiduciary duties of directors and senior officers shows the pervasiveness of a strict ethic in this area of the law. In my opinion, this ethic disqualifies a director or senior officer from usurping for himself or diverting to another person or company with whom or with which he is associated a maturing business opportunity which his company is actively pursuing; he is also precluded from so acting even after his resignation where the resignation may fairly be said to have been prompted or influenced by a wish to acquire for himself the opportunity sought by the company, or where it was his position with the company rather than a fresh initiative that led him to the opportunity which he later acquired.

The concept that the fiduciary duty continues after resignation was applied to a director in *Edgar T. Alberts Ltd. v. Mountjoy* (1977), 16 O.R. (2d) 682, 2 B.L.R. 178, 36 C.P.R. (2d) 97, 79 D.L.R. (3d) 108 (H.C.). Estey C.J.H.C. cited the judgment of the Supreme Court in the *Can. Aero* case, *supra*, with particular reference to the fact that the fiduciary duty "transcended the severance of the employee-employer relationship" [p. 117]. Applying the same concept to a defendant whose fiduciary duty arose because he had been a director of a company, Estey C.J.H.C. reached this conclusion at p. 119:

> In this case the defendant Mountjoy stood in a fiduciary relationship to the plaintiff and there was accordingly imposed upon him a "larger, more exacting duty" than a duty simply to respect his former employer's trade secrets and the confidentiality of its customer lists.

The *Alberts v. Mountjoy* decision is very similar in its fact to the instant case. The defendant Mountjoy was the general manager and director of Edgar T. Alberts Ltd., an insurance agency. He resigned his position as both director and general manager in order to establish a competitive insurance agency. He was not bound by any restrictive covenant towards Edgar T. Alberts Ltd. Immediately upon founding his new company, the defendant Mountjoy solicited and obtained general insurance business from many of the plaintiff's former customers. It was this direct solicitation of business from clients of the firm which he had served as general manager and director that Estey C.J.H.C. found illegal.

There is nothing to prevent an ordinary employee from terminating his employment and normally that employee is free to compete with his former employer. The right to compete freely may be constrained by contract. It would be improper too for an employee to purloin trade secrets or confidential information, including customer lists. But it is different for a director/officer/key management person who occupies a fiduciary position. Upon his resignation and departure that person is entitled to accept business from former clients but direct solicitation of that business is not permissible. Having accepted a position of trust, the individual is not entitled to allow his own self-interest to collide and conflict with fiduciary responsibilities. The direct solicitation of former clients traverses the boundary of acceptable conduct. The defendant Greer and the co-defendant Sussex should have been content to allow news of Greer's departure and the establishment of Sussex to reach the clientele of W. J. Christie, without resort to direct approach.

• • •

[ed: The Judge then explained why he was unwilling to follow the leading case authority cited by the defendants, and concluded as follows:]

I would, therefore, confirm the decision of the learned trial judge and hold the defendants liable to the plaintiffs for the damage flowing from the breach of fiduciary duty.

## DAMAGES

The learned trial judge assessed damages in favour of the plaintiff at $23 862. That sum corresponds exactly with the total revenues which would have been generated by the seven clients who transferred their business over the course of one year. $21 230 is the fee for property management and $2632 represents insurance commissions relative to those same clients.

• • •

[ed: The Judge discussed various arguments presented by both sides on the quantum of damages.]

In my opinion, the figure struck by the learned judge is a fair one, except that it should be discounted in some measure to take into account the cost of doing business. The figure should not be reduced by 65 per cent as urged by the defendants but, by the same token, the overhead costs should not be ignored as urged by the plaintiff.

After making a reasonable deduction to take this factor into account, a fair assessment of damages of $15 000. I would vary the judgment downward to that extent.

Since there is mixed success in this court, I would award no costs on the appeals.[2]

## NOTES

1. *Although a director's fiduciary obligations to the company are clearly established by the common law, provisions such as Sec. 117 of the* Corporations Act *in Manitoba are typically included in the legislation of the other provinces and the federal government.*

2. *Ordinarily the judge will award court costs to the winning party. (See* General Explanatory Notes *in Part I.) However, the judge exercised his discretion to refuse to award court costs since, although the defendant lost on the issue of liability, the plaintiff received a reduced damage award.*

# PART FIVE

# Credit Transactions

# A. Secured Transactions

[ed: Readers are reminded that the constitutional division of powers in Canada assigns "property and civil rights" to the provinces. Therefore, the legislation on secured transactions can vary widely from one province to another. Readers are cautioned to avoid general conclusions about the relevant law that may affect a secured transaction.]

## Carlson v. Avco Financial Services

[1974] 3 W.W.R. 80
Alberta District Court
January 28, 1974

TAVENDER D.C.J.: This is an inter-pleader issue[1] to determine the rights and priorities of the parties with respect to a motor vehicle. The parties filed an agreed statement of facts.

On 8th December 1971 one Veronica Weir, being the owner of a 1971 M.G.B. motor vehicle, granted a chattel mortgage to the respondent covering the said vehicle and other property. The chattel mortgage was duly registered on 13th December 1971. The serial number shown in the chattel mortgage was incorrect, and on 17th January 1973 an order was obtained from this Court correcting the said serial number and the order was duly filed on 24th January 1973.

In April 1972 the said Weir sold and delivered the said vehicle to one Simon Youens. In November 1972 Youens sold and delivered the said vehicle to one David A. Wiebe. On 10th May 1973 Wiebe sold and delivered the vehicle to the applicant Carlson. It is agreed that Youens, Wiebe and the applicant each purchased the vehicle in good faith, for valuable consideration and without personal knowledge of the existence or registration of the said chattel mortgage.

On 24th May 1973 the respondent through the Sheriff seized the said vehicle and the applicant filed a notice of objection to the seizure. The matter comes before me pursuant to the order of the Master[2] directing an issue to be tried to determine the respective rights of the parties herein.

The issue is clear—Is the title of the applicant subject to the chattel mortgage by reason of his having purchased the car after an order was obtained and filed correcting the serial number of the car in the chattel mortgage, or is he free to deal with the car it having been sold to his predecessors in title at a time when the chattel mortgage was defective?

The *Bills of Sale Act,* R.S.A. 1970, c. 29, provides:

3. 1. Every sale or mortgage not accompanied by an immediate delivery and an actual and continued change of possession of the chattels sold or mortgaged is absolutely void as against
   (a) creditors, and
   (b) subsequent purchasers or mortgagees claiming from or under the grantor in good faith, for valuable consideration and without notice, whose conveyances or mortgages have been duly registered or are valid without registration, unless the sale or mortgage is evidenced by a bill of sale duly registered.
  2. The sale or mortgage and the bill of sale, if any, evidencing the sale or mortgage take effect, as against creditors and such subsequent purchases or mortgages, only from the registration of the bill of sale...

10. 2. The description of a motor vehicle, aircraft or trailer in a bill of sale shall include the serial number of the motor vehicle, aircraft or trailer...[Am. 1971, c. 9, s. 2.]

24. 1. Notwithstanding any other provisions of this Act, a bill of sale or renewal statement not registered within the times prescribed in this Act may be registered at a later date and such registration has the same effect as registration within the prescribed times except that it does not affect rights which have accrued prior to the late registration.
   2. Subject to the rights of other persons accrued by reason of any omission or misstatement referred to in this subsection, a judge of the district court, on being satisfied that any omission or misstatement in any document filed under this Act was accidental or due to any other sufficient cause, may in his discretion order the omission or misstatement to be rectified on such terms and conditions, if any, as to security, notice by advertisement or otherwise, or as to any other matter or thing as the judge sees fit to direct. [Re-en, 1973, c. 13, s. 3.]

25. No defect or irregularity in the execution or attestation of a bill of sale or renewal statement, or in any affidavit accompanying a bill of sale or renewal statement or filed in connection with its registration, and no error of a clerical nature or in an immaterial or non-essential part of a bill of sale or renewal statement, invalidates or destroys the effect of the bill of sale or renewal statement or the registration thereof, unless, in the opinion of the court or judge before whom a question relating thereto is tried, such defect, irregularity, omission or error has actually misled some person whose interests are affected by the bill of sale.

Section 6 of the Act requires registration of a bill of sale, within 21 days from the date of its execution in the case of itinerant machines which include a motor vehicle and 30 days in the case of personal property.

In order for the respondent to succeed it must establish that its claim is protected by and under the *Bills of Sale Act*. The Act is clear that every sale or mortgage not accompanied by an immediate delivery and an actual and continued change of possession of the chattels *is absolutely void* as against subsequent purchasers *claiming from or under* the grantor in good faith, for valuable consideration and without notice whose conveyances have been duly registered or are valid without registration unless the sale is evidenced by a bill of sale duly registered. The respondent is caught by this provision because its claim is under a chattel mortgage where there was no change of possession. The evidence is that the subsequent purchasers each acted in good faith, for valuable consideration and without notice. In each case the vendor "sold and delivered" the vehicle to his purchaser and no bill of sale or registration was required.

The respondent took a chattel mortgage from Weir and registered it, but it was defective in that it did not contain the correct serial number of the vehicle. The Act specifically requires the serial number to be shown in the chattel mortgage and the saving section of the Act with respect to defects and irregularities is therefore not applicable.

As against the vehicle the chattel mortgage had to be registered within 21 days of the date of its execution. I think there is not doubt but that when the vehicle was sold to Youens the chattel mortgage was absolutely void as against him. It was similarly absolutely void as against Wiebe.

After the sale to Wiebe and before the sale to the applicant the respondent obtained an order from this Court correcting the serial number in the chattel mortgage and this order was duly filed. For certain purposes the chattel mortgage then became a valid bill of sale. Was it a valid chattel mortgage so as to defeat the title of the applicant?

In my view of the wording of s. 24(2) is clear and decisive. "Subject to the rights of other persons accrued by reason of any…misstatement…" a judge may rectify the bill of sale. The Legislature has used the broad term "rights". I think it is very clear and there can be no doubt about it that the "rights" Youens acquired were the rights of use of the vehicle and sale or mortgage of it. He acquired all the rights of ownership and was free to deal with the vehicle as he wished. Any other interpretation would restrict and diminish his "rights" which the statute specifically protects. It follows that Youens had the right to give a good title and any subsequent purchaser or mortgagee under him also acquired a good title. The rectifying order therefore did not affect the "rights" of the applicant to ownership of the vehicle.

Counsel for the respondent argued that once the rectifying order was obtained and registered the chattel mortgage then became a valid bill of sale from that moment and took effect prospectively. I do not subscribe to this view. All the rights of ownership had "accrued" to Youens previously and all persons claiming "from or under" him acquired a good title.

I have no doubt about the applicant's title to the vehicle. He acquired a good title and all the rights incident to it.

The respondent's chattel mortgage is ineffective insofar as the vehicle is concerned and it has no claim to it.

The applicant will have his costs of these proceedings including the costs of the inter-pleader order on col. 1, no limiting rule to apply.

NOTES

1. *An inter-pleader issue is one in which two or more persons claim the same thing of a third who makes no claim to it himself but who does not know which of the claimants has legal right to the matter. The third party can force the other parties to litigate the matter and obtain a court decision deciding who has rightful title.*
2. *The Master is an officer of the court appointed to assist the judges; he handles routine matters and applications.*

# Re Hutchinson

*[1977] 4 W.W.R. 547*
*B.C. Supreme Court*
*May 5th, 1977*

CASHMAN L.J.S.C.: This is an application by the trustee in bankruptcy for an order pursuant to s. 59(4) of the *Bankruptcy Act*, R.S.C. 1970, c. B-3[1] that the trustee be at liberty to dispose of a 1975 Chrysler Cordoba, Serial No. SS22N5R309508, free of any lien, right, title or interest of the Bank of British Columbia, and for an order that the said bank deliver possession of that vehicle forthwith to the trustee in bankruptcy.

On or about 8th September 1975 the bankrupt executed a chattel mortgage in favour of the Bank of British Columbia (hereinafter referred to as the "bank") for the sum of $6900 on a 1975 Chrysler Cordoba described in the chattel mortgage as having Serial No. SS22N5RS09508. The serial number of the Chrysler Cordoba which in fact belonged to the bankrupt has the serial number, SS22N5R309508. The misdescription on the chattel mortgage is in one digit; the "S" following the "R" ought to have been a "3" in order to properly describe the motor vehicle.

The bank has possession of the motor vehicle and filed a proof of claim with the trustee, appending to it the chattel mortgage as Ex. A to the proof of claim. The assignment of the bankrupt was made on 31st January 1977 and the proof of claim was sworn 11th March 1977.

The trustee takes the position that, because the motor vehicle described in the chattel mortgage has a different serial number to that which the motor vehicle in fact possesses, the chattel mortgage is null and void insofar as the trustee is concerned within the meaning of s. 16 of the *Bills of Sale Act*, 1961 (B.C.) c. 6. That section provides that:

> 16. 1.  Where a bill of sale…[is] not registered in accordance with the *Bills of Sale Act* applicable thereto and formerly in force or is not registered in accordance with this Act, as the case may be, the bill of sale is, as against
> > (*a*)  the liquidator, assignee, receiver, or trustee of the estate and effects of the person, any of whose personal chattels are comprised in the bill of sale or are under assignment for the benefit of his creditors;…
>
> null and void with regard to the property in or right to possession of any of the personal chattels comprised in the bill of sale.

The trustee relies upon s. 3 [am. 1962, c. 7, s. 2; 1973, c. 7, s. 3] of the *Bills of Sale Act* and in particular subss. (2) and (3) thereof, which read as follows:

> 2.  the description of a motor-vehicle in a bill of sale shall include the vehicle identification number consisting of such sequence of numbers, or of numbers and letters, as are impressed upon or fixed to the vehicle by its maker.
> 3.  For the purposes of subsection (2), the vehicle identification number shall not be insufficient or defective where the motor-vehicle is particularly described in a manner that sets it apart from any other motor-vehicle.

In my view subs. (3) cannot be applicable in the circumstances here, although it was urged upon me by counsel for the bank that it was applicable, and I come to that conclusion because there does not appear to me to be anything set out in the bill of sale which would sufficiently describe this particular motor vehicle in a manner which sets it apart from any other Chrysler Cordoba, aside from the serial number itself, which is defective. That being so, it is my view that subs. (3) is not applicable to the case at bar.

The trustee searched in the motor vehicle registry and found no encumbrances to be registered against this vehicle, having searched it for the correct serial number.

No cases apparently have been decided on the present s. 3. However, there were cases decided under the former section, which read slightly differently. This section read as follows:

> 2.  Where a bill of sale comprises a motor-vehicle, the description therein of the motor-vehicle shall include the serial number thereof, and the Registrar-General may disallow or cancel the registration in his office of a bill of sale that does not comply with this subsection.

The cases decided under that subsection decided that there must be strict compliance with the requirements of the statute. That is set out in the British Columbia Supreme Court case of *Ostler v. Industrial Acceptance Corpn. Ltd.* (1963), 45 W.W.R. 673, 42 D.L.R. (2d) 750, a decision of Hutcheson J., who held that a mistake in the serial number of a motor vehicle in respect of which a conditional sale contract has been registered amounts to non-compliance with the requirements of the *Conditional Sales Act*, 1961 (B.C.), c. 9.

The British Columbia Court of Appeal agreed with that and came to consider the *Bills of Sale Act* having the particular s. 3(2) set forth immediately above. That is the case *Active Petroleum Products Ltd. v. Duggan* (1970), 72 W.W.R. 486, 14 C.B.R. (N.S.) 194, 10 D.L.P. (3d) 599. The effect of that judgment is that there must be strict compliance with the requirements of s. 3, and it was, it ought to be noted, a unanimous judgment of that court.

The section has been amended to some extent but the requirements of a number are still in the present section, although the present section refers to it as a vehicle identification number rather than a serial number. Save and except for that distinction, the requirements of the section appear to me to be essentially the same as they were at the time those two cases were decided.

The present *Conditional Sales Act* contains a section which appears to be identical with the present s. 3 of the *Bills of Sale Act*, and that section was discussed among other matters in a recent decision in our Court of Appeal in *Hawker Siddeley Can. Ltd., Can-Car Trailer Sales Division v. Sigurdson*, [1975] 3 W.W.R. 60, 19 C.B.R. (N.S.) 240, 52 D.L.R. (3d) 116. That case, however, was decided on a question of "delivery of possession" and is not particularly helpful on this aspect. However, that particular parallel section was discussed by the Court of Appeal and for other reasons was not given effect to. It should be noted, however, that Carrothers J.A. at p. 69 said as follows:

> If it is the registration of the second lease-option that governs, judicial authority would indicate that the misdescription in the second lease-option by one digit in a ten-digit number of the vehicle identification number called for by s. 3(2) of the Act might be fatal and give rise to non-compliance.

While that appears to be "obiter dicta,"[2] nonetheless it is in line with the decisions of our courts under the prior statute.

Counsel for the bank relies upon s. 24 [re-en. 1962, c. 7, s. 9], which reads as follows:

> 24. A defect, omission, or irregularity in a bill of sale, affidavit, or statement required to be filed or registered under this Act or a *Bills of Sale Act* previously in force does not invalidate the bill of sale or any renewal statement in respect thereto, or the registration thereof, unless the Court or Judge before whom the matter is heard finds that the defect, omission, or irregularity has actually misled or was likely to mislead some person whose interests are affected by the bill of sale.

It should be noted that there was a similar provision in force at the time the *Ostler* and *Active Petroleum* cases were decided.

It is suggested that this section applies here because the trustee in fact was aware the bank had a chattel mortgage and that certainly appears to be so from the affidavit of the trustee filed in these proceedings because he says that he was informed that there was a chattel mortgage; but he was also informed that it was not known whether the chattel mortgage had been registered. Consequently, the trustee conducted a search and found that there was no chattel mortgage registered against the motor vehicle bearing the correct serial number, and consequently he agreed to act as trustee in bankruptcy for the bankrupt. It was of some importance to the trustee to know that this chattel formed part of the estate of the bankrupt free and clear of encumbrances because it is the only property upon which any money could be realized.

Counsel for the bank submits that, because of this knowledge, the bank is therefore entitled entitled to the benefit of s. 24. I do not agree.

In my view the provisions of s. 3, containing as they do the mandatory words "shall include", mean exactly what they say and the misdescription, even by one digit, in a serial number is a defect which cannot be cured by the application of s. 24 to the mandatory provisions of s. 3.

In the result the trustee is entitled to the order sought with costs.

NOTES

1. *The* Bankruptcy Act *is federal legislation and therefore applies in all the provinces and territories of Canada.*
2. *"Obiter dicta" means a statement of law made in a previous case that was not the legal principle that determined the outcome of that case. Thus, a statement of law that is* obiter dicta *is not a binding precedent for future legal decisions.*

# B. Bankruptcy

## Re Holmes/Re Sinclair

*(1975) 60 D.L.R. (3d) 82*
*Ontario Supreme Court (in Bankruptcy)*
*May 22, 1975*

HENRY, J.: These two petitions in bankruptcy were tried together as the debt alleged to be owing to the petitioning creditor, the Huron and Erie Mortgage corporation, is the joint debt of Mr. Holmes and Miss Sinclair. The evidence shows that these persons operated a chequing account in the St. Clair West branch of the petitioning creditor in Toronto. Apparently the account was used primarily for real estate investments and related transactions. This account became overdrawn for the main reason that several cheques were deposited in the account and were subsequently returned N.S.F.[1] After the account had been in an overdraft position for some time, the two debtors on November 5, 1974, jointly acknowledged their indebtedness in respect of the overdraft in writing, and at the same time they gave a joint demand note to the petitioning creditor for the amount outstanding, which was $46 418.97. They also agreed to a programme of periodic payments to repay the debt. The first payment of $1000 was made. In spite of demands made by the company upon the debtors, nothing further has been paid on the debt.

I am satisfied that the petitioning creditor has proved the following allegations in the petitions against each of the debtors—that the debt exceeds $1000; that the amount is as stated in the petitions, less the $1000 paid on account; that the debtors reside within the jurisdiction of this Court; that they have defaulted on this obligation within the six-month period prescribed; and that the proposed trustee is qualified and available. I am, however, not satisfied that the essential act of bankruptcy alleged has been proved.

Paragraph 3 of each petition alleges that the debtor has ceased to meet his liabilities generally as they became due. This is the only act of bankruptcy alleged. Under the juris-prudence, the *Bankruptcy Act*, R.S.C. 1970, c. B-3, being a *quasi*-criminal statute, the act of bankruptcy and every allegation in

217

the petition must be strictly proved: *Re Elkind* (1966), 9 C.B.R. (N.S.) 274. This requires that evidence be placed before the Court to prove all the allegations of fact made in the petition, whether or not they are put in issue by the debtor in his notice of dispute, including what might be regarded as merely formal facts. All the elements necessary to found a receiving order must be pleaded in the petition and all allegations made therein must be strictly proved by the petitioning creditor.

In the case of each of these petitions, the petitioning creditor has proved the debt owing to it beyond question, but it stops there. Only two witnesses were called—both employees of the petitioning creditor. No evidence that I could regard as admissible was led to disclose the existence or identity of any creditor of these debtors. Clearly the witnesses believed there were other creditors, but no attempt was made to bring proper evidence of the situation before the Court. Instead, counsel submitted that the receiving order should be made on the ground that the present state of the law allows me to grant a receiving order where there is proof of default to only one creditor. In making this submission Mr. Gringorten referred me to the judicial decisions in *Re Raitblat* (1925), 28 O.W.N. 237 [1925] 2 D.L.R. 1219, 5 C.B.R. 714; affirmed 28 O.W.N. 292, [1925] 3 D.L.R. 446, 5 C.B.R. 765; *Le Comité de L'Industrie de la Construction de la Region de Montreal v. Colonello Construction Inc.* (1967), 10 C.B.R. (N.S.) 19; *Kaneb v. Canadian Int'l Paper Co.* (1968), 12 C.B.R. (N.S.) 41; *Re Dixie Market (Nurseries) Ltd.* (1971), 14 C.B.R. (N.S.) 281; *Re Polyco Distributors Ltd.* (1971), 14 C.B.R. (N.S) 285; and *Re King Petroleum Ltd.* (1973), 2 O.R. (2d) 192, 42 D.L.R. (3d) 322, 19 C.B.R. (N.S.) 16.

I have carefully considered these decisions and it is clear that the Courts, in Ontario at least, have granted a receiving order on the basis of a default to one credit in special circumstances. These circumstances are:

(a)  the creditor is the only creditor of the debtor, and the debtor has failed to meet repeated demands of the creditor; in these circumstances he should not be denied the benefits of the *Bankruptcy Act* by reason only of his unique character; or

(b)  the creditor is a significant creditor and there are special circumstances such as fraud on the part of the debtor which make it imperative that the processes of the *Bankruptcy Act* be set in motion immediately for the protection of the whole class of creditors; or

(c)  the debtor admits he is unable to pay his creditors generally, although they and the obligations are not identified.

I find on the evidence that these circumstances do not exist here.

Because this Court has in some of the recent decisions referred to, such as *Dixie Market, Polyco* and *King Petroleum,* made a receiving order on proof of failure to meet a liability to a single creditor, it is not to be taken to have established a new principle that a petitioning creditor need only prove default with respect to the debt owing to him. Those decisions in my judgment do not lay down such a principle; they are as I see it, merely the application to particular facts of the general rule (exemplified by the decision in *Re Elkind, supra*), that when relying on an act of bankruptcy described in s. 24(1) ( *j* ) the petitioning creditor must strictly establish that, in the words of the statute, the debtor "ceases to meet his liabilities generally as they become due"; in all of them the Court was influenced either by the existence of other creditors, or of one of the special circumstances I have set out above. In the non-exceptional case, as in the case at bar, that situation cannot be ordinarily proved by having regard to the experience of one creditor only, even though he may be a major creditor. Resort to the statutory machinery of the *Bankruptcy Act*, rather than to the remedies to enforce a debt or claim in the ordinary Courts, is intended by Parliament to be for the benefit of the creditors of a debtor as a class, and the act of bankruptcy described in s. 24(1) ( *j* ) is in my judgment, an act that singles out the conduct of the debtor in relation to the class, rather than to the individual (as is the case under s. 24(1) (*e*)). It is for this reason that the Court must be satisfied that there is sufficient evidence from which an inference of fact can fairly be drawn that creditors generally are not being paid. This requires as a minimum some evidence that liabilities other than those incurred towards the petitioning creditor, have ceased to be met. The Court ought not to be asked to draw inferences with respect to the class on the basis of one creditor's experience where evidence of the debtor's conduct towards other members of the class could, with reasonable diligence, be discovered and produced. The Court's intuition is no substitute for the diligence of the petitioning creditor.

In the case before me, the petitioning creditor has not established conduct of the debtors towards other creditors. I am, in effect, asked to infer that there is a group of creditors who have not been paid. It is not possible to say, on the evidence, whether they exist at all, or are few or numerous, or whether their claims individually or in total are significant or, most important, to say whether the debtors have *ceased* to meet their liabilities *generally*.

The petitions will therefore be dismissed. I am bound to point out, however, that on the evidence the debtors have behaved in a most irresponsible manner towards the petitioning creditor, although on the evidence I do not find it was fraudulent. They have undertaken to discharge their indebtedness by a programme of payments which they have virtually ignored without explanation. They have put up security that is heavily encumbered. They have opposed the petitions in part by suggesting that if time were allowed, assets could be liquidated to discharge their debt, when, as appears from the evidence, this is patently not so. They have not seen fit to attend personally in Court to support by their testimony the position they have taken in the notice of dispute. They succeed here, not by reason of any merit in their position, but by reason of failure of the petitioning creditor to discharge the onus upon it.

In these circumstances there will be no order for costs and the dismissal of the petitions is without prejudice[2] to this or another creditor presenting a new petition.

NOTES

1. *"N.S.F." means non-sufficient funds and is used by financial institutions to signify when the drawer of a cheque does not have enough money in his account to cover the amount of the cheque.*
2. *"Without prejudice" in this context means that the dismissal of the petitions in this case cannot be used to legally prevent or hinder the filing of any subsequent petition.*

# Re Shickele

*[1977] 5 W.W.R. 421*
*British Columbia Supreme Court*
*June 30, 1977*

MACDONALD L.J.S.C.: This is an issue directed to be tried before myself by an order of Arkell L.J.S.C. dated 14th December 1976 to determine whether the transfer of land and premises hereinafter described from Jeffrey Gordon Shickele to Alena Sharon Shickele is void as against the trustee on the ground that the same is a settlement contrary to the provisions of s. 69(2) of the *Bankruptcy Act*, R.S.C. 1970, c. B-3, hereinafter referred to as "the *Bankruptcy Act*".

In the years 1971 through 1973, Mr. Shickele was employed as an accountant in Bill McAulliffe Motors Ltd. in Kamloops, British Columbia. Mr. Wettering, president of Bill McAulliffe Motors Ltd., sometime in 1972 started up a business under the name Gerven Motors Ltd., and Mr. Shickele was engaged as accountant with the new firm. In the summer of 1973 Mr. Wettering, Dr. Clark, and Mr. Shickele decided to incorporate a new company, Gerven Motors (1973) Ltd., and buy out Gerven Motors Ltd. They each invested the sum of $20 000 in the new company at this time. Mr. Shickele carried on as accountant and manager and was more or less in charge of the day-to-day operations of the business. At the time these three parties entered into this business Mr. Shickele owned a half interest in his home at 1630 Westmount Drive in the city of Kamloops. He was, however, not able or in a position to raise the $20 000 required for this investment so Dr. Clark loaned Mr. Shickele $20 000 and Mr. Shickele gave Dr. Clark a promissory note in the amount of $20 000 bearing interest at 10 per cent, payable on demand. At the time that Dr. Clark loaned Mr. Shickele the $20 000 he advised Dr. Clark that he had an equity in his house along with his wife.

The business Gerven Motors (1973) Ltd. started out in a loss position and the company continued to lose money. The three shareholders held a meeting in March 1974 and I am satisfied that at this meeting Mr. Wettering suggested that they should consider liquidating the company. At this time Mr. Shickele was more optimistic and felt that they should carry on, and I am satisfied he felt things would improve. The matter was discussed and apparently all three eventually decided to carry on the business. All three shareholders had guaranteed the indebtedness of Gerven Motors (1973) Ltd. at the Canadian Imperial Bank of Commerce. I am satisfied from the evidence of the manager of that bank that as of 11th April 1974 Gerven Motors (1973) Ltd. was indebted to the bank in the approximate amount of $71 000 and that each one of the shareholders as guarantor of the company's indebtedness to the bank was indebted to the bank in this amount. I am also satisfied that on 11th April 1974 Mr. Shickele owed Dr. Clark the sum of $20 000 on the demand promissory note. It was clear from the evidence that in the spring of 1974 Mr. Shickele was not indebted in any amount to other creditors and that his current bills were being paid on a month-to-month basis. On 11th April 1974 Mr. Shickele transferred his share in the matrimonial home, which he held as a joint tenant with his wife to his wife, Alena Sharon Shickele. I am satisfied that at the time the house was transferred to Mrs. Shickele it was their intention that she would carry on as sole owner of the house. The consideration that was shown in the deed of land was $1 plus other good and valuable consideration. It was clear from the evidence that the wife did not pay the husband anything for the husband's interest in the property. Mr. Shickele did not advise Mr. Wettering or Dr. Clark of the conveyance. I would find that Mrs. Shickele had paid the down payments on the house in the amount of $2000. I would also find that Mr. Shickele, apart from a few months, had made the monthly payments on this mortgage up until this date. I would find that in 1974 Mr. Shickele's equity in the matrimonial home was approximately $10 000. In the spring of 1974 and before 11th April 1974 Mrs. Shickele was aware that her husband was indebted to a substantial amount. I am satisfied at this time that the marriage was not going well for a number of reasons, one of which was that the husband did not communicate with his wife and did not advise her of the steps he had taken when he got involved with Gerven Motors Ltd. She eventually found out and became aware that he had incurred substantial indebtedness and, understandably, she felt kept out of the picture, as she put it. In all likelihood, had he taken the trouble to consult with her, he would not find himself in the predicament in which he is today. She stated she felt strongly that the house was hers, and that in view of the marital situation it should be transferred to her.

• • •

Gerven Motors (1973) Ltd. carried on in business until the end of 1974. The financial position of the company became progressively worse. In December 1974 the shareholders held a meeting and decided to close out the business. The company was eventually wound up the following June, and at that time the company's loss was $140 000; $134 000 of this was owed to the

Canadian Imperial Bank of Commerce. Mr. Wettering agreed and did pay out the $140 000 and it was arranged at that time between Mr. Wettering, Dr. Clark and Mr. Shickele that, as Mr. Shickele had no means with which to pay off one-third of the liability that he was responsible for under the guarantees, he, Mr. Wettering and Dr. Clark would pay $60 000 each and that Shickele was to absorb $20 000 of the loss and that he would pay off the note to Dr. Clark. Mr. Shickele did not pay anything on Dr. Clark's note. On 9th March 1976 Mr. Shickele executed an assignment for the general benefit of creditors under the provisions of the *Bankruptcy Act*. At this time he had just commenced work with an insurance agency in Kamloops and was earning approximately $1000 per month. He did not advise either Mr. Wettering or Dr. Clark of the assignment.

Dealing first with the trustee's claim that the transfer of Mr. Shickele's interest in the matrimonial home to Mrs. Shickele was fraudulent and void as against the trustees as a settlement within the provisions of s. 69(2) of the *Bankruptcy Act*—section 69(2) of the *Bankruptcy Act* reads as follows:

2. Any settlement of property, if the settlor becomes bankrupt within five years after the date of the settlement, is void against the trustee if the trustee can prove that the settlor was, at the time of making the settlement, unable to pay all his debts without the aid of the property comprised in the settlement or that the interest of the settlor in the property did not pass on the execution thereof.

The onus of proof under s. 69(2) of the *Bankruptcy Act* is upon the trustee. The first question to be resolved here is, has the trustee proved a settlement of property by Mr. Shickele on his wife?

• • •

[ed: Mr. Justice MacDonald then reviewed a number of case precedents dealing with the meaning of the term "settlement" as per the Bankruptcy Act.]

This court would conclude that the word "settlement" as contained in s. 69(2) of the *Bankruptcy Act* refers to a voluntary disposition of property to and for the benefit of an individual with the intention that it be retained by that individual either in its original form or in such a form that can be traced. I would find that the transfer of Mr. Shickele's joint interest in the matrimonial home to his wife was a settlement within the meaning of s. 69(2) of the *Bankruptcy Act*. I would find that Mr. Shickele became bankrupt within five years of this settlement. The onus is then on the trustee to prove that Mr. Shickele was, at the time of making the settlement, unable to pay all his debts without the aid of his equity in the matrimonial home, which was transferred to his wife.

I have found that at the time he made the transfer Mr. Shickele was keeping up with his day-to-day bills and that he did not appear to have any liabilities other than what he owed on the guarantee of Gerven Motors (1973) Ltd.'s indebtedness to the Canadian Imperial Bank of Commerce and on his note to Dr. Clark. The liabilities to the bank on the guarantee were approximately $71 000, and to Dr. Clark, $20 000. It is important here to note that the words used here are "all his debts", not his current debts. Counsel for Mr. Shickele has argued that as Mr. Shickele at the time of settlement was able to pay his day-to-day current debts and as no demand had been made on the promissory note or on the guarantee at that time, it cannot be said that Mr. Shickele could not pay his debts without the aid of the property comprised in the settlement. As to the argument that these contingent liabilities—and I refer to the bank guarantee—are not to be considered as a debt within s. 69(2) of the *Bankruptcy Act*, the court refers itself to *Re Ridler; Ridler v. Ridler* (1882), 22 Ch. D. 74, where Lord Selborne L.C. says at p. 80:

> The arguments on behalf of the respondents turned much on the proposition that when a person is liable on a guarantee he is not to be regarded for the present purpose as owing a debt of that amount, without taking into account the assets of the principal debtor as well as his own. There is a fallacy in this. To hold that a guarantor can make a voluntary settlement of the whole of his property and support it by shewing that when he made it the person guaranteed had assets enough to pay the amount guaranteed, would go far to defeat the contract of suretyship. We must look at the matter as if the event had already happened the possibility of which the parties must have had in contemplation when the guarantee was given of the debtor being unable to pay.

On the basis of this authority and on the evidence, there can be no question that as of 11th April 1974 the plaintiff, along with each of the other two shareholders, was indebted to the bank on this guarantee in the amount of approximately $71 000. Apart altogether from this indebtedness, there was his indebtedness to Dr. Clark on the demand note. As I have stated, in s. 69(2) of the *Bankruptcy Act* the court is concerned with the words "all his debts". Debt has been described in the Canadian edition of the Standard College Dictionary as follows: "That which one owes as money, goods, or services. The obligation to pay or render something to another. The condition of owing something."

In Ballantyne's Law Dictionary a debt is described as follows: "A sum of money which is payable is a debt without regard to whether it is payable presently or in a future time."

There can be no question here that this $20 000 was a debt that Mr. Shickele owed to Dr. Clark on 11th April 1974. The fact that a demand had not been made on the promissory note up to that time did not make it any the less a debt. It is abundantly clear that Mr. Shickele could not meet this debt of $20 000 on 11th April 1974 without the aid of his equity in the matrimonial home, which he conveyed to his wife on that day. His equity in that house was $10 000, and the only other asset that he had of any consequence was a rifle worth $150. In the circumstances, this court would rule that on 11th April 1974, Mr. Shickele was unable to pay all his debts without the aid of the property comprised in the settlement. It remains to be decided whether or not the settlement was one that was made in favour of a purchaser in good faith and for valuable consideration under s. 69(3) of the *Bankruptcy Act*. On the question of whether or not there was valuable consideration for the conveyance from Mr. Shickele to his wife, the consideration shown in the deep was $1 plus other good and valuable consideration. It was clear from the evidence that there was no other good and valuable consideration. The wife did not agree to assume payments under the mortgage and her husband has carried on paying these mortgage payments to date. The wife, in consideration of the sum of $1, received a $10 000 equity in this house. I would conclude, therefore, that there was no valuable consideration to this settlement. With reference to the question of good faith, s. 69(3) (*b*) of the *Bankruptcy Act* reads as follows:

> 3.   This section does not extend to any settlement made...
> (*b*)   in favour of a purchaser or incumbrancer in good faith and for valuable consideration.

In *Re MacKeen,* 10 C.B.R. 311, [1929] 1 D.L.R. 528 at 530 (N.S.), Jenks J. stated: "The onus of proving good faith is upon the person desiring to avail himself of the protection of the saving clause. See *Ex parte Tate* (1876), 35 L.T. 531; *Koop v. Smith* (1915), 8 W.W.R. 1238, 51 S.C.R. 554, 25 D.L.R. 355.

> The quite general statements contained in the affidavits of MacKeen and his wife are in my opinion not sufficient to discharge this burden and taking all the circumstances together, I am clearly of opinion that the conveyance to the wife of the whole of the debtor's real property for a past and inadequate consideration when the debtor was involved as this debtor was, in a transaction which cannot stand as against the trustee in bankruptcy. My inference from the facts and circumstances of the case is that the conveyance in question was not made "in favour of a purchaser or incumbrancer in good faith and for valuable consideration," (s. 60(3) (b)) and I so find.

I understand s. (60)(3) (*b*) of the *Bankruptcy Act,* R.S.C. 1927, c. 11, contained a saving clause setting out that the section did not apply to settlements made in good faith and for valuable consideration, as does s. 69(3) (*b*) of the *Bankruptcy Act,* 1970. I would hold that the onus is upon Mr. and Mrs. Shickele, here, to prove that the settlement of the husband's interest in the matrimonial home upon his wife was made in good faith.

I have found that in April 1974 Mr. Shickele was indebted to the Canadian Imperial Bank of Commerce in the amount of $71 000 on the guarantee, and indebted to Dr. Clark in the amount of $20 000. In March, Mr. Wettering wanted to close the business down. Mr. Shickele was more optimistic of the company's future and the other two went along with his suggestion that they carry on. However, the fact remains that, apart altogether from the indebtedness to the bank at this time, he did owe $20 000 to Dr. Clark, and the only asset of any substance he had to meet this indebtedness with was his equity in the home, the equity he mentioned to Dr. Clark when he made the loan. Mr. Shickele stated on discovery that his wife was upset when she found out he owed a substantial amount of money. He also stated on discovery and at the trial that his wife felt at this time he was jeopardizing her position. His wife confirmed in her testimony that she knew he was indebted at the time of the settlement in a substantial amount. It was apparent from the evidence that the marriage was not going well and that her husband's financial position was compounding the situation. In cross-examination she was asked if she knew if her husband's interest in the matrimonial home could be attached. She said she had not given this matter serious thought. Looking at Mr. Shickele's statement on discovery and his evidence on trial, particularly his statement that his wife thought he was jeopardizing her position, one thing does become apparent and this is that she felt insecure because of the way that the marriage was going and, I am satisfied, as well because of her husband's financial position. I do not doubt that one of the considerations of the husband was that it would help the marriage if he transferred his equity to his wife; however, that does not change the fact that he was transferring the only asset he had to satisfy his indebtedness at that time, an indebtedness of which he was very much aware. Mr. Shickele's statement that he was confident that the company would eventually succeed is hard to understand in light of the company's indebtedness at that time and the fact that Mr. Wettering wished to liquidate the company at that time and take the loss, rather than carry on and incur further loss. Mr. Shickele may have had hopes that the company could succeed at this time; however, he must have been aware that there was a good chance the company would not succeed and could well go deeper into debt, as it eventually did. The settlement must be in good faith. They both acted to allay the wife's fears for her security, and they acted in the full knowledge that the husband was substantially indebted, and I am satisfied they both knew that the equity in the matrimonial home was the husband's only asset of any significance. To act in good faith in these circumstances would mean that Mr. and Mrs. Shickele acted in an honest belief that what they were doing was without detriment to others, in particular, to the husband's creditors. The husband certainly—and perhaps to a lesser extent, his wife—must have known there was something wrong here, that what they were doing would be to the detriment of the husband's creditors. I cannot find that Mrs. Shickele has satisfied the onus placed upon her to show that the settlement was made in good faith and for valuable consideration.

I find and declare that the transfer by Jeffrey Gordon Shickele of a one-half undivided interest in those lands and lying and being in the city of Kamloops, province of British Columbia, more particularly known and described as Lot 53, District Lot 257, K.D.Y.D., Plan 16614, to Alena Sharon Shickele by deed of land dated 11th April 1974 is void as against the trustee on the ground that the same was a settlement contrary to the provisions of s. 69(2) of the Bankruptcy Act.

In view of the court's finding, I see no necessity to deal further with the trustee's application for a declaration that the transfer herein was a fraudulent conveyance within the provisions of s. 2 of the *Fraudulent Conveyances Act,* R.S.B.C. 1960, c. 155.

The trustee is awarded his costs on the trial of the issue. As to the costs on the original motion, any further directions in this regard will have to be given by the chambers judge who dealt with the motion.

# Re 52181 Manitoba Ltd. (Auto Re-Nu)

*[1983] 5 W.W.R. 270*
*Manitoba Court of Appeal*
*May 25, 1983*

[ed: The concurring judgment of Matas J. A. has been omitted.]

HUBAND J.A. (HALL J.A. concurring): This case involves a question of priorities in a bankruptcy situation.

A dispute arose between the two principal shareholders of a company, 52181 Manitoba Ltd. The shareholders agreed to wind up the company, and for that purpose the firm of Deloitte Haskins & Sells Limited was approached and agreed to act as liquidator. A court order appointing Deloitte to that position was made on 17th July 1981. Among other things, the order provided that "The liquidator's fees are to be a first charge as against the company's assets..."

Clause 10 of the order directed the liquidator to apply to the court for direction "...if at any time the liquidator determines that the corporation is unable to pay or adequately provide for the discharge of its obligations."

Shortly after its appointment the liquidator did indeed ascertain that the company had insufficient funds to pay its liabilities.

On the 13th August 1981 the liquidator returned to court to report the insolvency of the company, and to obtain direction. Wilson J. of the Court of Queen's Bench requested that the liquidator call a meeting of creditors of the company. Such a meeting was convened by the liquidator on 27th August 1981, as a result of which one of the creditors indicated that it would petition 52181 Manitoba Ltd. into bankruptcy.

By mid-September, however, that particular creditor changed its mind, realizing that the cost of doing so would exceed the return to that creditor in the bankruptcy proceedings.

Since no one else would take the obvious and appropriate step, the liquidator, Deloitte, came before the courts again, suggesting that it be directed to make an assignment into bankruptcy of 52181 Manitoba Ltd. On 28th September 1981, Morse J. of the Court of Queen's Bench directed that notice be given to all known creditors with claims in excess of $1000. That was done.

Four weeks later, on 28th October 1981, Solomon J. of the Court of Queen's Bench made the order directing Deloitte to put the company into bankruptcy.

Bankruptcy proceedings were initiated on 5th November 1981, and from that point onward Deloitte was functioning as trustee in bankruptcy, rather than as liquidator under the consent order made 3½ months before.

In bankruptcy proceedings, the first meeting of creditors was held on 24th November 1981, and inspectors were appointed. The inspectors met on 24th November and again the next day, and it was determined that an auction sale should be held to dispose of the assets of the bankrupt company. Tentative arrangements were made for an auction sale on 28th November, but, to generate greater publicity, the auction sale was postponed to 5th December 1981.

After the auction sale was held, the assets of the bankrupt company were all in liquid form, and division among creditors could be contemplated.

There was all too little to go around. It was clear that after a secured creditor had taken what was due to it, there would be insufficient funds to satisfy all of the claims of preferred creditors, let alone unsecured creditors who do not enjoy a preferred position.

The total amount of money realized came to $17 328.89, but of that amount the Bank of Nova Scotia obtained $8289.65 by virtue of security held by the bank. Accordingly, $9039.24 was available for distribution among competing claimants.

In his decision [reported at [1982] 6 W.W.R. 67, 44 C.B.R. (N.S.) 302, 18 Man. R. (2d) 284] Wilson J. gave first priority to Revenue Canada whose claim amounted to $1000.98. He then allowed the fees of Deloitte for having acted as liquidator, between 27th July and 26th October 1981, in the sum of $5500. Next came the legal fees which were incurred as a disbursement by the liquidator during the same period, amounting to $1098.38. When these amounts are paid, (assuming for the moment that it is appropriate to do so) there is only $1340.20 available for distribution. The learned trial judge held that the next claim, in order of priorities, was that of Deloitte for its fees and proper disbursements as trustee in bankruptcy. As a result, nothing will be available for other creditors including the landlord of the premises occupied by the bankrupt company. The landlord advanced a claim for several thousand dollars and reasserts its position on appeal. It is argued that at least part of the landlord's claim should be included as the liquidator's disbursements during the period prior to bankruptcy. Part of the landlord's claim should be treated as a proper disbursement of the trustee in bankruptcy subsequent to the assignment in bankruptcy. Finally, the landlord argues that the trustee in bankruptcy is personally responsible for rent during the period 5th November to 28th November, even though the amount available for distribution is considerably less than the rental claim.

There is no argument that Revenue Canada is entitled to first priority on the moneys available for distribution. The claim of Revenue Canada falls within the category discussed in *Dauphin Plains Credit Union Ltd. v. Xyloid*

*Indust. Ltd.*, [1980] 1 S.C.R. 1182, [1980] 3 W.W.R. 513, 33 C.B.R. (N.S.) 107, 108 D.L.R. (3d) 2527, 3 Man. R. (2d) 283, 31 N.R. 301.

In my view, it is entirely proper to next allow the fee of the liquidator, together with his disbursements, including legal costs, during the period prior to the assignment in bankruptcy. The liquidator was functioning under a court order making his fees the first charge against the company's assets. The liquidator's proper disbursements (for legal fees for example) fall within the ambit of that protection.

The bankrupt company rented space in a building where it kept auto parts, that being the nature of the business. From the date the order was made appointing Deloitte as liquidator, no further business was conducted. The liquidator did not attempt to operate the company as a going concern.

The landlord, Westbar Holdings Ltd., was formally notified of the liquidation by way of a letter dated 28th July 1981. At the outset the landlord seemed content to have the liquidation proceed in the expectation that its claim for rent would be dealt with in the course of the liquidation.

On 18th August the landlord, through a letter from its legal counsel, claimed a "preferred lien" on goods and chattels in the premises, to recover rent for the months of July and August 1981, in the amount of $8147.74. The same letter, directed to the liquidator, requested that the premises be vacated by 31st August.

When it became clear to the liquidator that the company was insolvent, and when the court ordered that creditors be notified, the landlord was invited to attend the initial meeting of creditors.

On 3rd September 1981, or thereabouts, the landlord changed the locks on the premises and indicated that storage would be charged at the rate of $150 per day. The liquidator did not question the right of the landlord to advance a claim for storage but suggested that the per diem amount was excessive. In the present proceedings the landlord has reduced the storage claim from $150 per day to $20.55 per day, which amounts to a total of $1315 for the period from 3rd September 1981, to 5th November 1981, when the assignment in bankruptcy ended the liquidation proceedings.

At no time did the landlord distrain for rent.

I see no basis upon which the rent for the months of July and August, or the storage charges thereafter up to 5th November, can be added to the liquidator's fees and disbursements. The liquidator did not make any contractual arrangements with the landlord to use the premises or to pay occupational rent. There is authority for the proposition that a liquidator, being a trustee, is entitled to be indemnified for fees and disbursements and deduct them from the estate before turning over the assets to the trustee in bankruptcy when an assignment in bankruptcy is made: see *Re Holden; Ex parte Official Receiver* (1887), 20 Q.B.D. 43 (Div. Ct.). In any event, the liquidator's position is protected by the order which appointed him.

The landlord, however, is not entitled to have his claim for rent, or occupational rent, included as a liquidator's disbursement when the evidence does not support the conclusion that such items were proper disbursements voluntarily incurred by the liquidator during the course of the liquidation.

That does not mean, of course, that the landlord's claim for rent prior to bankruptcy is invalid. What it does mean is that his claim must be dealt with under the statutory scheme for the determination of priorities under s. 107(1) of the *Bankruptcy Act*, R.S.C. 1970, c. B-3, and, as we shall see, that is of no assistance to the landlord.

The goods and chattels of the bankrupt company remained on the landlord's premises from 5th November, when the assignment in bankruptcy was made, until 5th December, when the auction sale took place. During this period the landlord claims occupational rent for 23 days at $142.01 per day, or a total of $3266.23. The landlord does not claim beyond 28th November, because the delay in holding the auction sale was at the landlord's request. Once again, the landlord's only hope of obtaining payment is by having this claim for occupational rent included as a disbursement of the trustee. The landlord would thus be entitled to more than a share of the $1340 which is left, because the landlord would then claim to be entitled to full indemnity from the trustee on a contractual basis, whether there are funds in the bankrupt estate to pay or not.

Once again, the evidence simply does not support a claim for occupational rent during the time of the bankruptcy. The solicitor for the landlord was appointed as one of the inspectors in the bankruptcy proceedings. In the inspector's meeting held on 24th and 25th November, 1981, there was no discussion about occupational rent, and no authority was given to the trustee in bankruptcy to willingly incur a debt, as a disbursement of the trustee, for occupational rent or storage charges.

Once again, the validity of a claim for occupational rent is not challenged. What is contested is the right of the landlord to have such a claim imported as a disbursement obligation of the trustee, in the absence of evidentiary support for that conclusion. Once again, the landlord is left with his remedy (in this case a non-remedy) under s. 107(1) of the *Bankruptcy Act*.

Section 107(1) establishes priorities in bankruptcy and reads as follows:

107 1. Subject to the rights of secured creditors, the proceeds realized from the property of a bankrupt shall be applied in priority of payment as follows:
(*a*) in the case of a deceased bankrupt, the reasonable funeral and testamentary expenses incurred by the legal personal representative of the deceased bankrupt;
(*b*) the costs of administration, in the following order,
(i) the expenses and fees of the trustee,
(ii) legal costs;
(*c*) the levy payable under section 118;
(*d*) wages, salaries, commissions or compensation of any clerk, servant, travelling salesman, labourer or workman for services rendered during three months next preceding the bankruptcy to the extent of five hundred dollars in each case; together with in the case of a travelling salesman, disbursements properly incurred by him in and about the bankrupt's business, to the extent of an additional three hundred

dollars in each case, during the same period; and for the purposes of this paragraph commissions payable when goods are shipped, delivered or paid for, if shipped, delivered or paid for within the three-month period, shall be deemed to have been earned therein;

(e) municipal taxes assessed or levied against the bankrupt within two years next preceding his bankruptcy and that do not constitute a preferential lien or charge against the real property of the bankrupt, but not exceeding the value of the interest of the bankrupt in the property in respect of which the taxes were imposed as declared by the trustee;

(f) the landlord for arrears of rent for a period of three months next preceding the bankruptcy and accelerated rent for a period not exceeding three months following the bankruptcy if entitled thereto under the lease, but the total amount so payable shall not exceed the realization from the property on the premises under lease, and any payment made on account of accelerated rent shall be credited against the amount payable by the trustee for occupation rent;

(g) the fees and costs referred to in subsection 50(2) but only to the extent of the realization from the property exigible thereunder;

(h) all indebtedness of the bankrupt under any Workmen's Compensation Act, under any Unemployment Insurance Act, under any provision of the *Income Tax Act* or the *Income War Tax Act* creating an obligation to pay to Her Majesty amounts that have been deducted or withheld, *pari passu*;

(i) claims resulting from injuries to employees of the bankrupt to which the provisions of any Workmen's Compensation Act do not apply, but only to the extent of moneys received from persons or companies guaranteeing the bankrupt against damages resulting from such injuries;

(j) claims of the Crown not previously mentioned in this section, in right of Canada or of any province, *pari passu* notwithstanding any statutory preference to the contrary.

The costs of administration, including the trustee's expenses take priority over the landlord's claim for rent under para. (f), hence the effort to have occupational rent included as an expense of the trustee.

No doubt a trustee can make arrangements with a landlord under which he agrees to pay either storage charges or occupational rent as part of the administration of the bankrupt estate. Even without agreement between them, the trustee in bankruptcy might so conduct himself as to incur the cost of occupational rent as an administrative expense, but that did not happen in this case.

The case of *Rosen v. Archambault* (1959), 37 C.B.R. 184 (Que. S.C.), is of assistance. The factual situation was not dissimilar to the facts in the present case. After an assignment in bankruptcy was made, the trustee acted with reasonable promptitude in arranging a meeting of creditors and subsequently obtaining authorization from inspectors to surrender up the premises to the landlord. The landlord made a claim for occupation rent as a liability of the trustee in bankruptcy in the course of his administration. Collins J. of the Quebec Superior Court, in Bankruptcy, rejected the claim, and said at p. 186:

It is obvious that some period of time must be allowed to a trustee to 'turn around' in the liquidation of a bankrupt estate. It was reasonable for the trustee (the present defendant) to attempt to find out first whether it was possible to assign his rights in the lease to a third party for the benefit of the creditors in general before surrendering the lease. A trustee cannot retain a lease indefinitely without becoming liable for occupation rent. The question is one of fact in the present matter, the Court is of the opinion that the trustee did not maintain his rights in the lease any longer than it was necessary to determine what should be done under the circumstances for the general benefit of the creditors.

In the instant case, the learned trial judge came to the correct decision, and the appeal by the landlord is dismissed with costs.

*Appeal dismissed.*